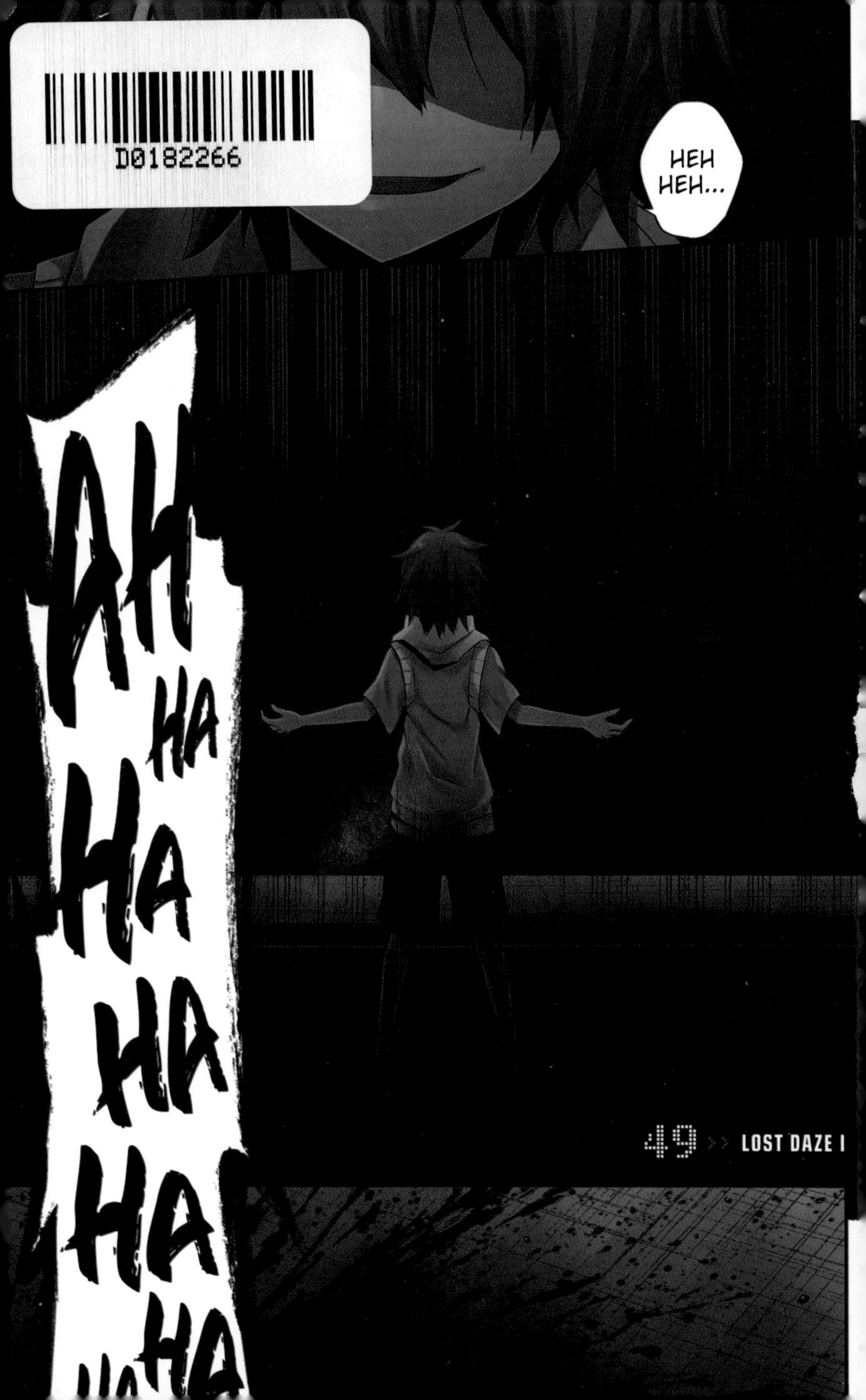
HEH HEH...
49 >> LOST DAZE I
AH HA HA HA HA HA HA HA HA

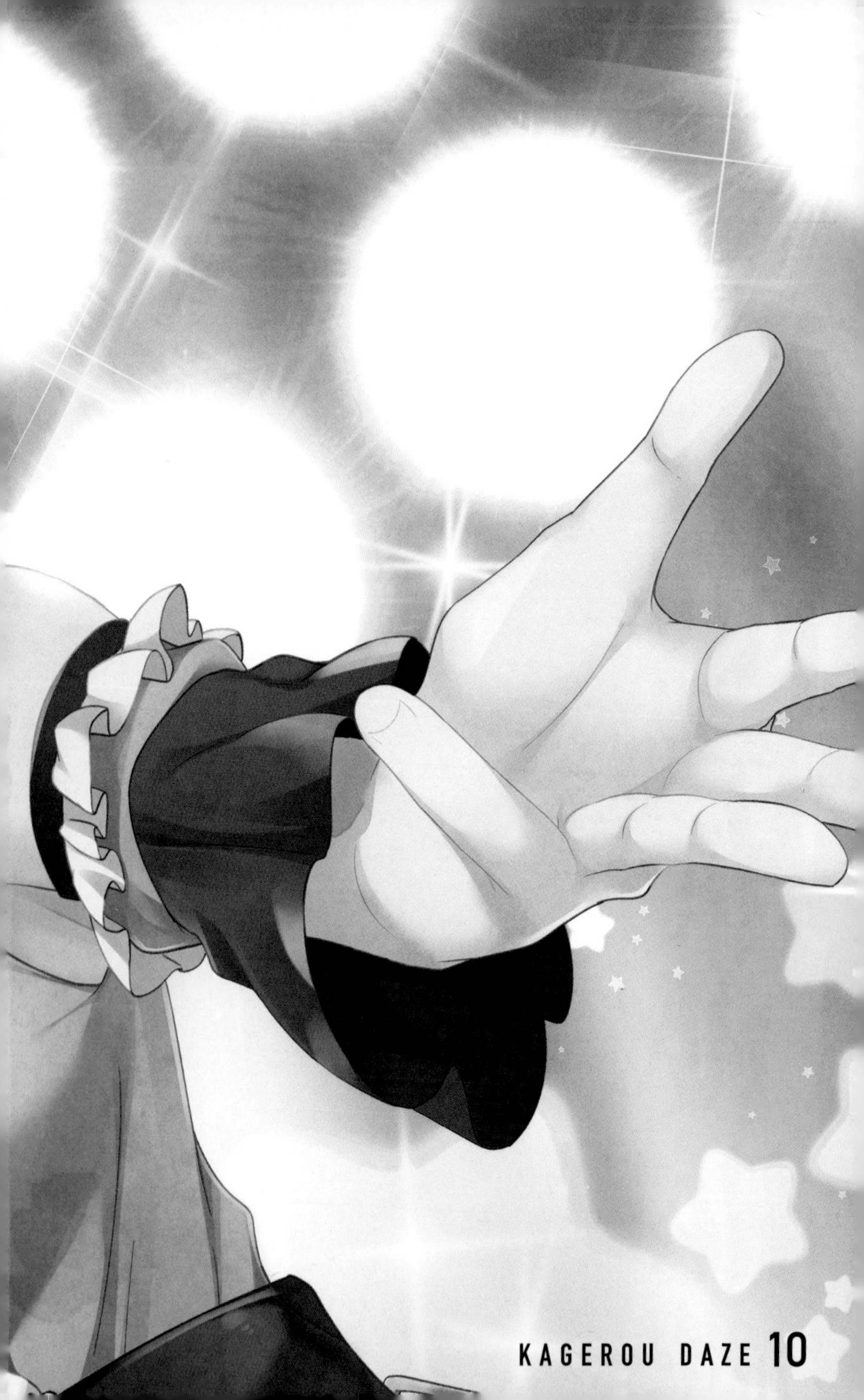
KAGEROU DAZE 10

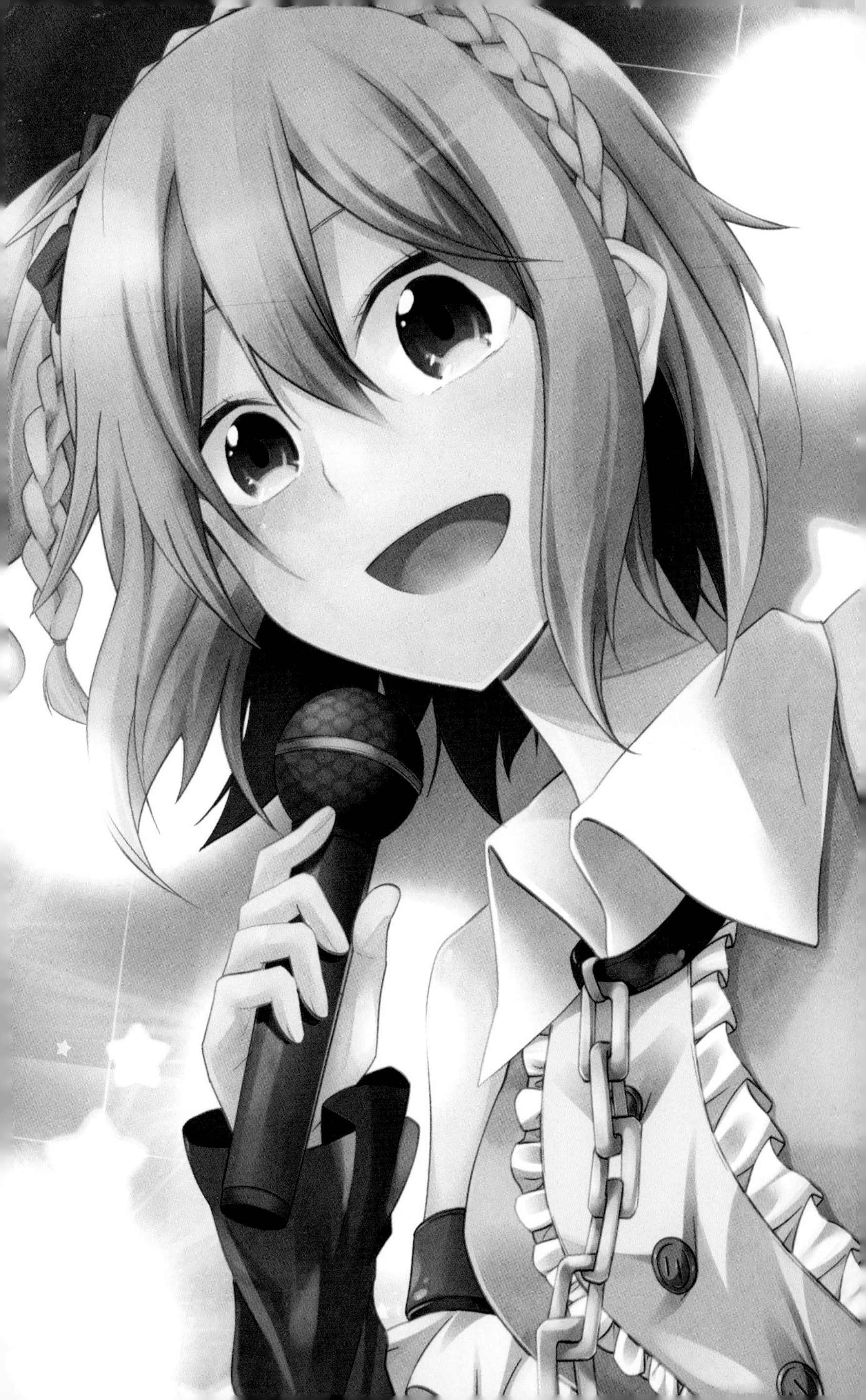

KAGEROU DAZE 10

CONTENTS

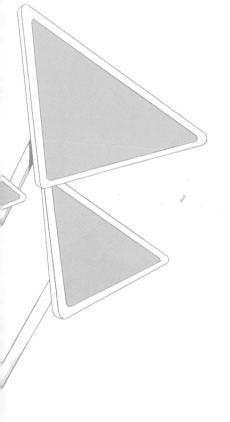

CHARACTERS

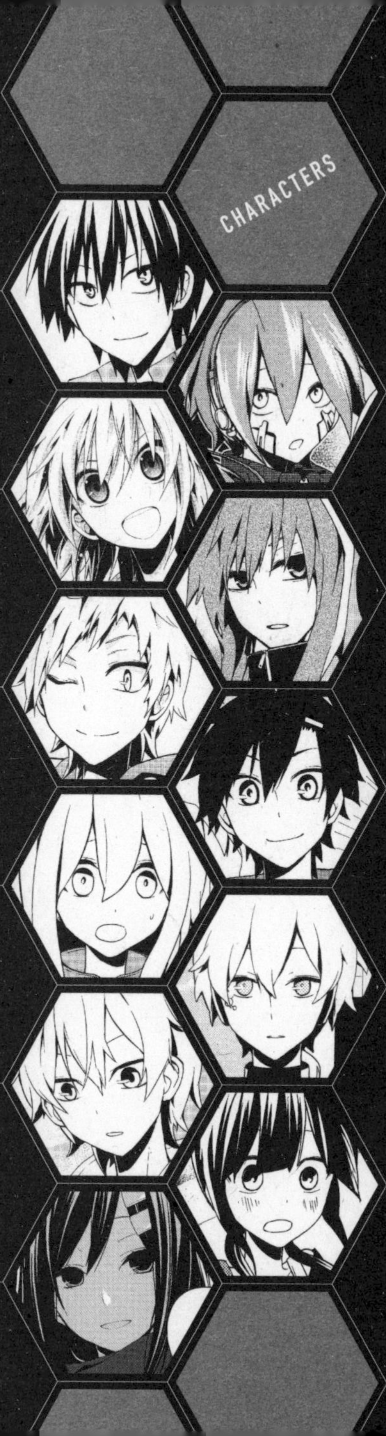

SHINTARO

A teenage boy who's been holed up in his house for the past two years.

ENE (Takane Enomoto)

An innocent, naive "digital girl" who's taken up residence in Shintaro's computer.

MOMO

An ultra-popular singer with the "drawing eyes" ability. Shintaro's sister.

KIDO

Leader of the Mekakushi-dan. Possesses the "concealing eyes" ability.

KANO

Friends with Kido and Seto since childhood. Possesses the "deceiving eyes" ability.

SETO

A young man engaged in assorted part-time work. Possesses the "stealing eyes" ability.

MARIE

A young Medusa whose "locking eyes" ability lets her freeze people in their tracks.

KONOHA (Haruka Kokonose)

A young man who's lost his memory.

HIBIYA

A boy who's come to visit the neighborhood with Hiyori.

HIYORI

A girl who's come to visit Shintaro's neighborhood. A big fan of Momo.

AYANO

A mysterious girl who approached Hibiya. Capable of projecting memories and emotions directly into people's brains.

STORY

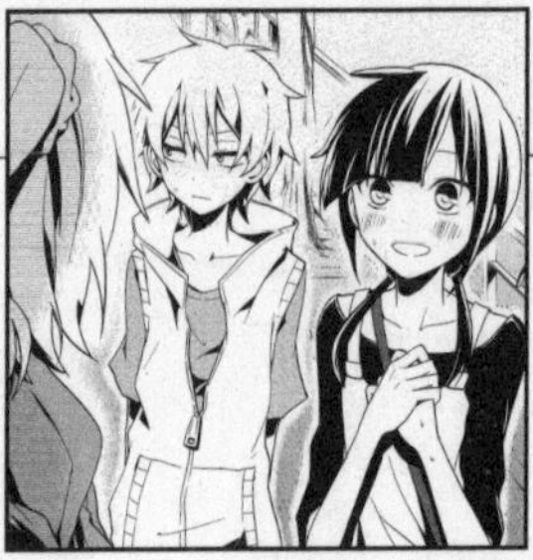

The tale of the events of August 14 and 15—

Shintaro and Momo run into a pair of children, Hibiya and Hiyori. They soon become friends, but after relaying a cryptic message to Momo over the phone, Hiyori disappears. They later discover Hibiya alone and unconscious, but he has lost his memory of the recent past. On the same day, Shintaro and Momo come across Kido and Kano, who claim to be part of a secret organization. They are also pursuing Hibiya and Hiyori, and soon the entire group's goals, destinies, and anxieties crisscross—and it's all connected by a supernatural phenomenon known as "Kagerou Daze."

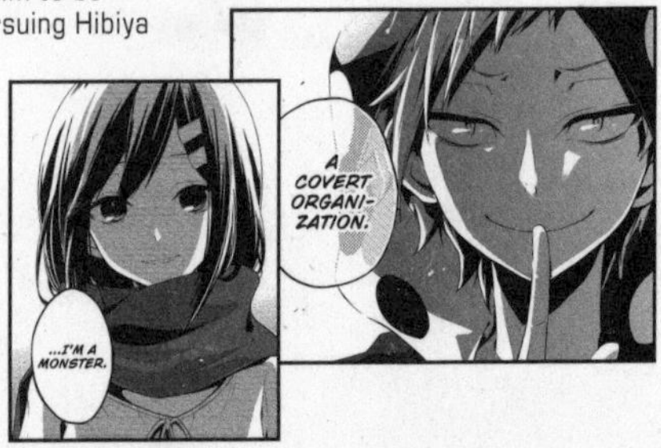
A COVERT ORGANI-ZATION.
...I'M A MONSTER.

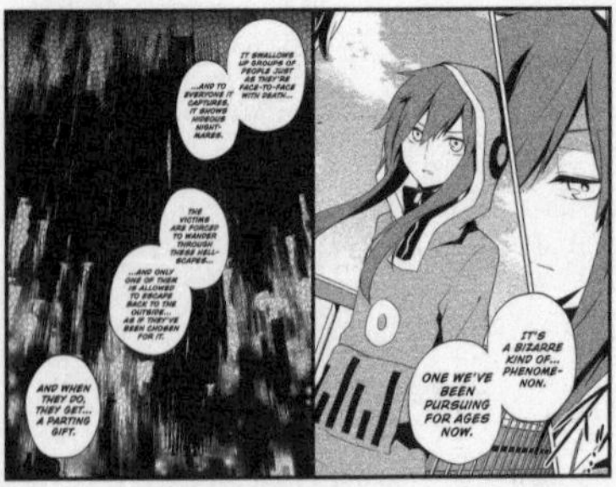
IT'S A BIZARRE KIND OF... PHENOME-NON.
ONE WE'VE BEEN PURSUING FOR AGES NOW.
IT SWALLOWS UP GROUPS OF PEOPLE JUST AS THEY'RE FACE-TO-FACE WITH DEATH...
...AND TO EVERYONE IT CAPTURES, IT SHOWS HIDEOUS NIGHT-MARES.
THE VICTIMS ARE FORCED TO WANDER THROUGH THESE HELL-SCAPES...
...AND ONLY ONE OF THEM IS ALLOWED TO ESCAPE BACK TO THE OUTSIDE... AS IF THEY'VE BEEN CHOSEN FOR IT.
AND WHEN THEY DO, THEY GET... A PARTING GIFT.

As Hibiya searches for the missing Hiyori, a mysterious girl approaches him. Using her ability to impart memories and emotions directly into anyone she wants, she reveals the truth behind the Kagerou Daze. She fears a snake with the "clearing eyes" ability is attempting to unite all the snakes that gave the rest of this group their own eerie skills into a single entity—and now it might be here, in the "worst possible form."

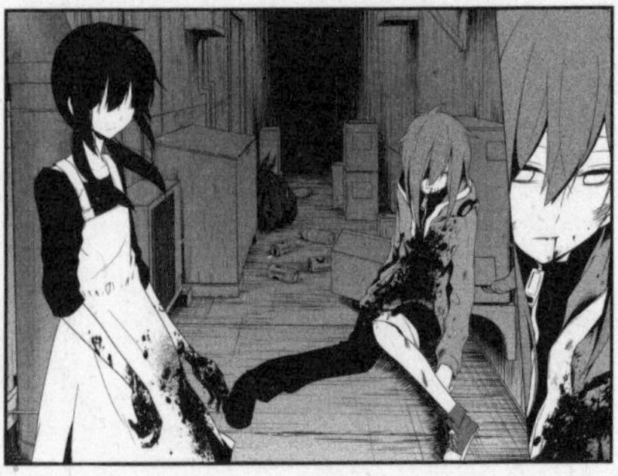

When Kano and Momo do find Hiyori, the scene is like something out of their worst nightmares: Hiyori, covered in blood, standing in front of a lifeless Kido. As he carries the fainted Momo back, Kano tells Ene about the lives of the Mekakushi-dan and how the snake has affected all of them.

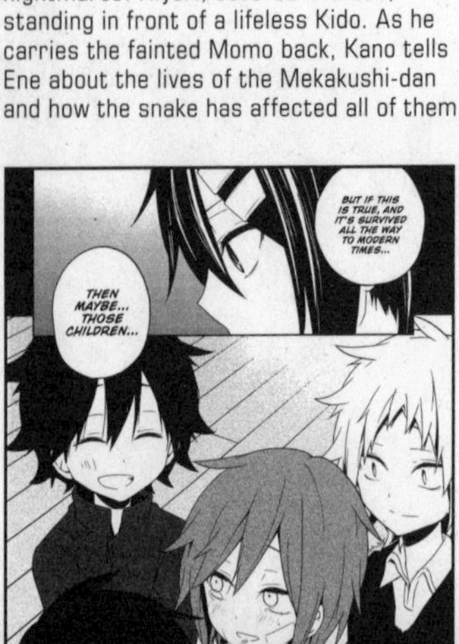
BUT IF THIS IS TRUE, AND IT'S SURVIVED ALL THE WAY TO MODERN TIMES...
THEN MAYBE... THOSE CHILDREN...

After awakening to their skills, Kido, Kano, and Seto spent their early years at a juvenile home. Ayaka, a researcher studying the Medusa myths of the past, decided to adopt the three of them, making them siblings to her own daughter, Ayano.

Kido, Kano, Seto, and Ayano formed the Mekakushi-dan, living as brothers and sisters despite no real blood relation. They are later joined by Marie, who stays after suddenly being brought to their doorstep.

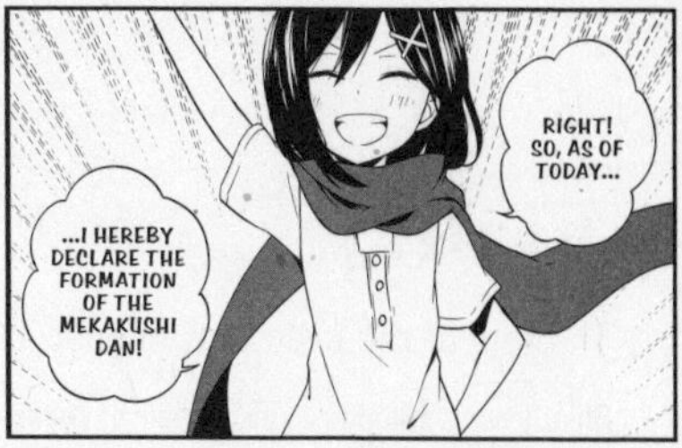
RIGHT! SO, AS OF TODAY...
...I HEREBY DECLARE THE FORMATION OF THE MEKAKUSHI DAN!

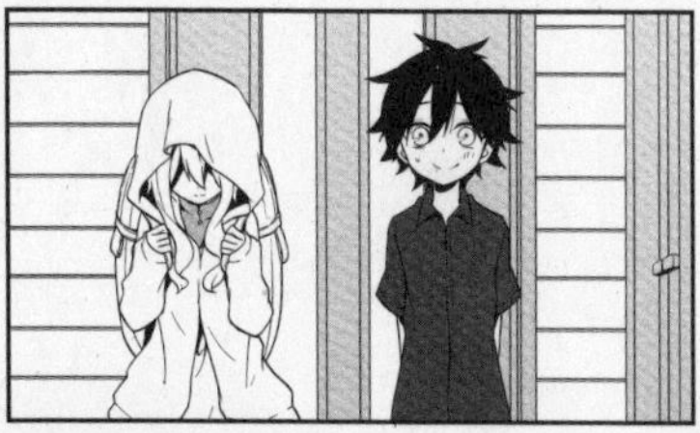

Once she realizes Marie is the child of a Medusa and that the children's abilities might affect their well-being—and their lives—Ayano resolves to protect her brothers and sisters.

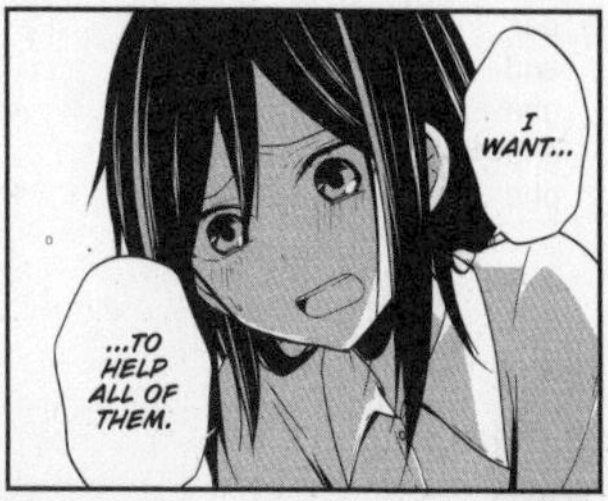
I WANT...
...TO HELP ALL OF THEM.

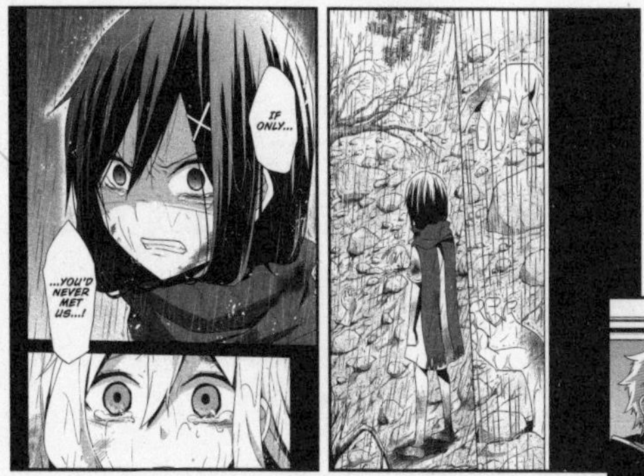
IF ONLY...
...YOU'D NEVER MET US...!

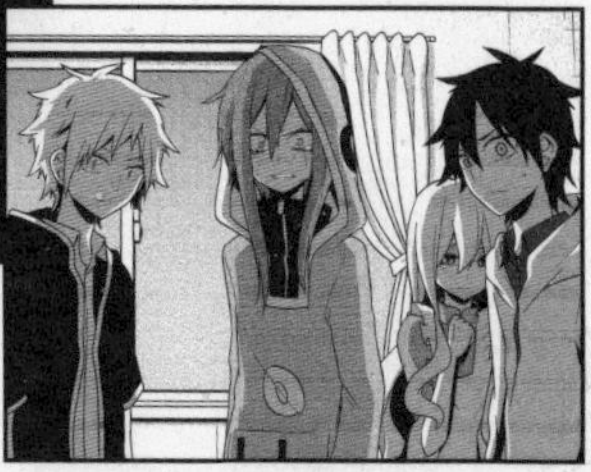

However, en route to Marie's home in search of clues that might explain the children's abilities, Ayano and her parents are killed in an accident. Swallowed up by the Kagerou Daze, Ayano gains her own snake ability along with an insight into the true nature of the Kagerou Daze. In light of what she has learned, Ayano determines the only way to put an end to the tragedy is to kill Marie. The other children vehemently refuse, but she presses on, chasing after the "clearing eyes" snake.

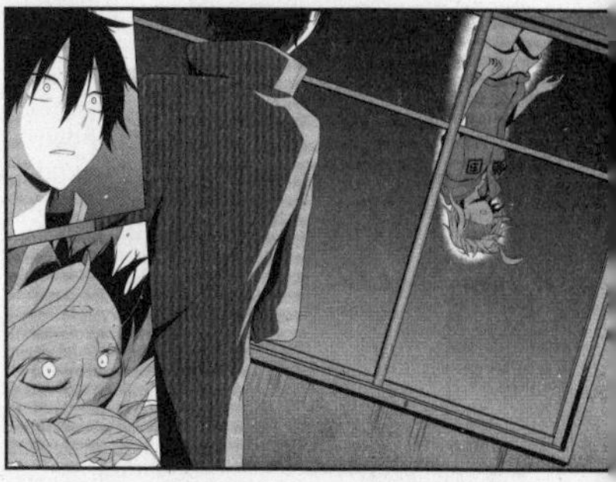

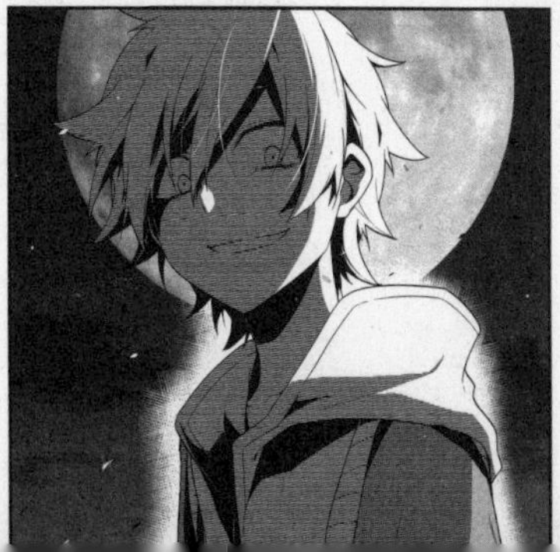

Meanwhile, Shintaro attempts to track down Momo, who has gone off to search for Hiyori. Kano tells him that the "focusing eyes" ability has housed itself within Hiyori, not Hibiya. At that moment, Shintaro spots Momo falling off of the building he's in—as Hibiya's maniacal laughter echoes from the roof...

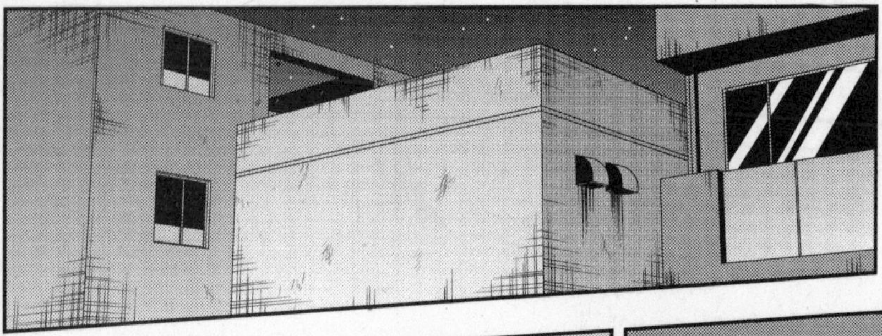
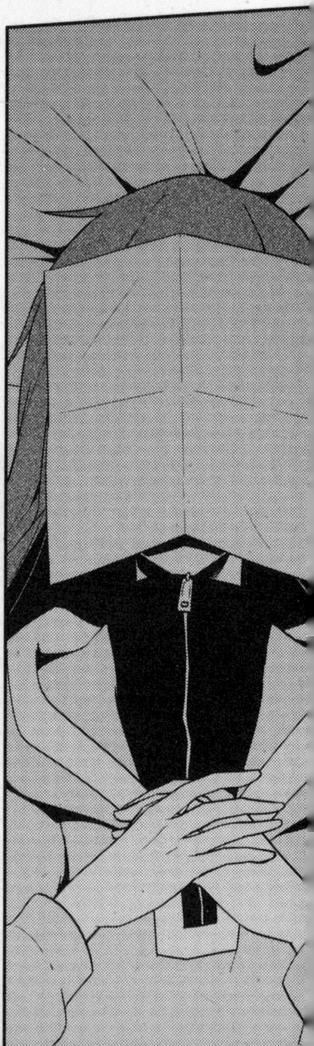
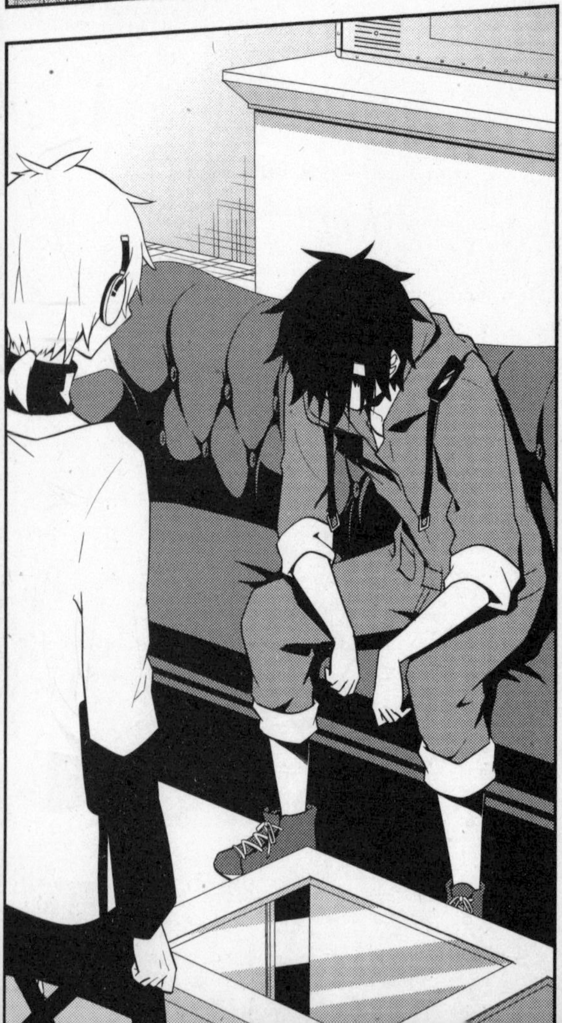

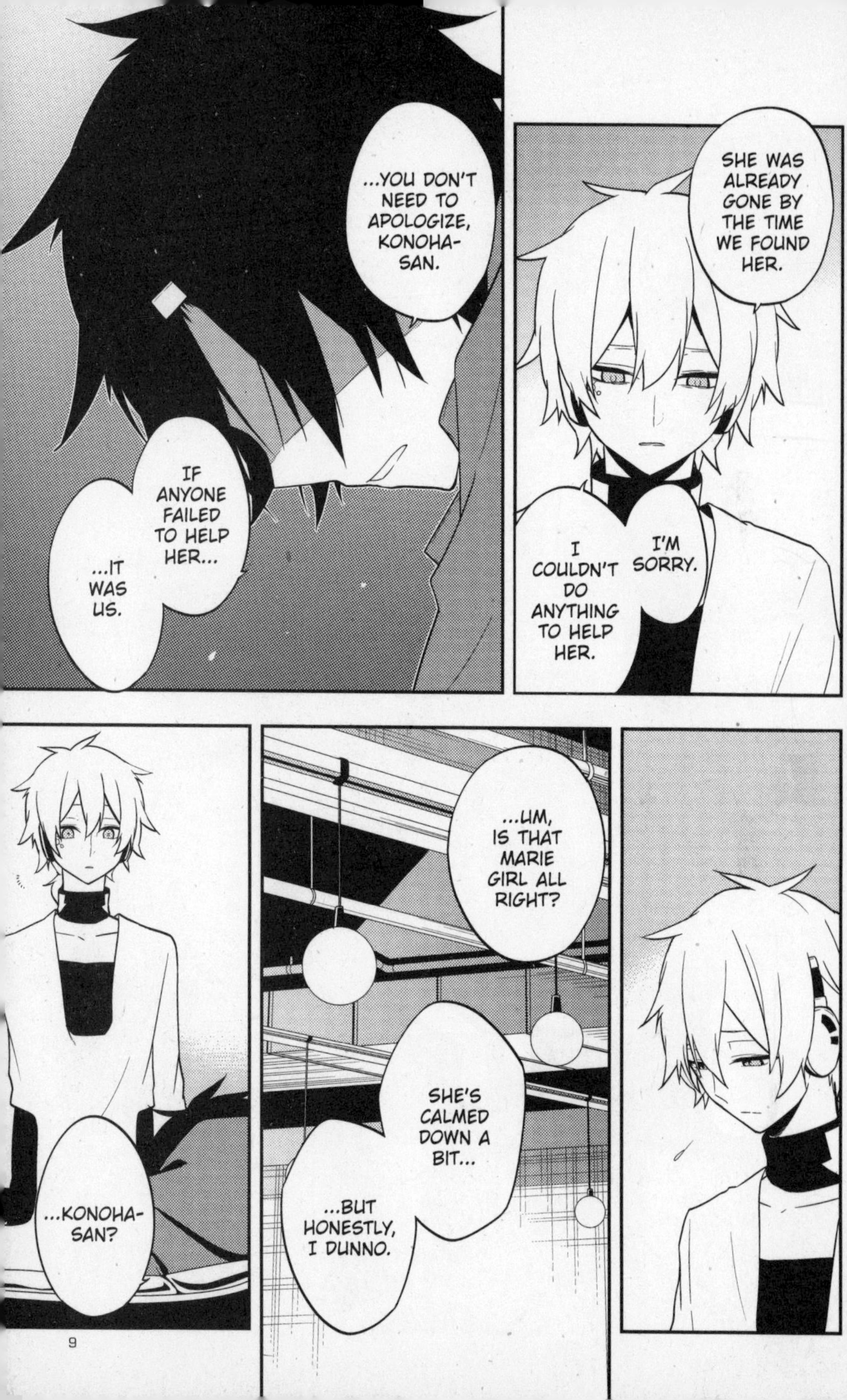
SHE WAS ALREADY GONE BY THE TIME WE FOUND HER.
I'M SORRY.
I COULDN'T DO ANYTHING TO HELP HER.
...YOU DON'T NEED TO APOLOGIZE, KONOHA-SAN.
IF ANYONE FAILED TO HELP HER...
...IT WAS US.
...UM, IS THAT MARIE GIRL ALL RIGHT?
SHE'S CALMED DOWN A BIT...
...BUT HONESTLY, I DUNNO.
...KONOHA-SAN?

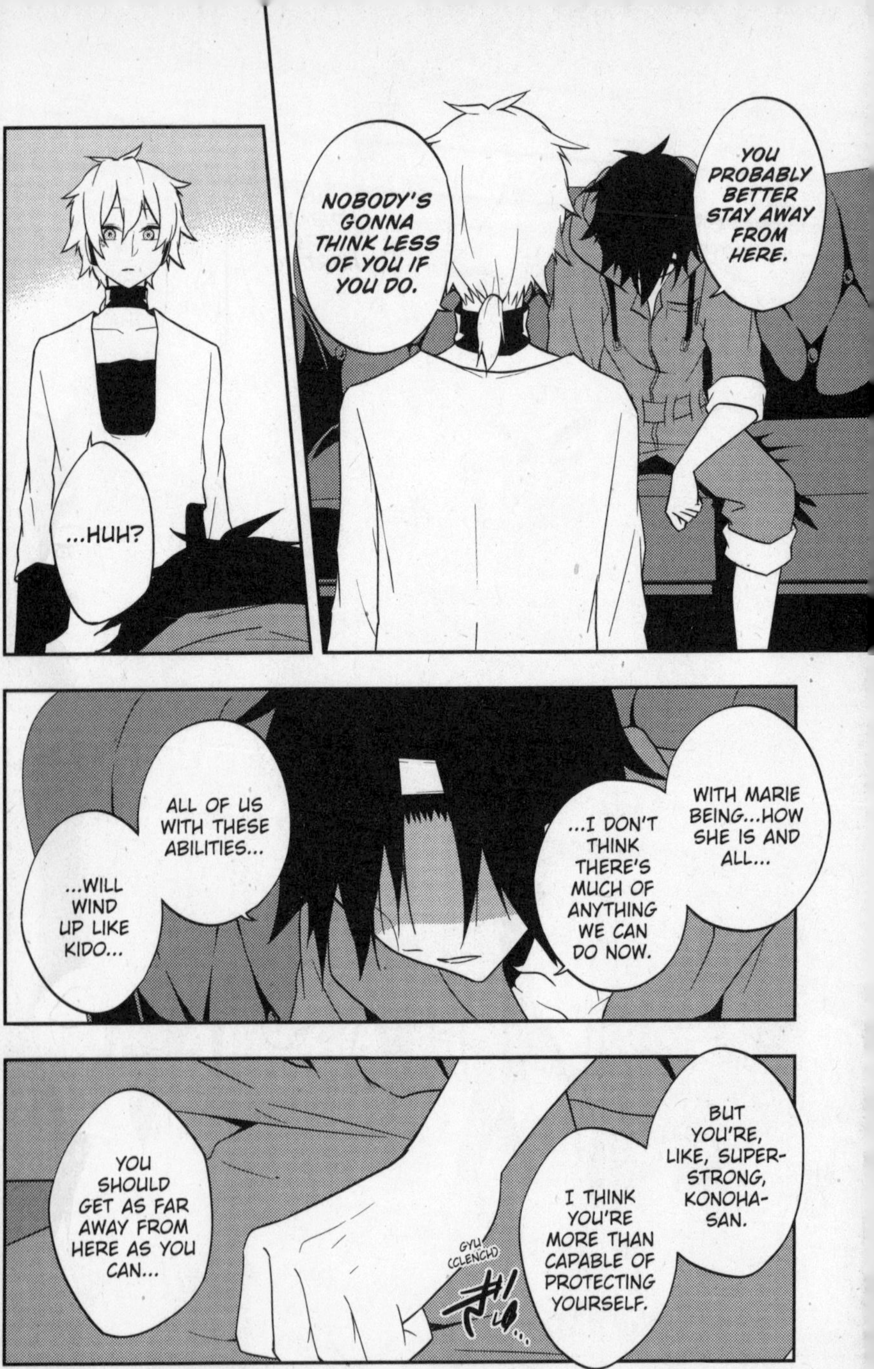
YOU PROBABLY BETTER STAY AWAY FROM HERE.
NOBODY'S GONNA THINK LESS OF YOU IF YOU DO.
...HUH?
WITH MARIE BEING...HOW SHE IS AND ALL...
...I DON'T THINK THERE'S MUCH OF ANYTHING WE CAN DO NOW.
ALL OF US WITH THESE ABILITIES...
...WILL WIND UP LIKE KIDO...
BUT YOU'RE, LIKE, SUPER-STRONG, KONOHA-SAN.
I THINK YOU'RE MORE THAN CAPABLE OF PROTECTING YOURSELF.
GYU (CLENCH)
YOU SHOULD GET AS FAR AWAY FROM HERE AS YOU CAN...

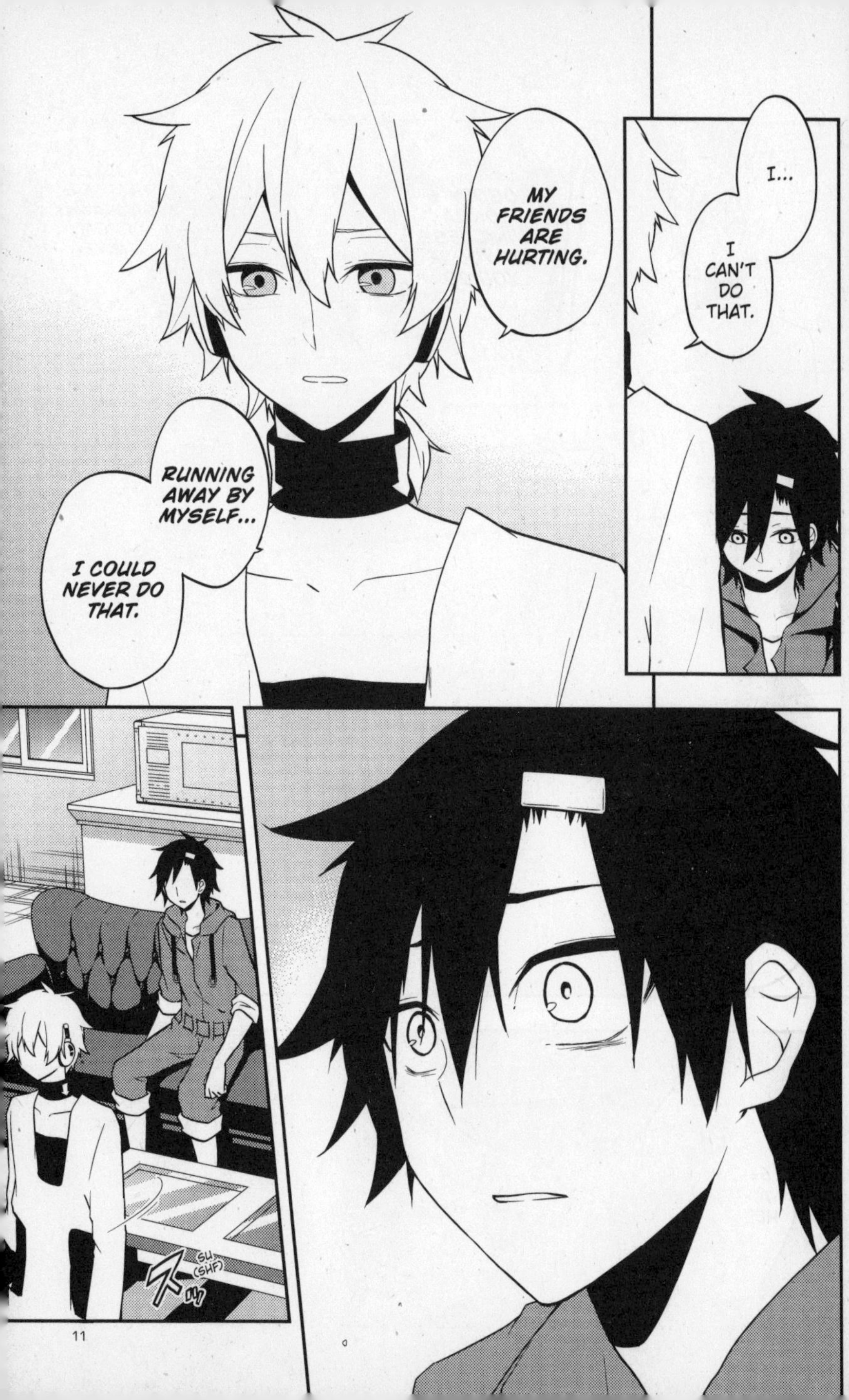
I...
I CAN'T DO THAT.
MY FRIENDS ARE HURTING.
RUNNING AWAY BY MYSELF...
I COULD NEVER DO THAT.
SU (SHF)

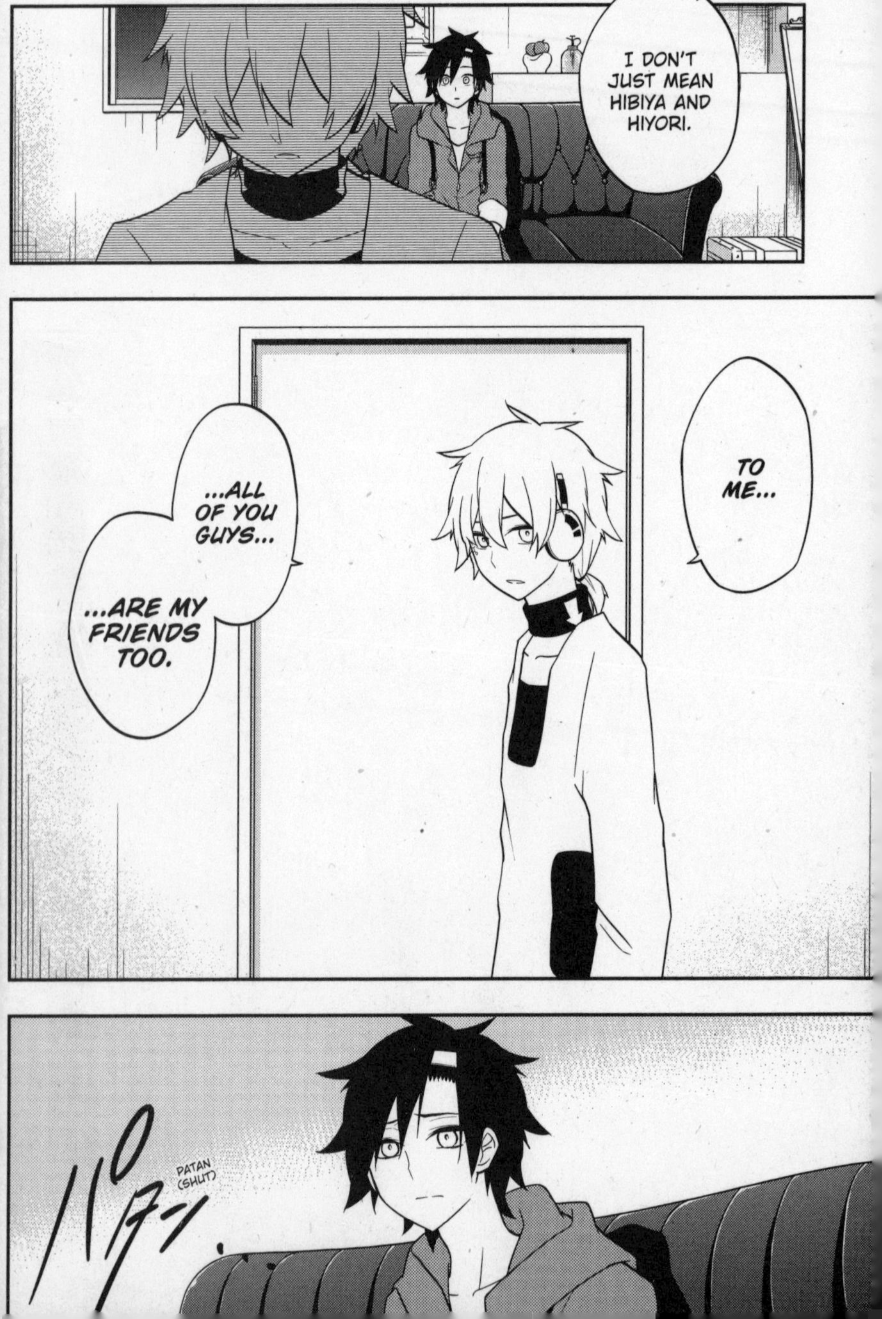
I DON'T JUST MEAN HIBIYA AND HIYORI.
TO ME...
...ALL OF YOU GUYS...
...ARE MY FRIENDS TOO.
パタン
PATAN (SHUT)

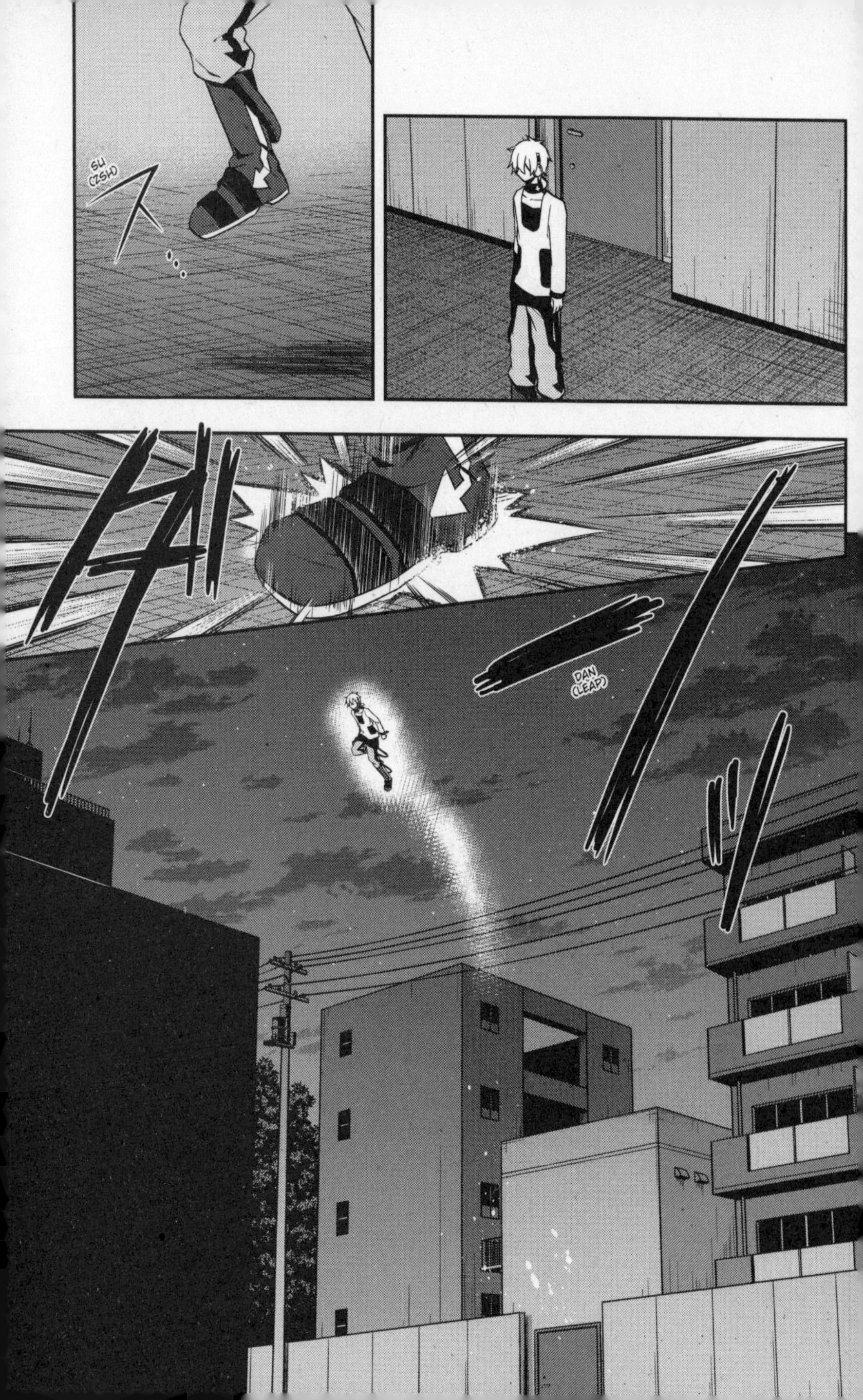
SU
(ZSH)
DAN
(LEAP)

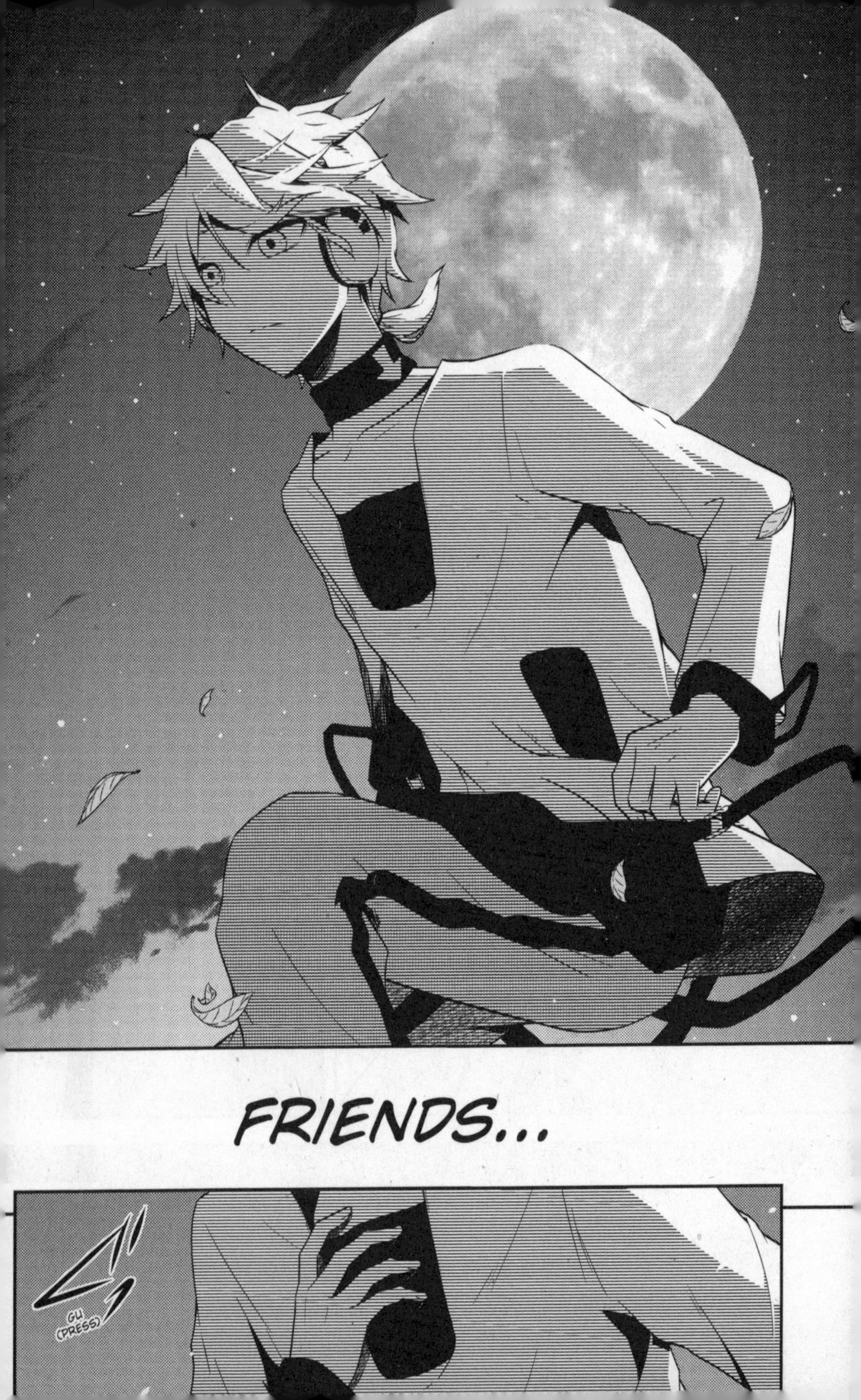
FRIENDS...
GU (PRESS)

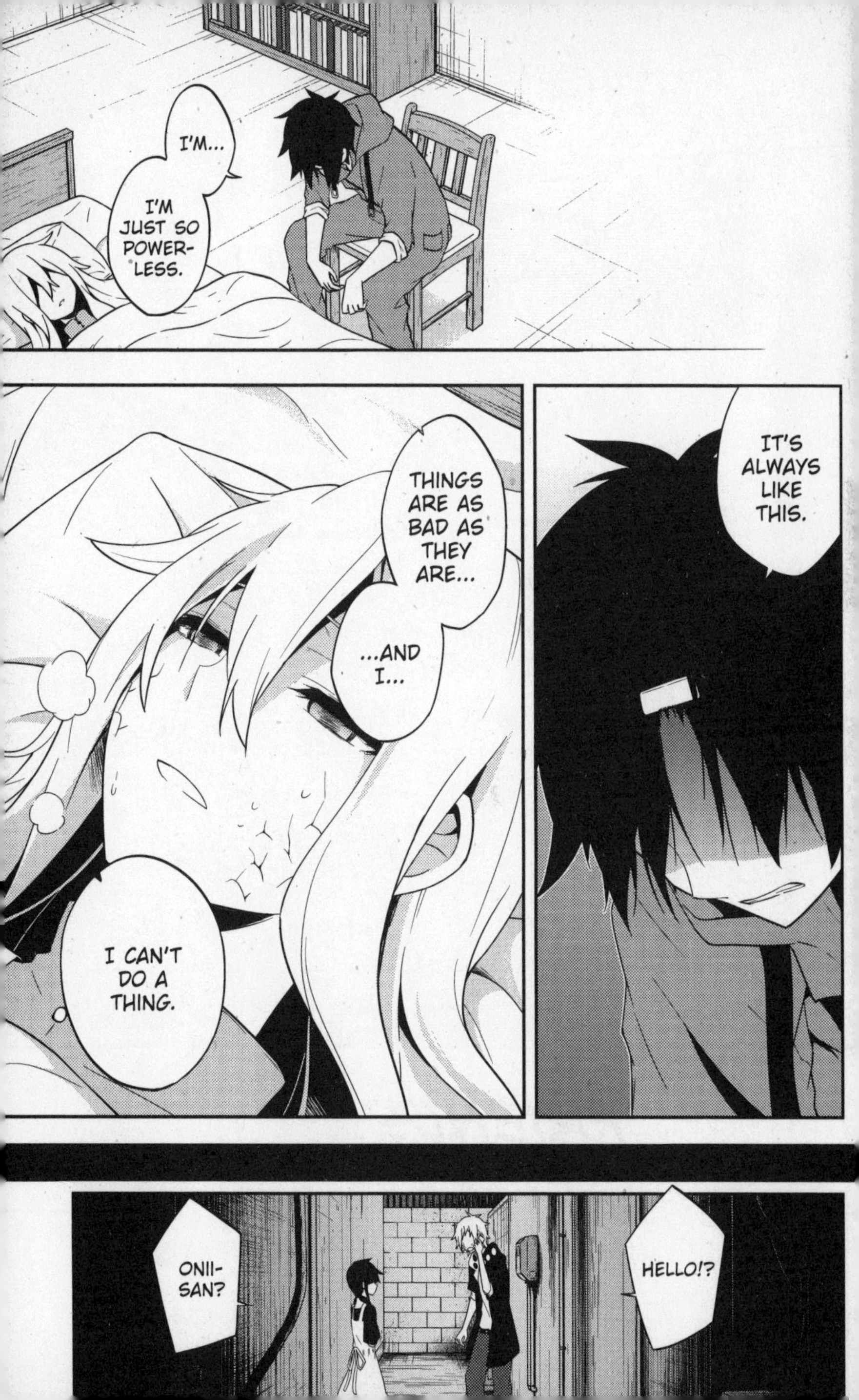
I'M...
I'M JUST SO POWER-LESS.
IT'S ALWAYS LIKE THIS.
THINGS ARE AS BAD AS THEY ARE...
...AND I...
I CAN'T DO A THING.
HELLO!?
ONII-SAN?

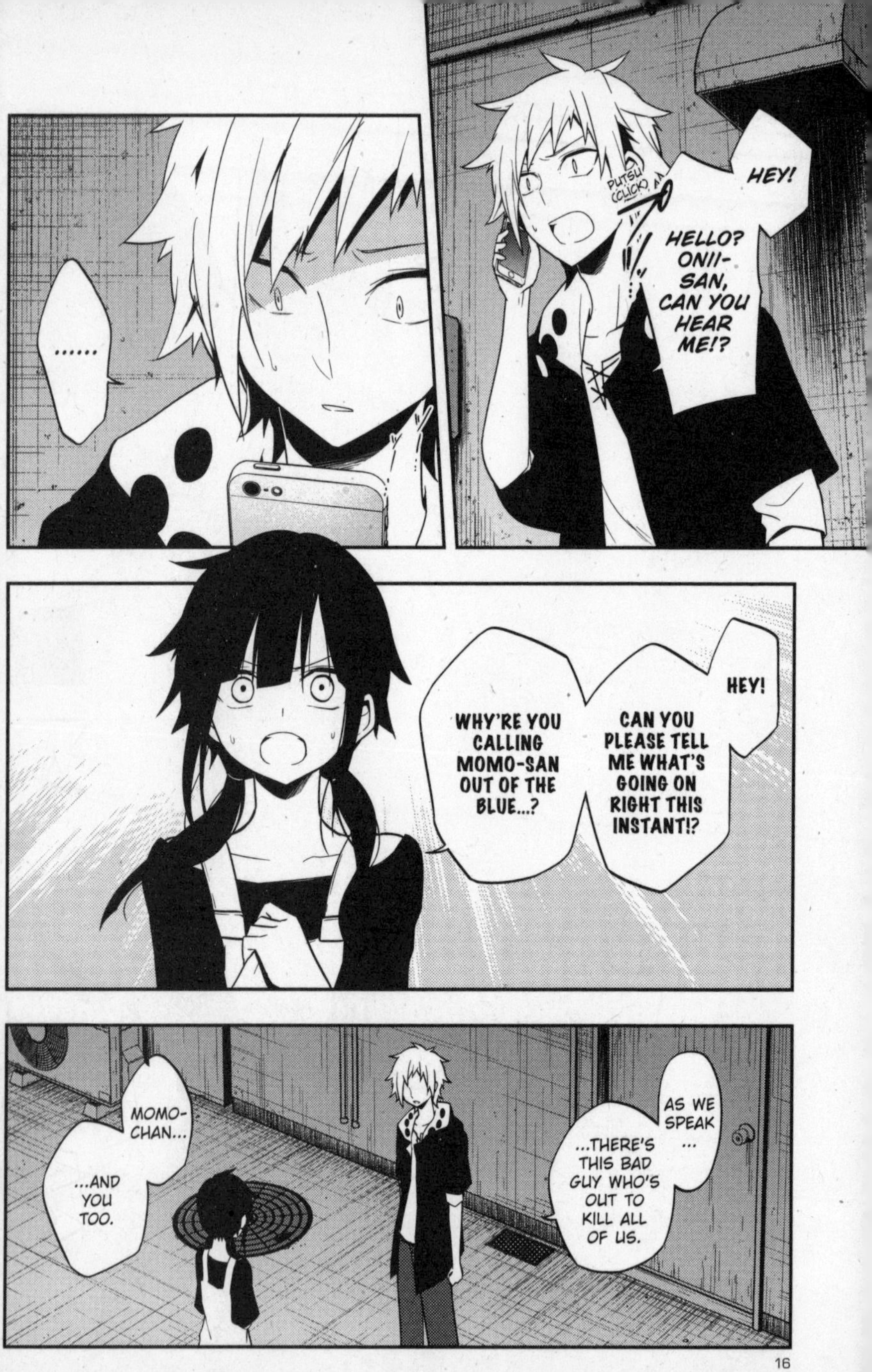
HEY!
PUTSU (CLICK)
HELLO? ONII-SAN, CAN YOU HEAR ME!?
......
HEY!
CAN YOU PLEASE TELL ME WHAT'S GOING ON RIGHT THIS INSTANT!?
WHY'RE YOU CALLING MOMO-SAN OUT OF THE BLUE...?
AS WE SPEAK...
...THERE'S THIS BAD GUY WHO'S OUT TO KILL ALL OF US.
MOMO-CHAN...
...AND YOU TOO.

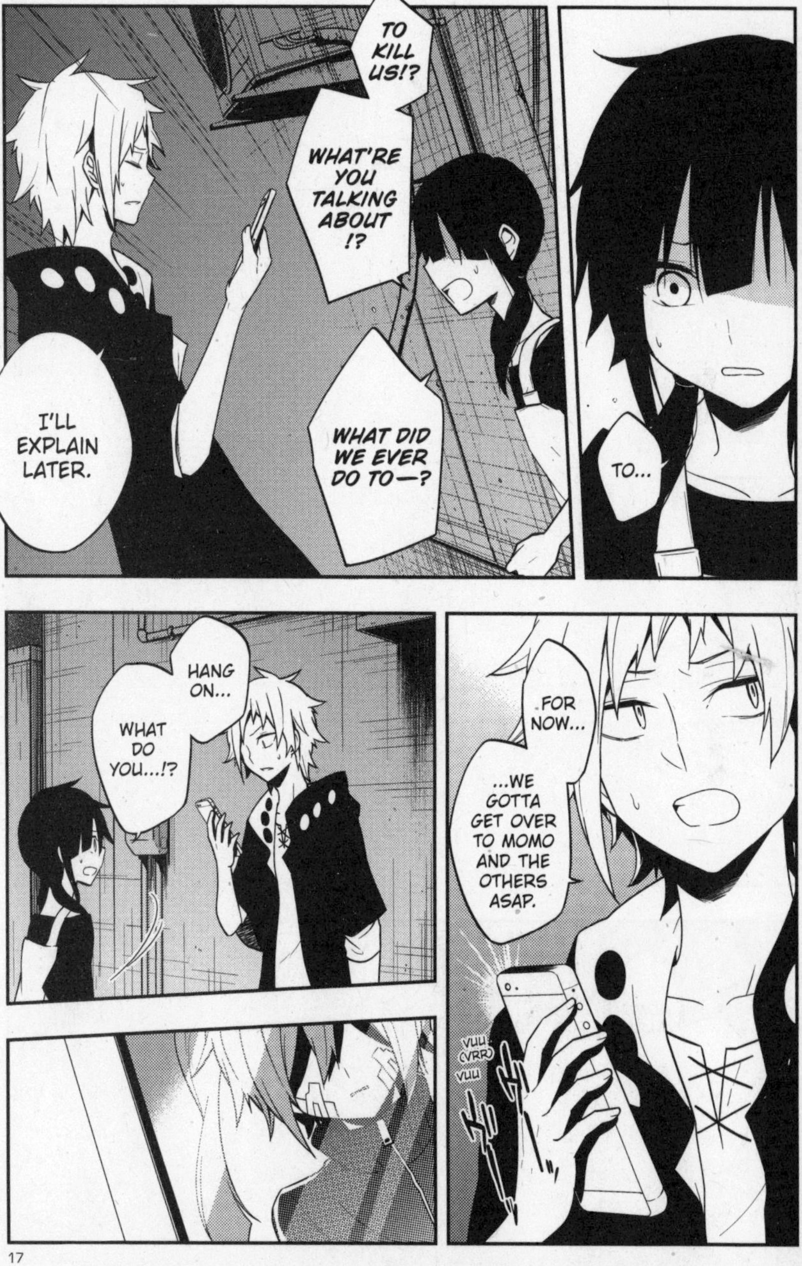
TO...
TO KILL US!?
WHAT'RE YOU TALKING ABOUT !?
WHAT DID WE EVER DO TO—?
I'LL EXPLAIN LATER.
FOR NOW...
...WE GOTTA GET OVER TO MOMO AND THE OTHERS ASAP.
VUU (VRR) VUU
HANG ON...
WHAT DO YOU...!?

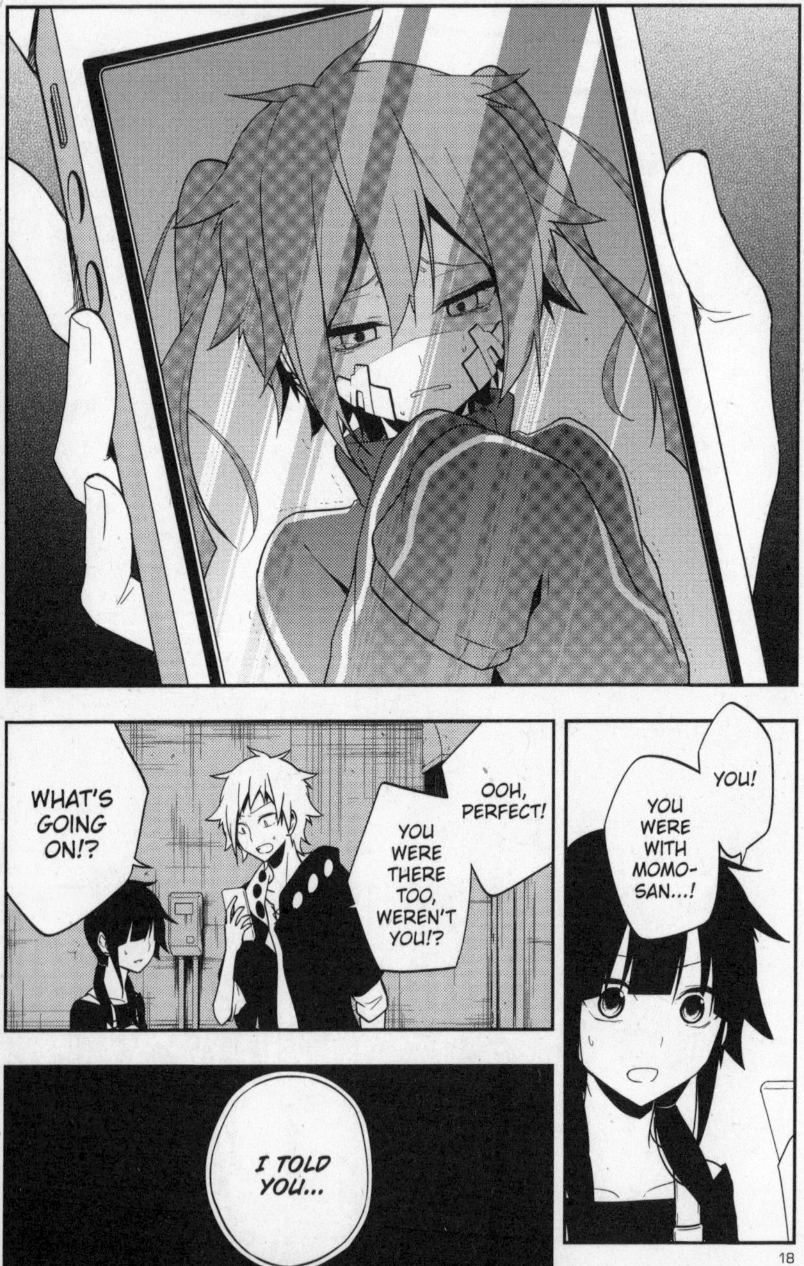
YOU!
YOU WERE WITH MOMO-SAN...!
OOH, PERFECT!
YOU WERE THERE TOO, WEREN'T YOU!?
WHAT'S GOING ON!?
I TOLD YOU...

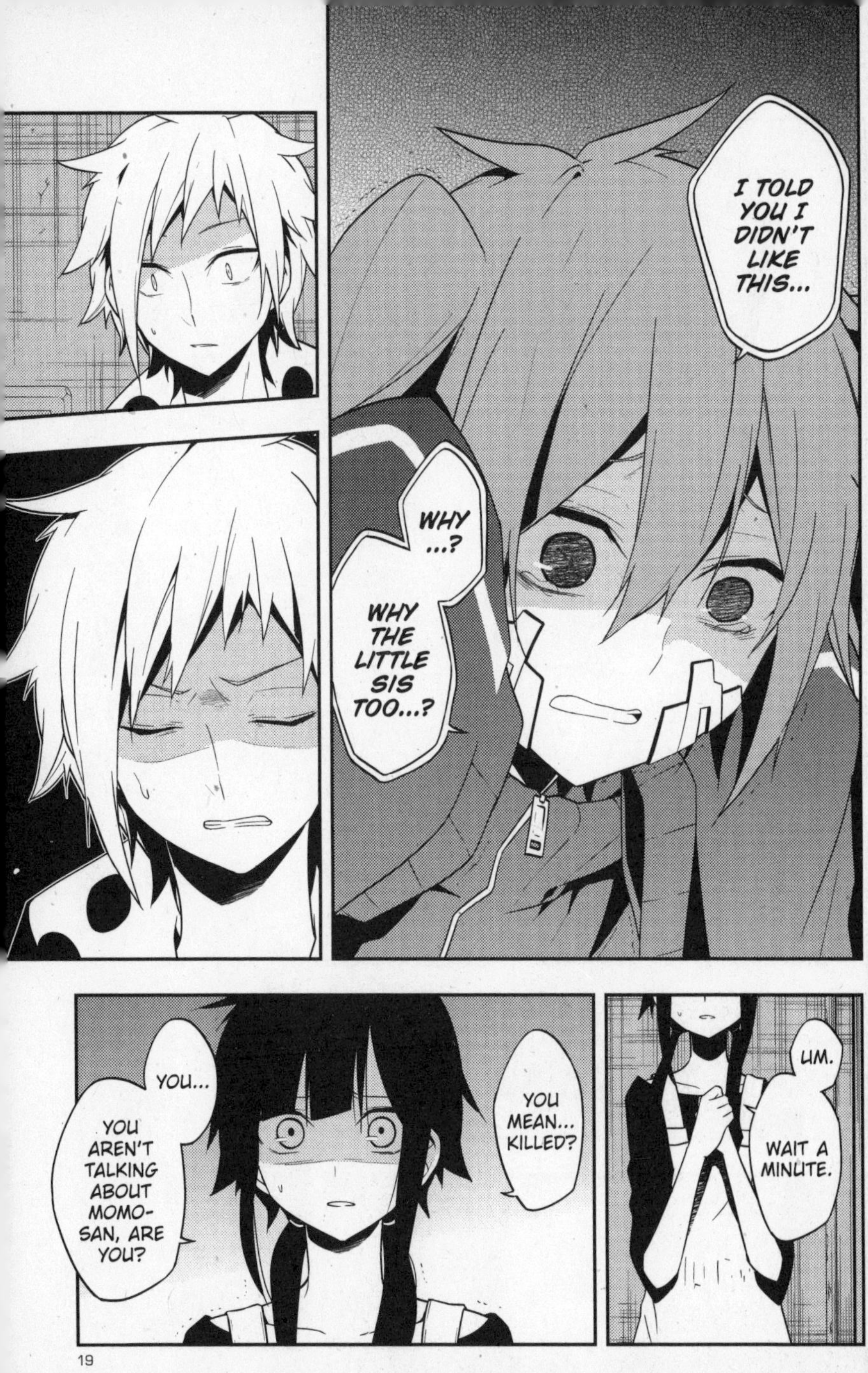
I TOLD YOU I DIDN'T LIKE THIS...
WHY ...?
WHY THE LITTLE SIS TOO...?
UM.
WAIT A MINUTE.
YOU MEAN... KILLED?
YOU...
YOU AREN'T TALKING ABOUT MOMO-SAN, ARE YOU?

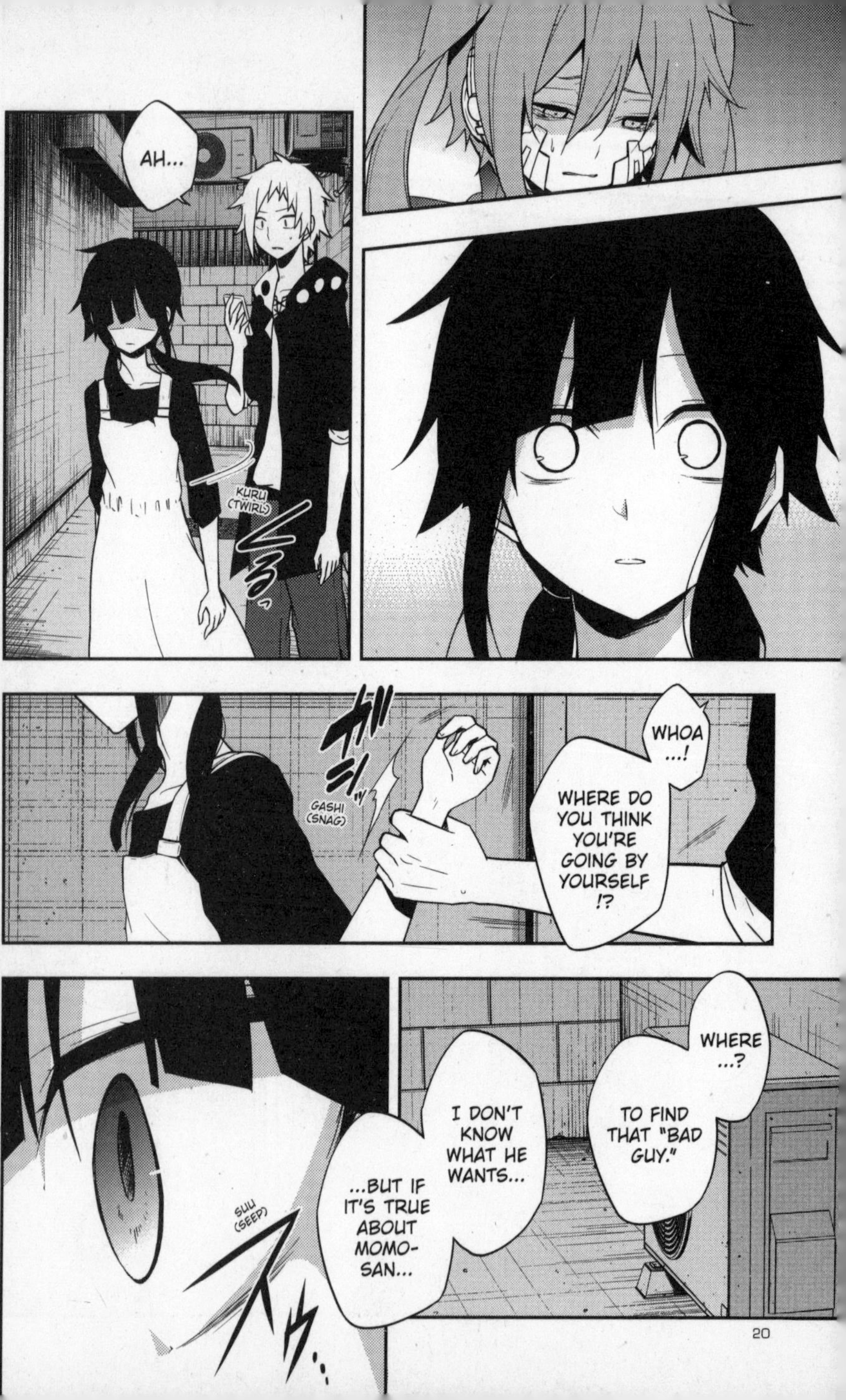
AH...
KURU (TWIRL)
WHOA ...!
WHERE DO YOU THINK YOU'RE GOING BY YOURSELF !?
GASHI (SNAG)
WHERE ...?
TO FIND THAT "BAD GUY."
I DON'T KNOW WHAT HE WANTS...
...BUT IF IT'S TRUE ABOUT MOMO-SAN...
SUU (SEEP)

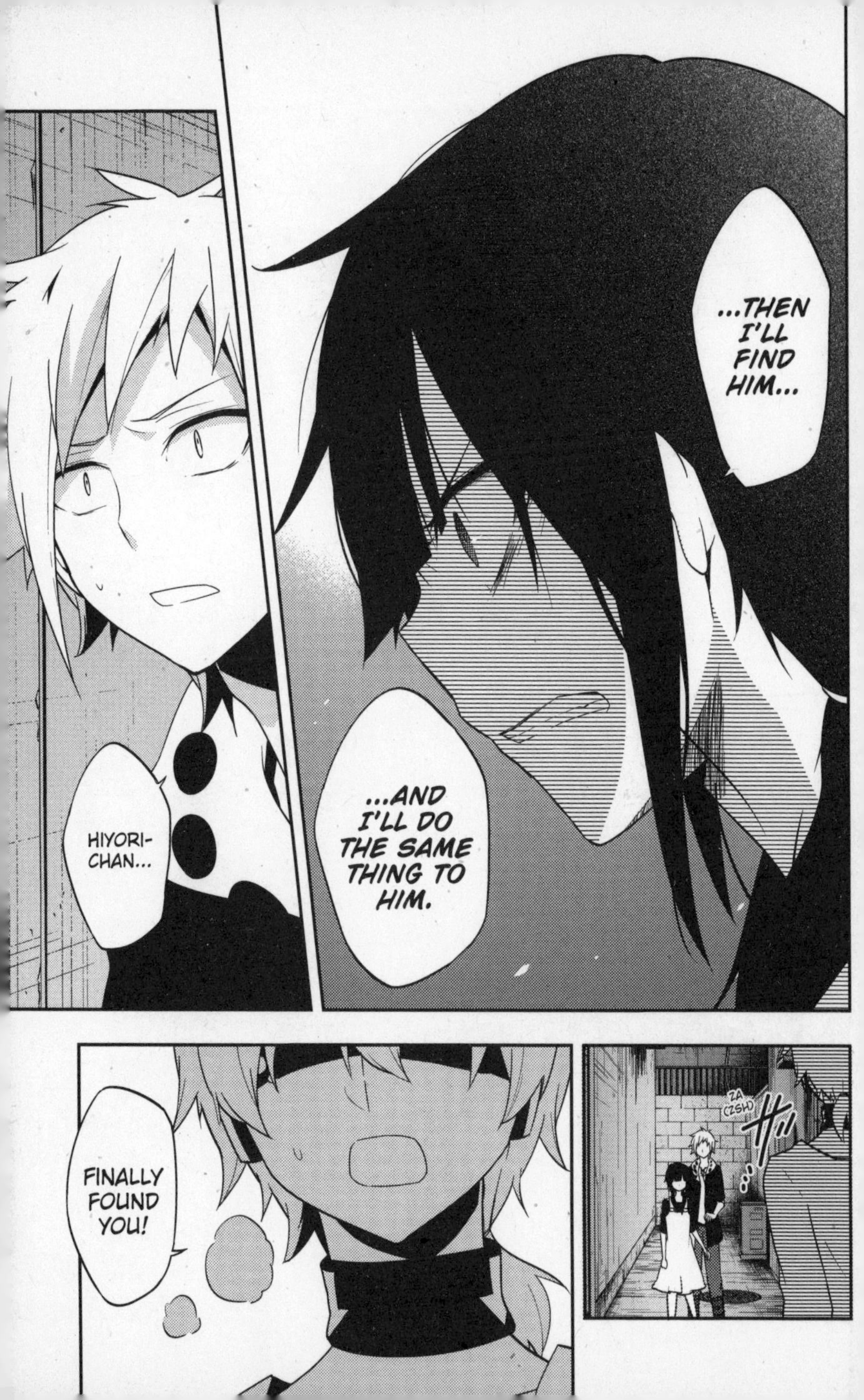
...THEN I'LL FIND HIM...
...AND I'LL DO THE SAME THING TO HIM.
HIYORI-CHAN...
ZA (ZSH)
FINALLY FOUND YOU!

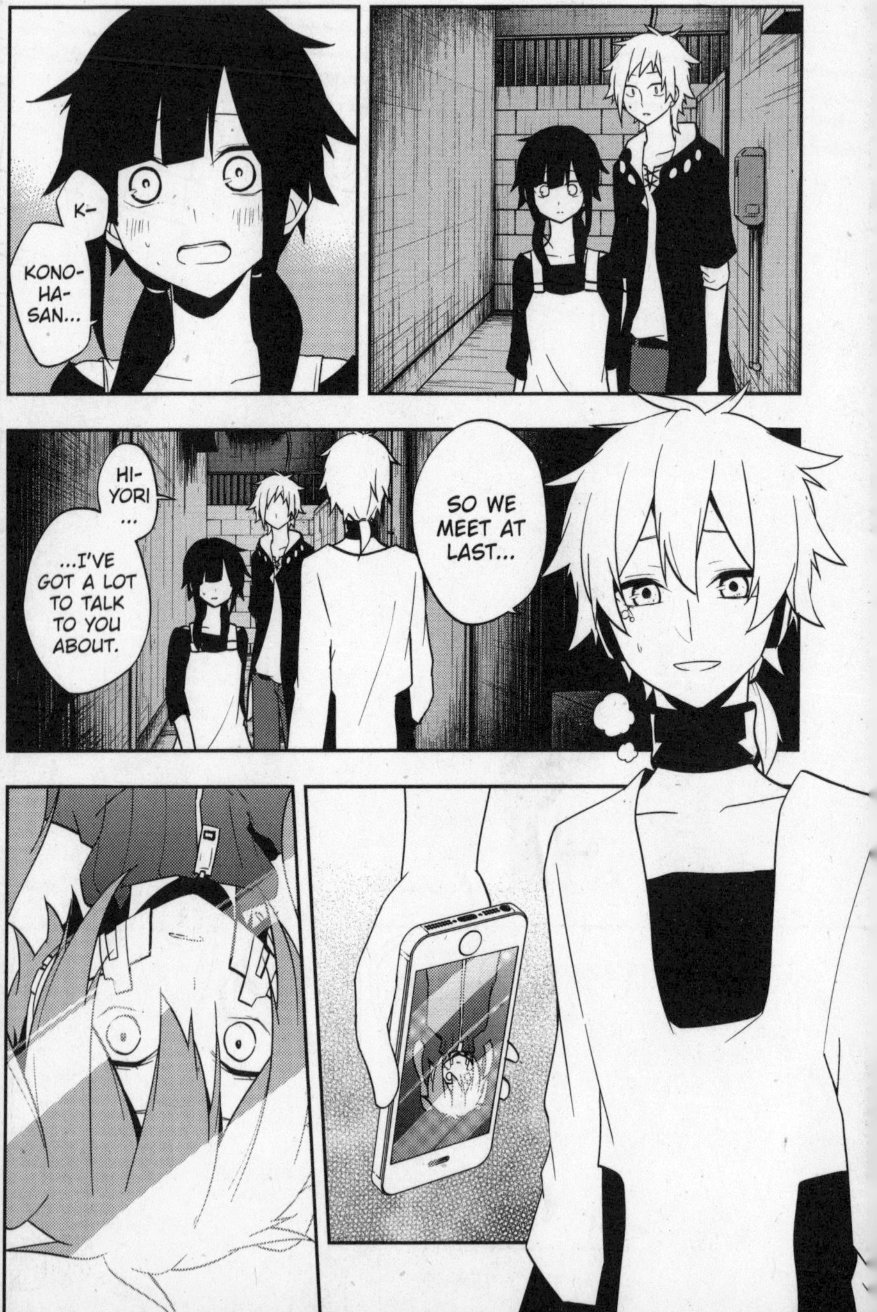
K–
KONO-HA-SAN...
SO WE MEET AT LAST...
HI-YORI ...
...I'VE GOT A LOT TO TALK TO YOU ABOUT.

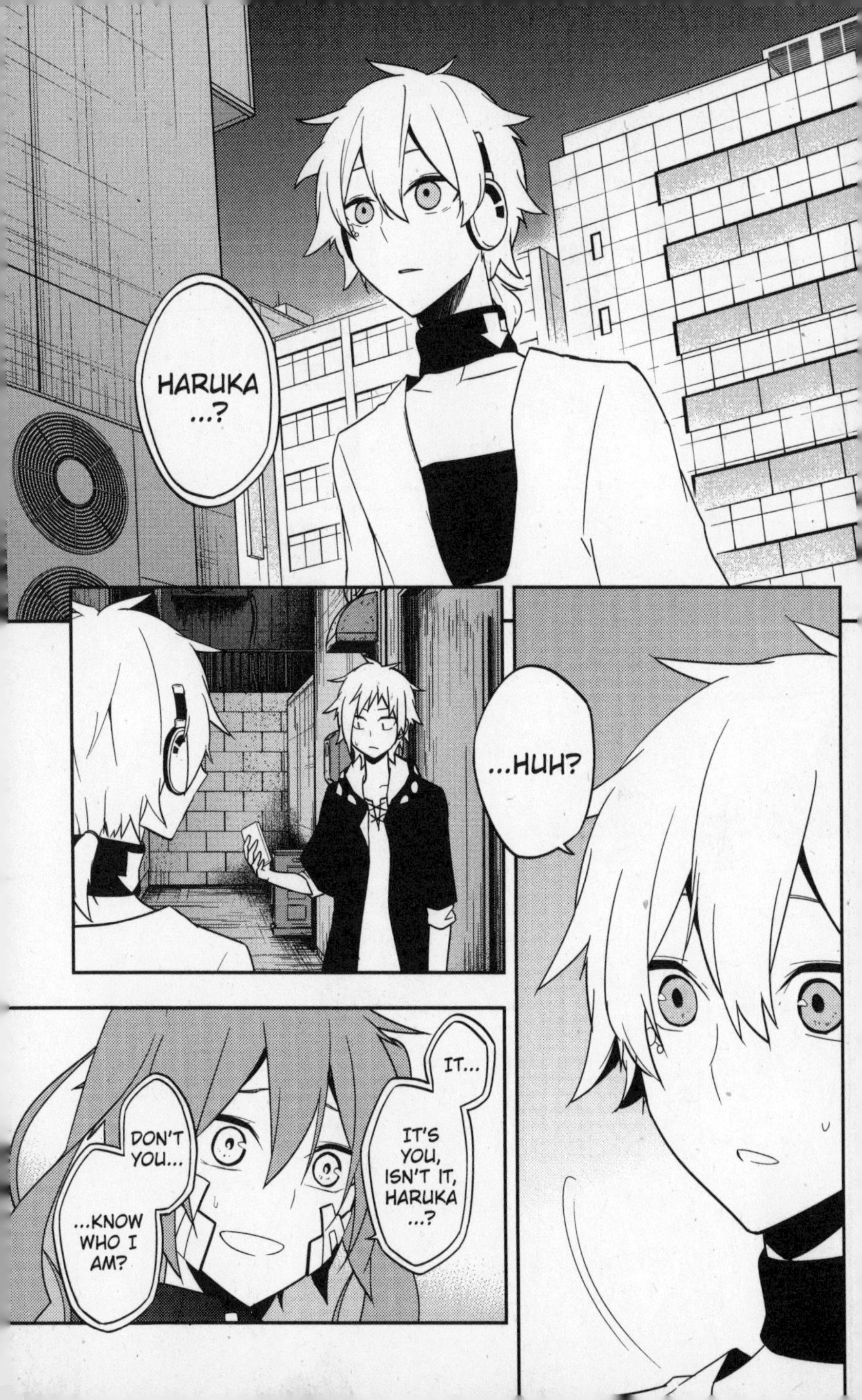
HARUKA ...?
...HUH?
IT...
IT'S YOU, ISN'T IT, HARUKA ...?
DON'T YOU...
...KNOW WHO I AM?

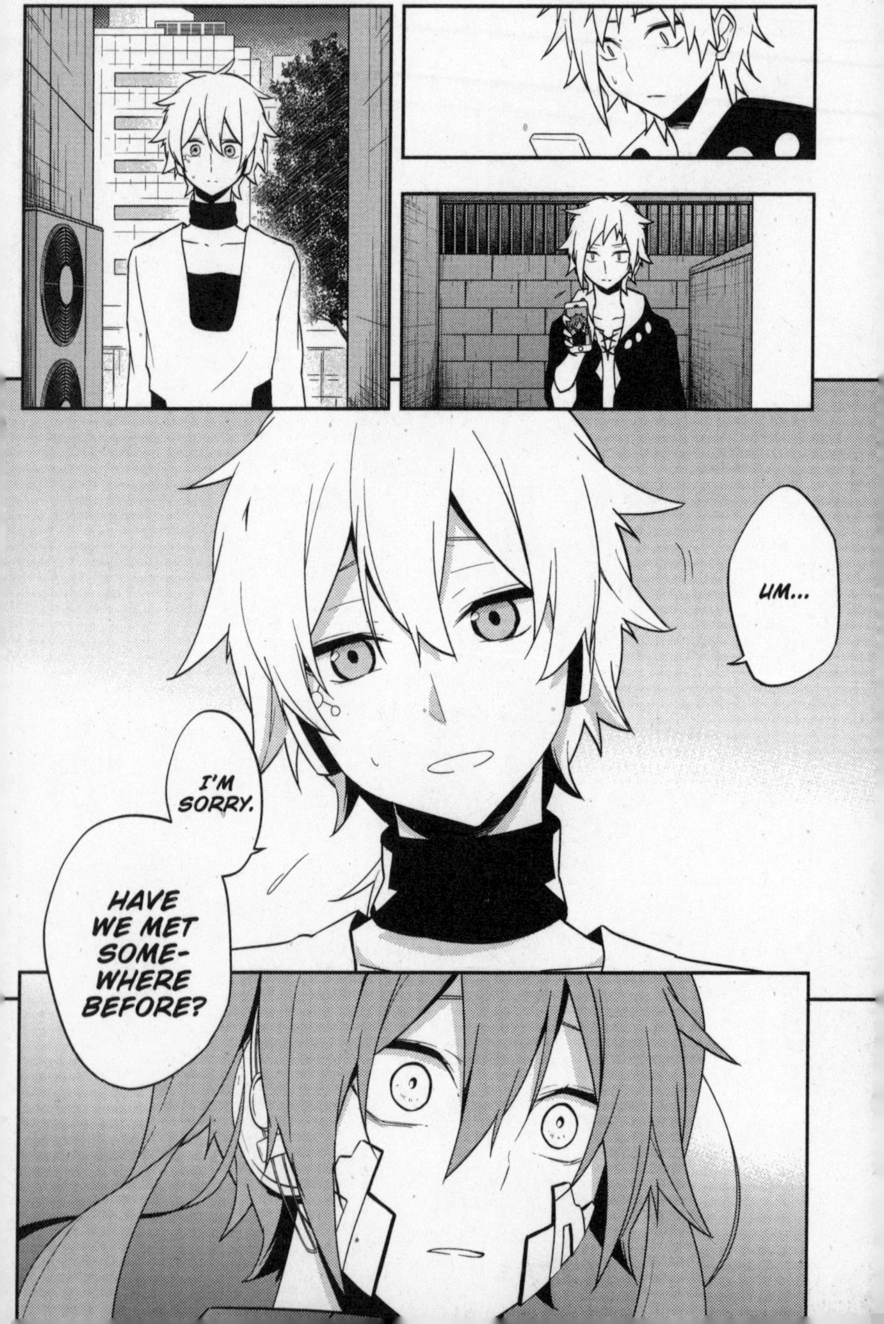
UM...
I'M SORRY.
HAVE WE MET SOME-WHERE BEFORE?

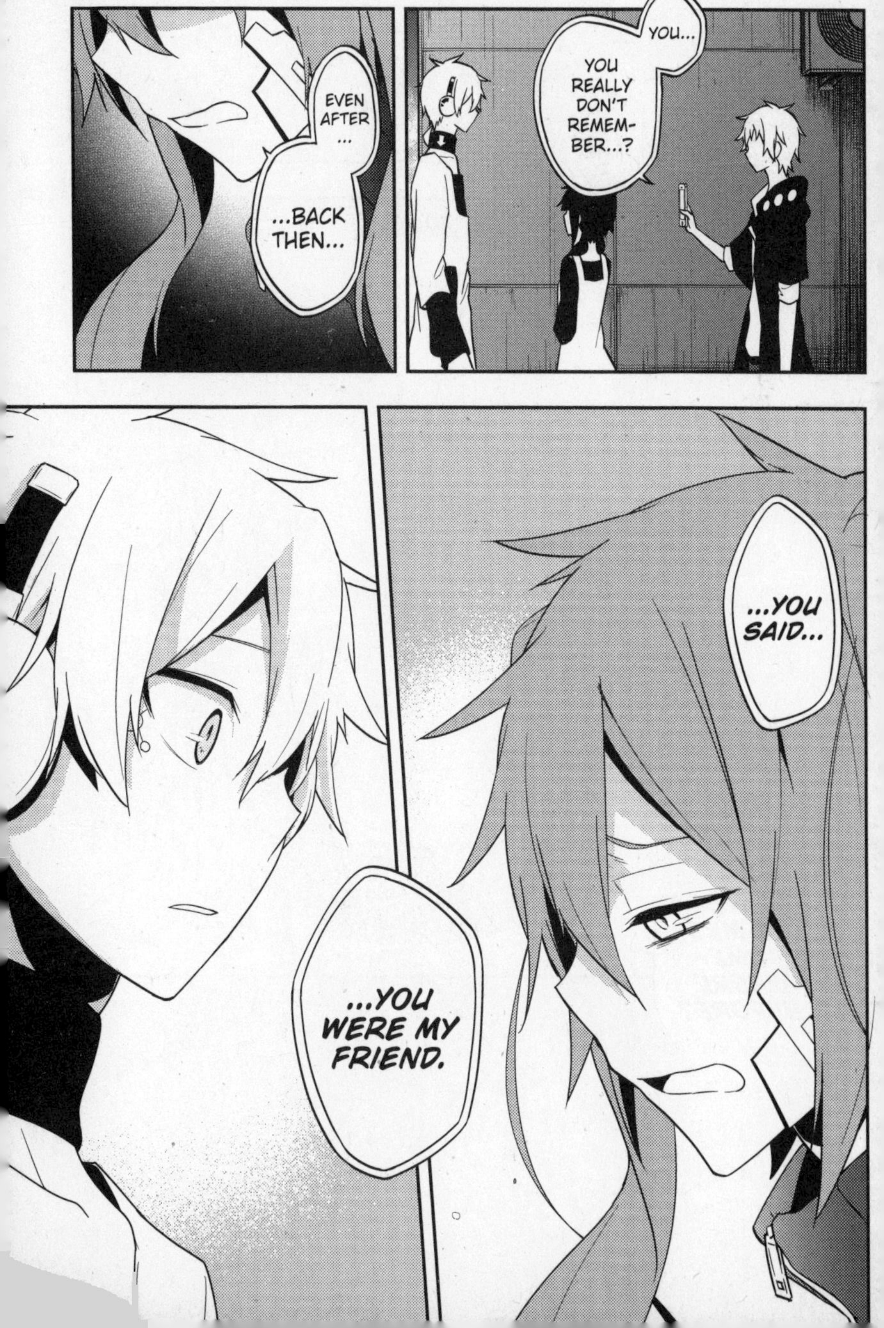
YOU...
YOU REALLY DON'T REMEM-BER...?
EVEN AFTER...
...BACK THEN...
...YOU SAID...
...YOU WERE MY FRIEND.

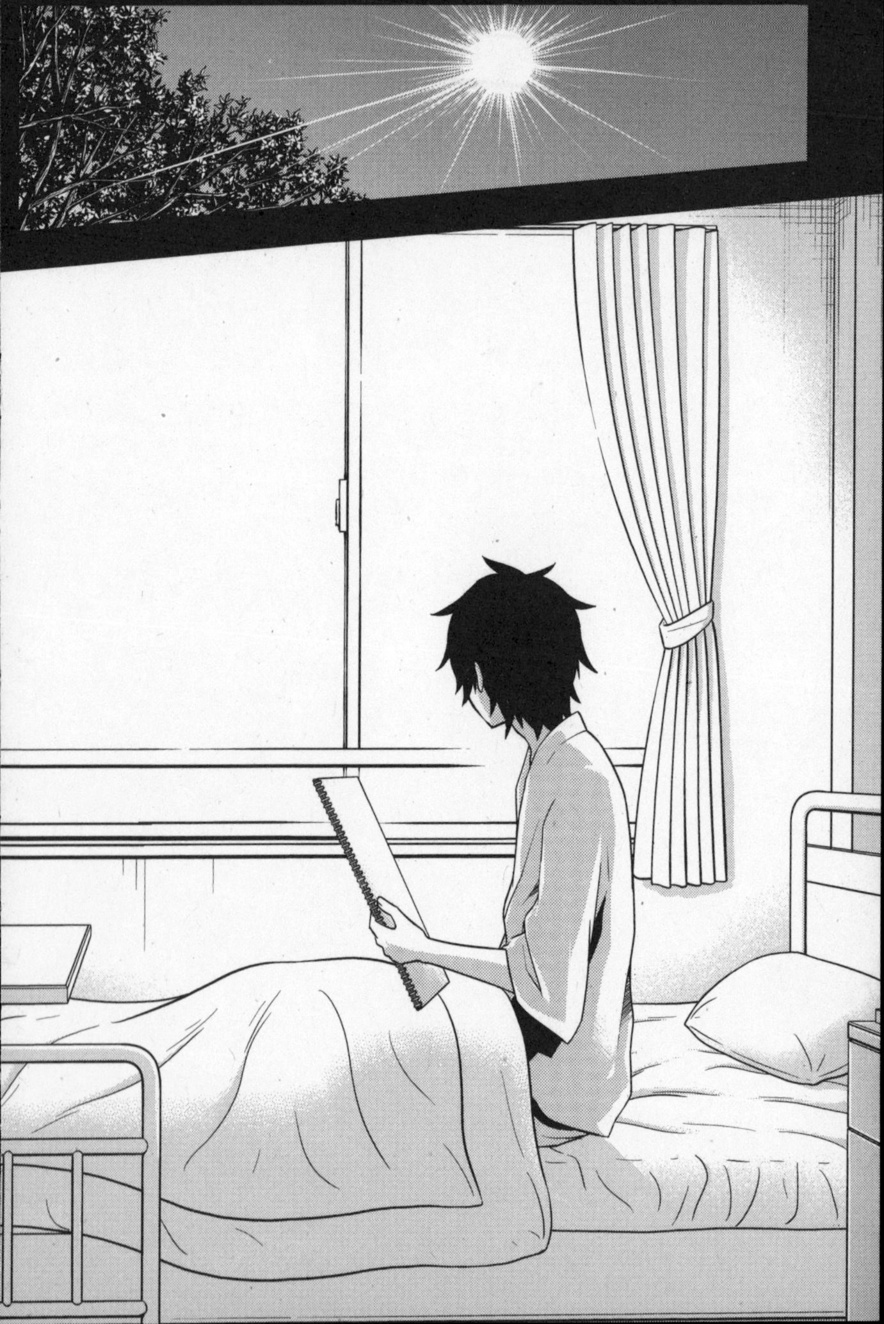

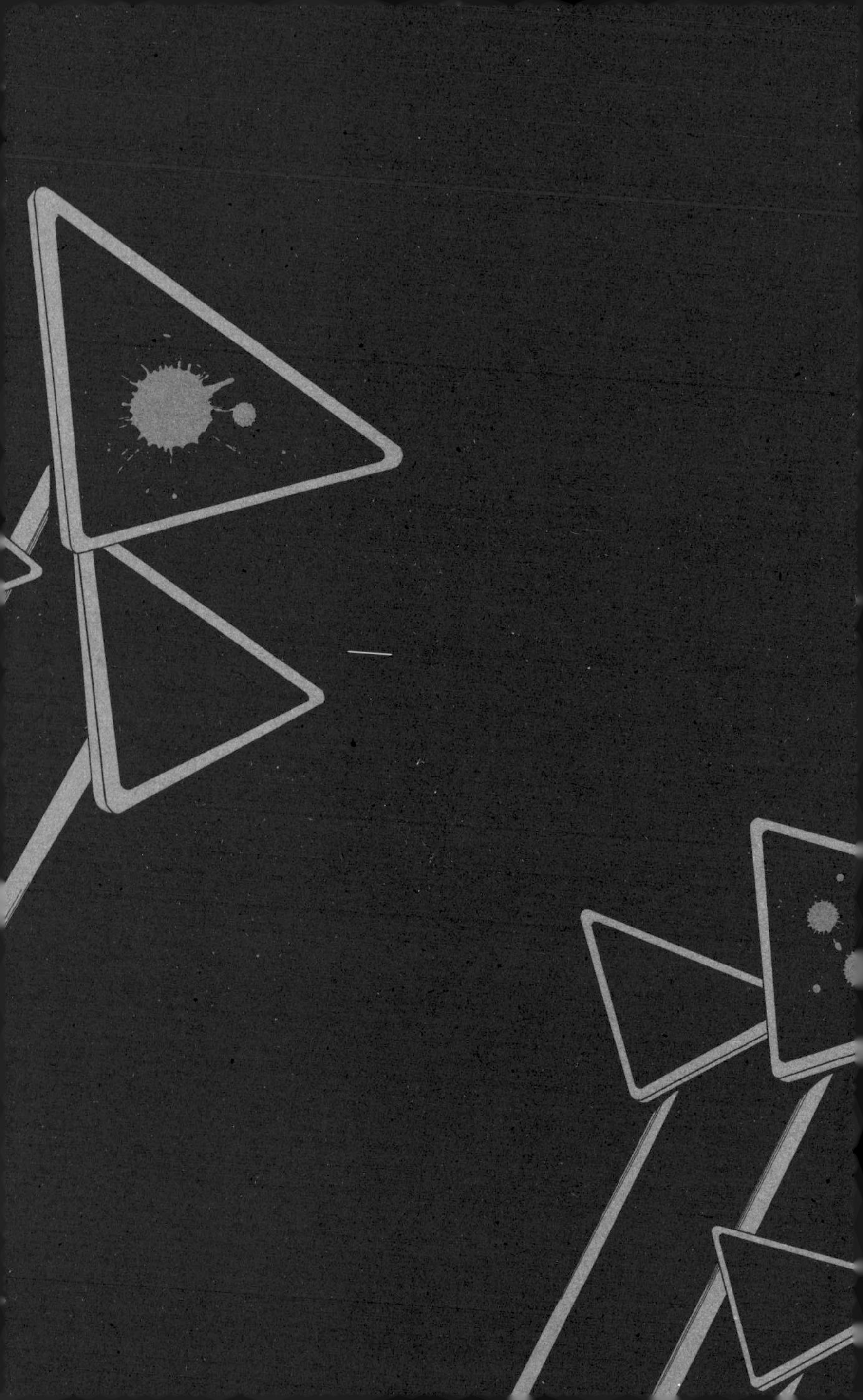

58 >> LOST DAZE II

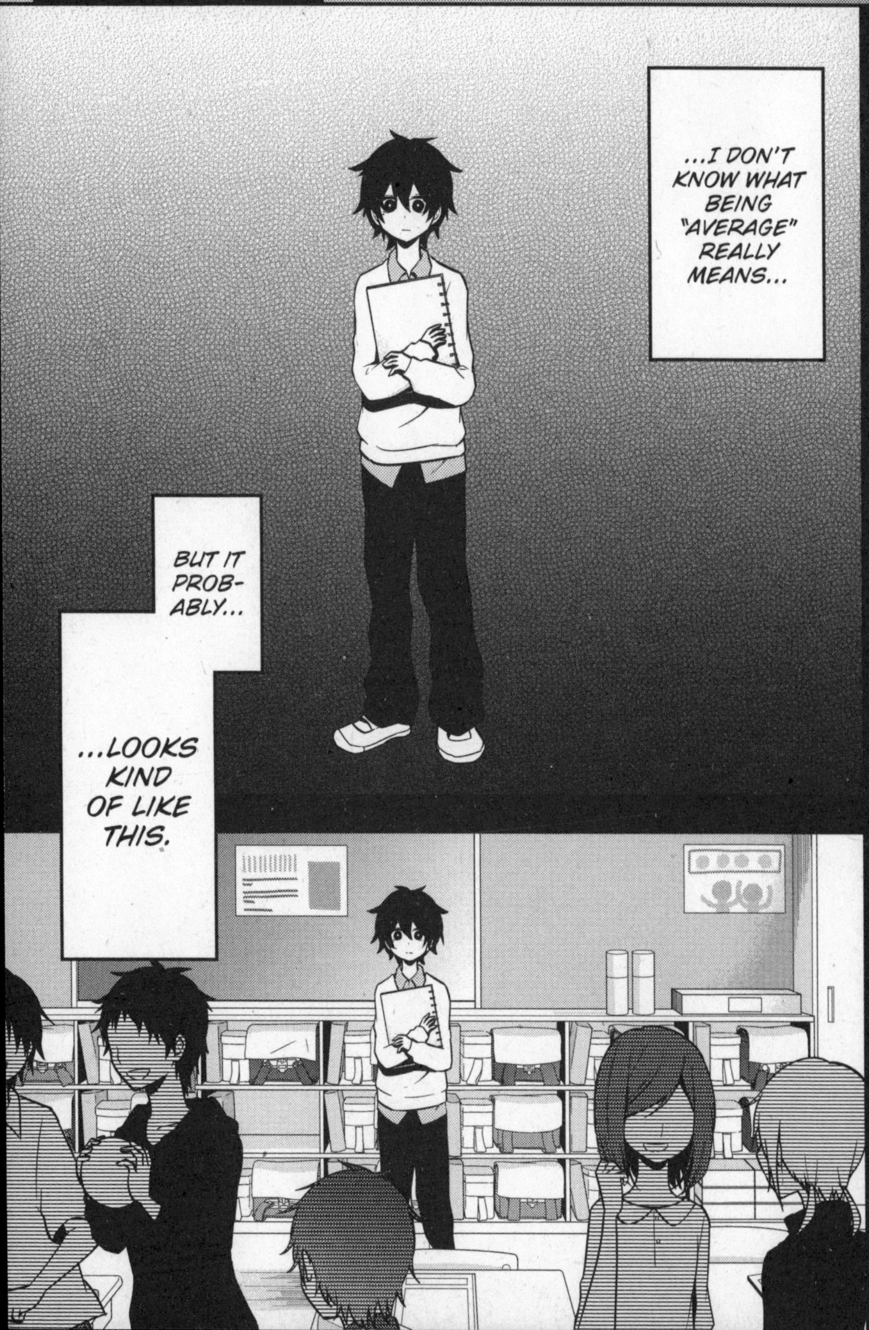
...I DON'T KNOW WHAT BEING "AVERAGE" REALLY MEANS...
BUT IT PROBABLY...
...LOOKS KIND OF LIKE THIS.

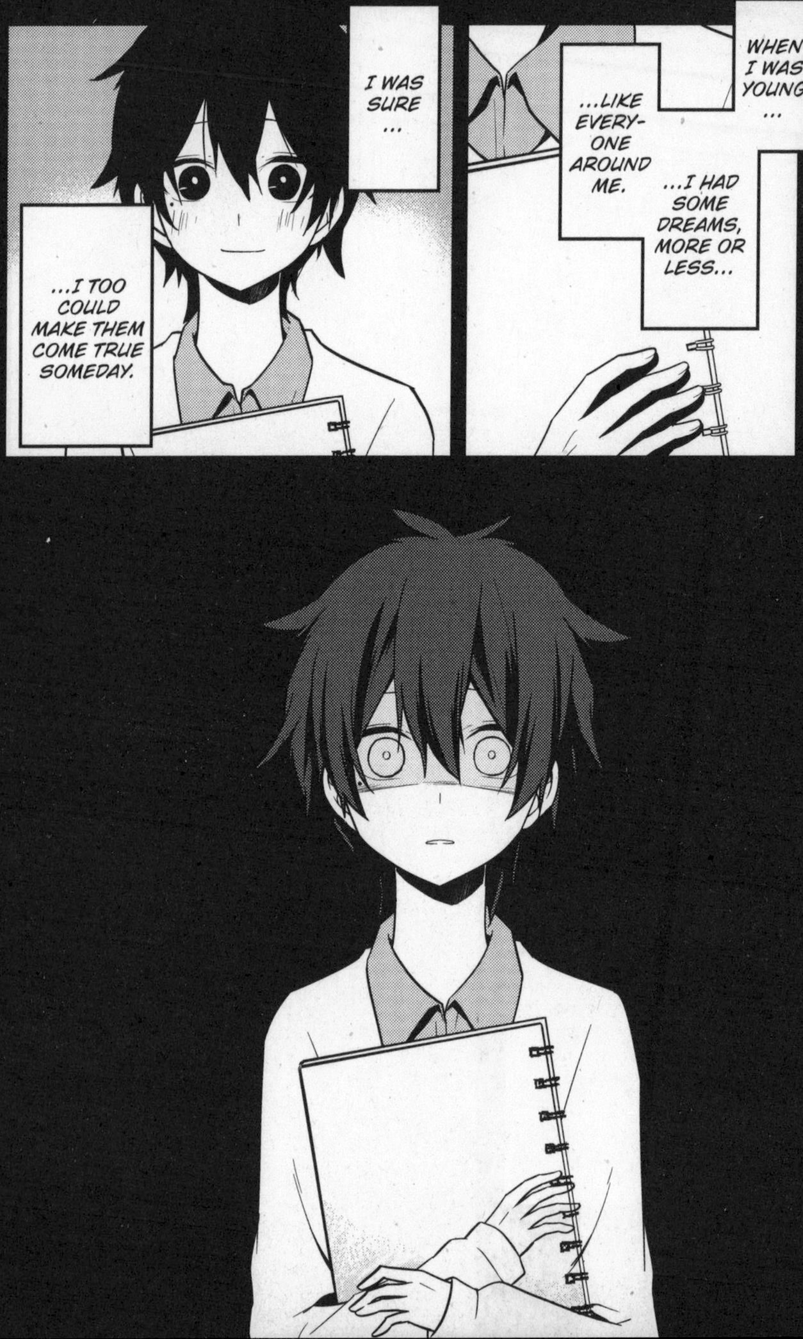
WHEN I WAS YOUNG...
...I HAD SOME DREAMS, MORE OR LESS...
...LIKE EVERY-ONE AROUND ME.
I WAS SURE...
...I TOO COULD MAKE THEM COME TRUE SOMEDAY.

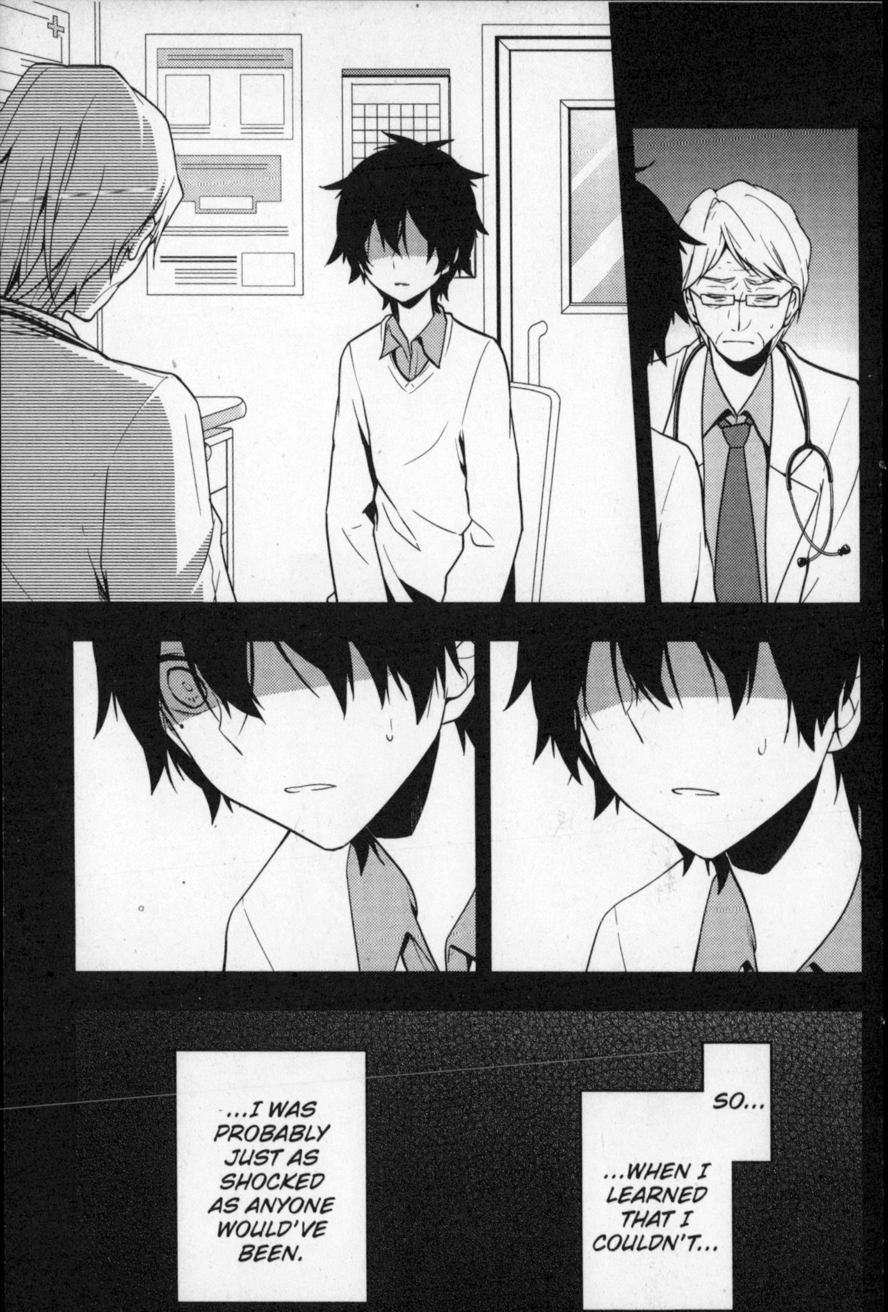
SO...
...WHEN I LEARNED THAT I COULDN'T...
...I WAS PROBABLY JUST AS SHOCKED AS ANYONE WOULD'VE BEEN.

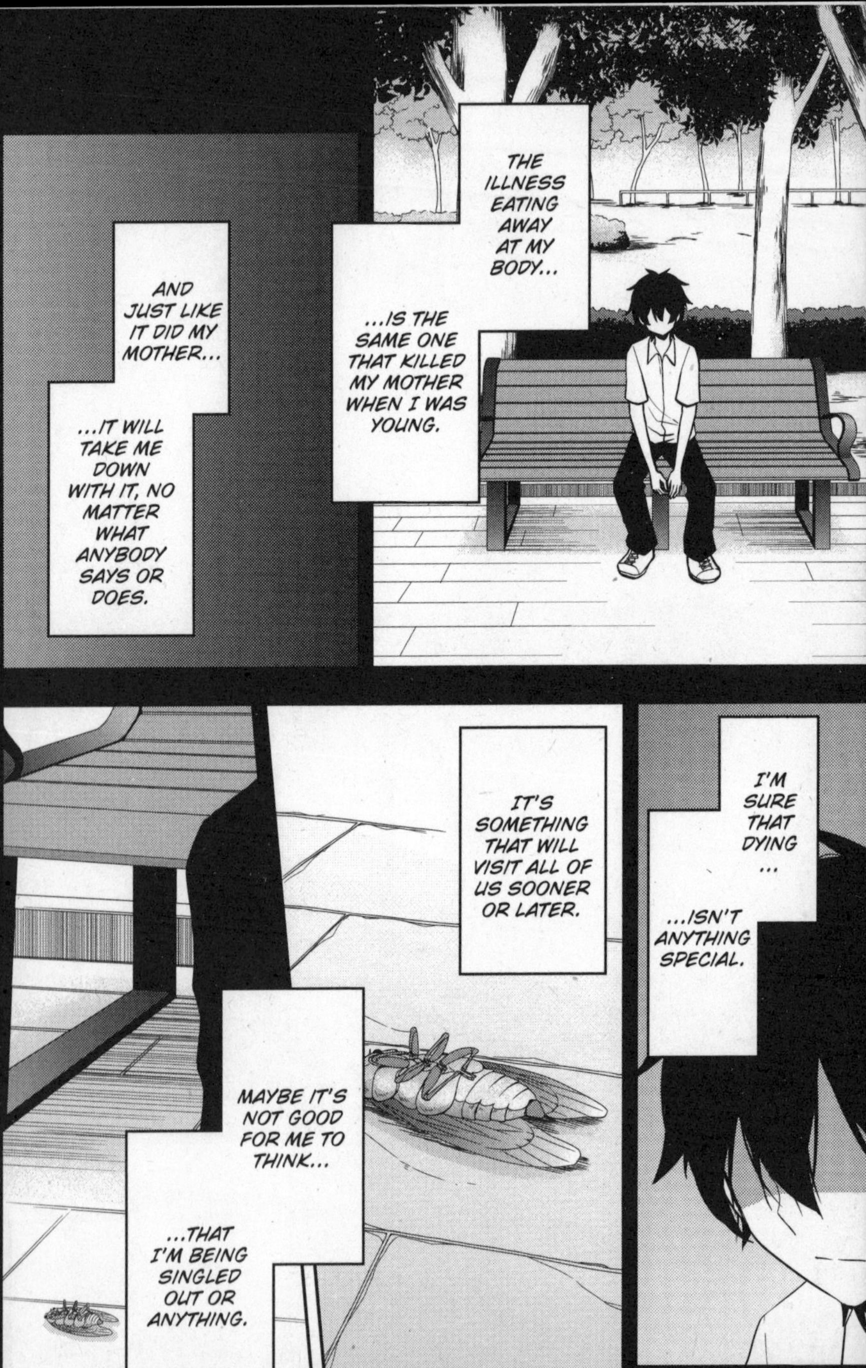
THE ILLNESS EATING AWAY AT MY BODY...
...IS THE SAME ONE THAT KILLED MY MOTHER WHEN I WAS YOUNG.
AND JUST LIKE IT DID MY MOTHER...
...IT WILL TAKE ME DOWN WITH IT, NO MATTER WHAT ANYBODY SAYS OR DOES.
I'M SURE THAT DYING...
...ISN'T ANYTHING SPECIAL.
IT'S SOMETHING THAT WILL VISIT ALL OF US SOONER OR LATER.
MAYBE IT'S NOT GOOD FOR ME TO THINK...
...THAT I'M BEING SINGLED OUT OR ANYTHING.

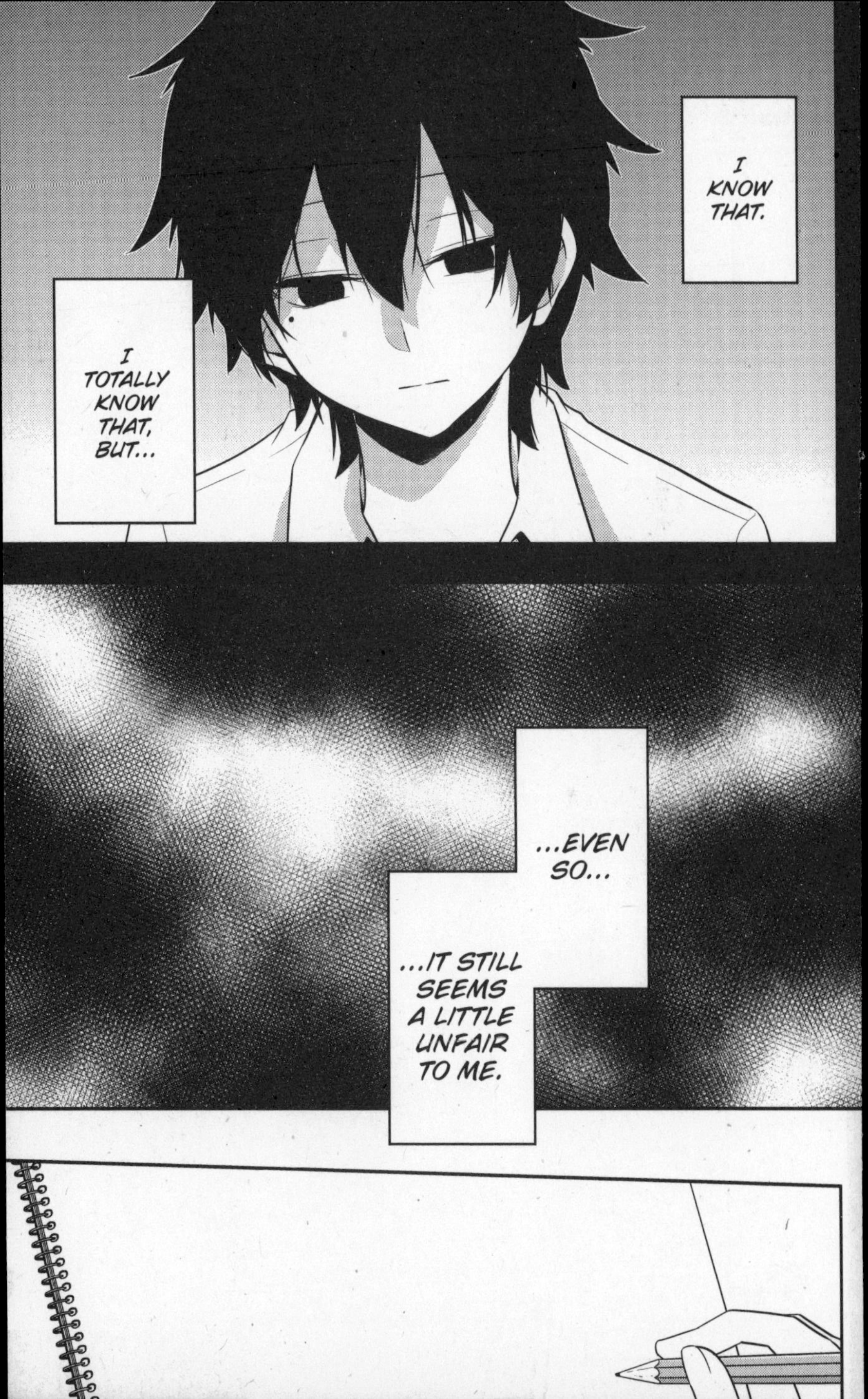
I KNOW THAT.
I TOTALLY KNOW THAT, BUT...
...EVEN SO...
...IT STILL SEEMS A LITTLE UNFAIR TO ME.

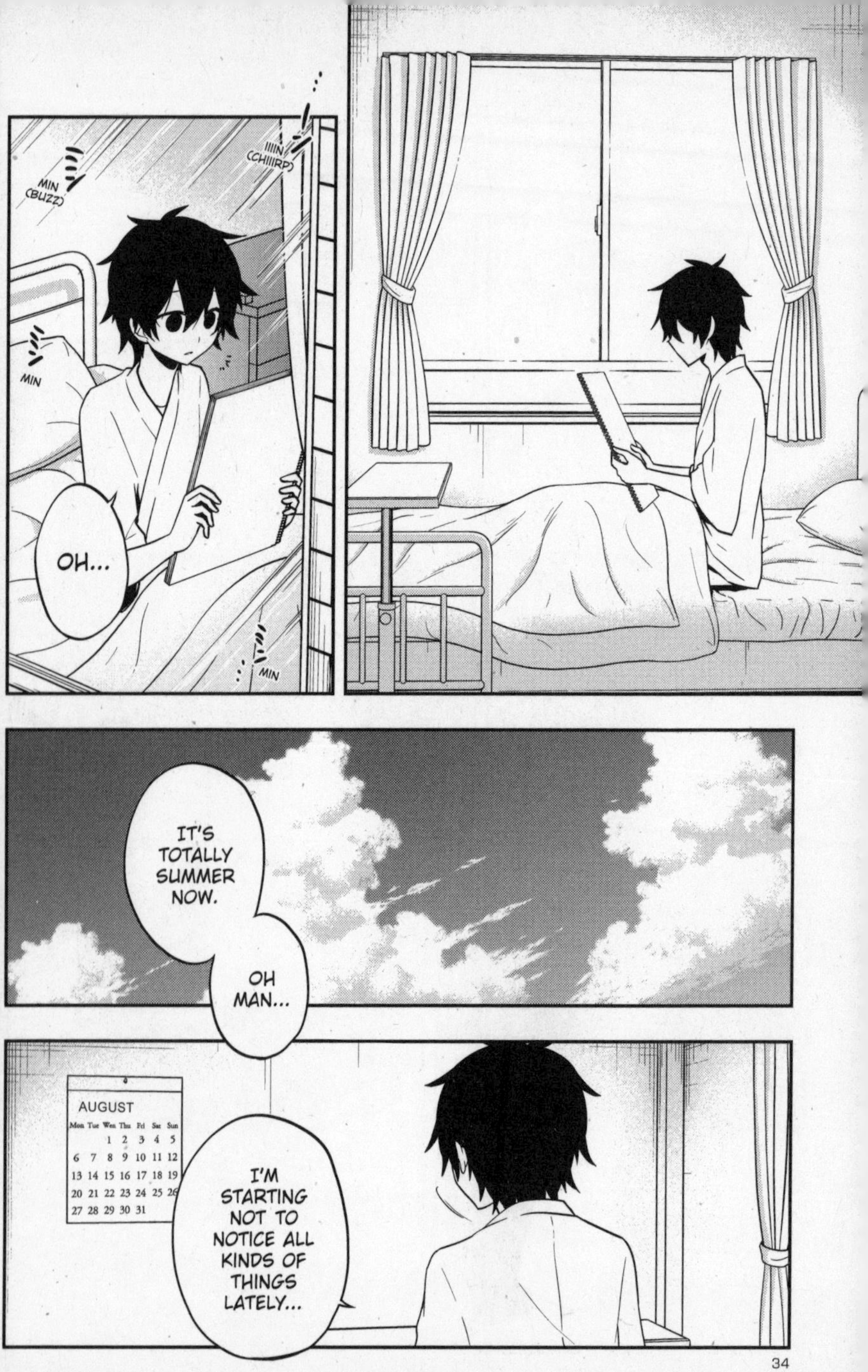

IIIIN (CHIIIRP)
MIN (BUZZ)
MIN
OH...
MIN
IT'S TOTALLY SUMMER NOW.
OH MAN...
I'M STARTING NOT TO NOTICE ALL KINDS OF THINGS LATELY...
AUGUST
Mon Tue Wen Thu Fri Sat Sun
1 2 3 4 5
6 7 8 9 10 11 12
13 14 15 16 17 18 19
20 21 22 23 24 25 26
27 28 29 30 31

AUGUST

MON TUE WED THU FRI SAT SUN
1 2 3 4 5

ONE YEAR
TO GO,
HUH...?

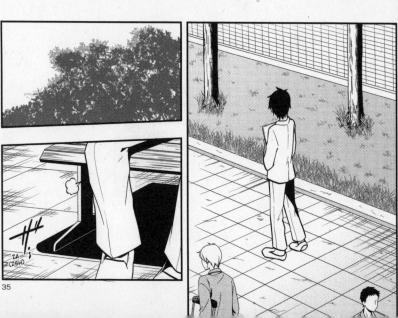

IT'S PRETTY HOT...

NOT TOO MANY PEOPLE EITHER...

WHEW...

SHA (SCRITCH)

SHA

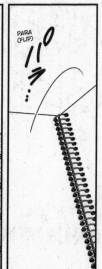

PARA (FLIP)

YOUR DRAWINGS ARE SO WONDERFUL, KOKONOSE-KUN!

SHA

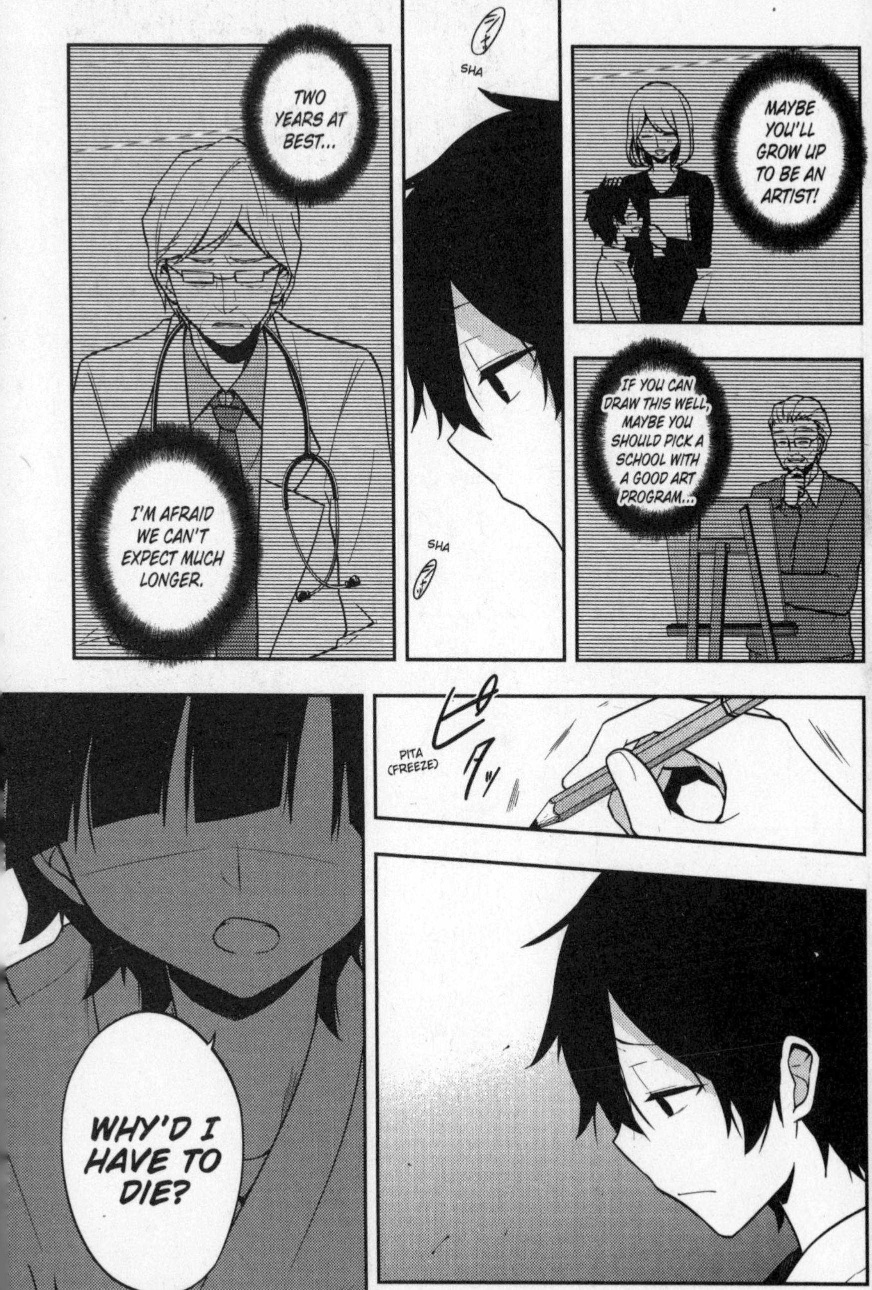
MAYBE YOU'LL GROW UP TO BE AN ARTIST!
IF YOU CAN DRAW THIS WELL, MAYBE YOU SHOULD PICK A SCHOOL WITH A GOOD ART PROGRAM...
SHA
SHA
TWO YEARS AT BEST...
I'M AFRAID WE CAN'T EXPECT MUCH LONGER.
PITA (FREEZE)
WHY'D I HAVE TO DIE?

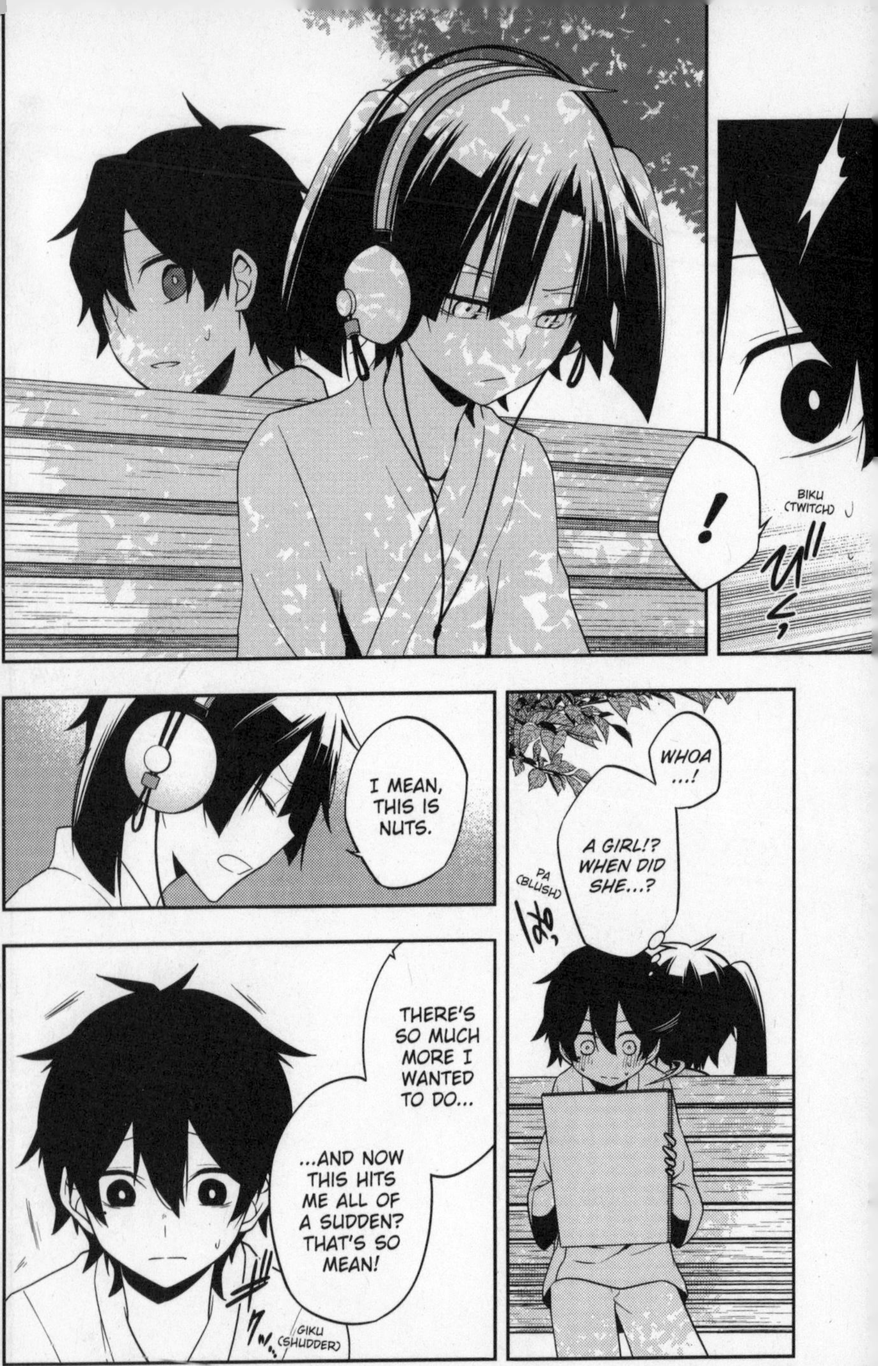

!
BIKU (TWITCH)
WHOA ...!
A GIRL!? WHEN DID SHE...?
PA (BLUSH)
I MEAN, THIS IS NUTS.
THERE'S SO MUCH MORE I WANTED TO DO...
...AND NOW THIS HITS ME ALL OF A SUDDEN? THAT'S SO MEAN!
GIKU (SHUDDER)

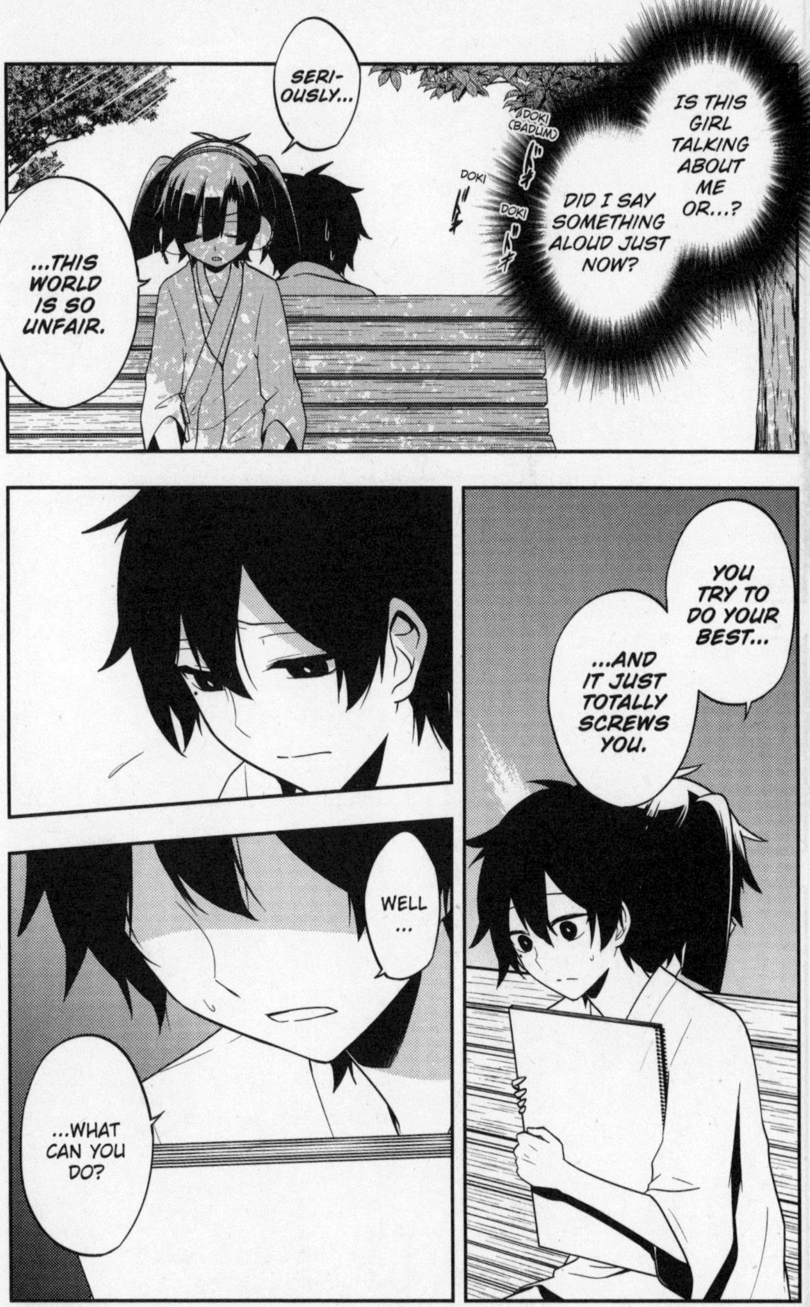
IS THIS GIRL TALKING ABOUT ME OR...?
DID I SAY SOMETHING ALOUD JUST NOW?
DOKI (BADUM)
DOKI
DOKI
SERI-OUSLY...
...THIS WORLD IS SO UNFAIR.
YOU TRY TO DO YOUR BEST...
...AND IT JUST TOTALLY SCREWS YOU.
WELL...
...WHAT CAN YOU DO?

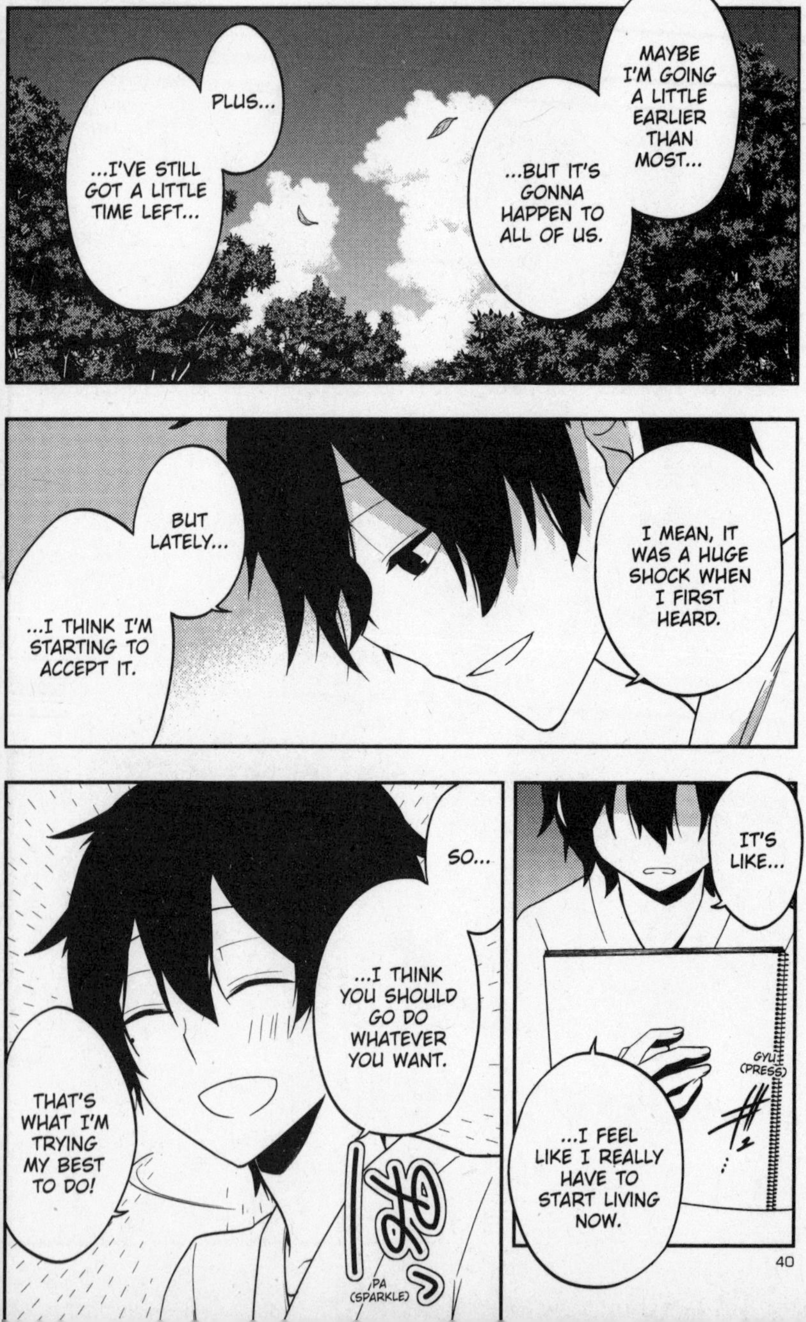

MAYBE I'M GOING A LITTLE EARLIER THAN MOST...
...BUT IT'S GONNA HAPPEN TO ALL OF US.
PLUS...
...I'VE STILL GOT A LITTLE TIME LEFT...
I MEAN, IT WAS A HUGE SHOCK WHEN I FIRST HEARD.
BUT LATELY...
...I THINK I'M STARTING TO ACCEPT IT.
IT'S LIKE...
...I FEEL LIKE I REALLY HAVE TO START LIVING NOW.
GYU (PRESS)
SO...
...I THINK YOU SHOULD GO DO WHATEVER YOU WANT.
THAT'S WHAT I'M TRYING MY BEST TO DO!
ぱっ
PA (SPARKLE)

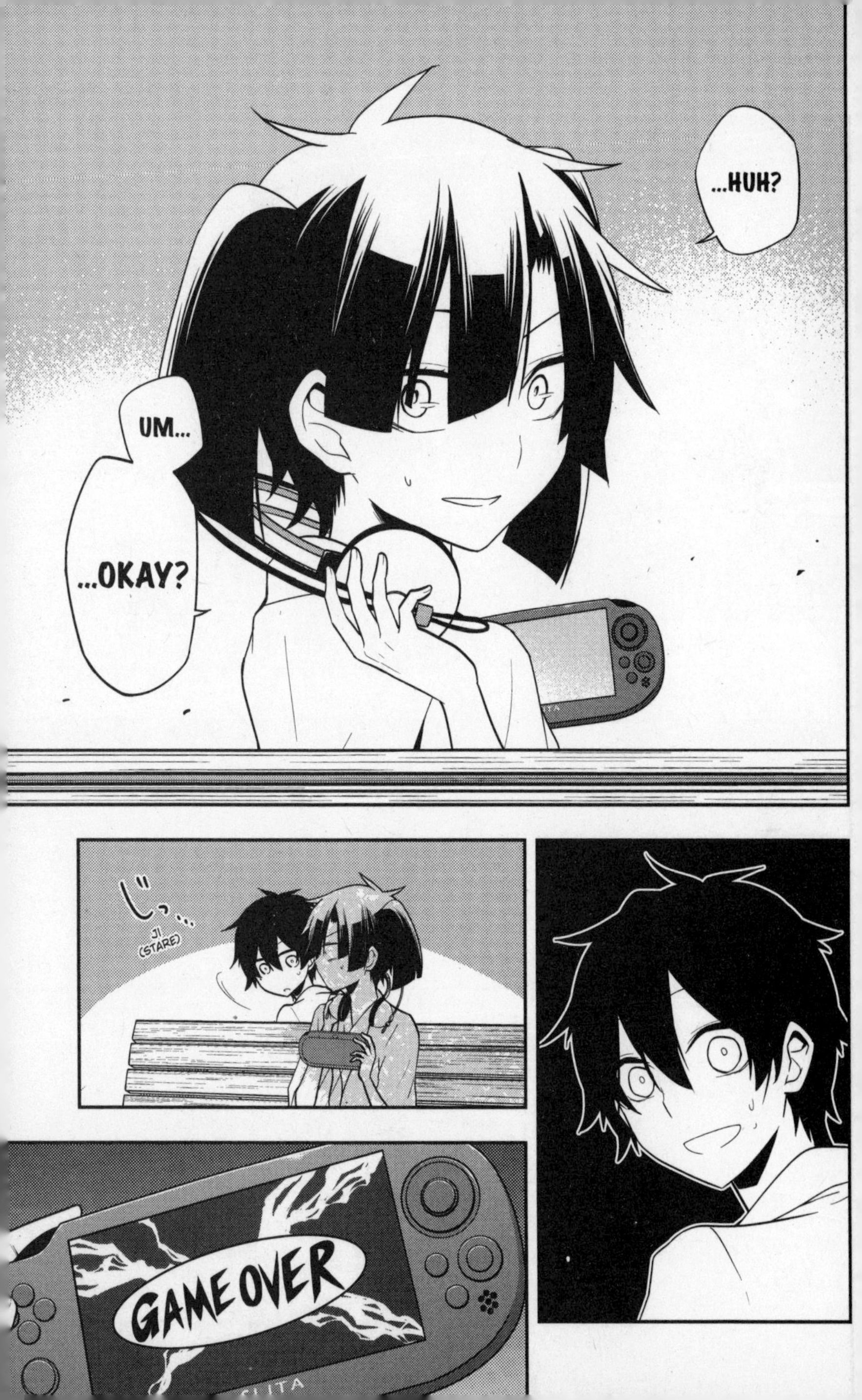
...HUH?
UM...
...OKAY?
じ...
JI (STARE)
GAME OVER

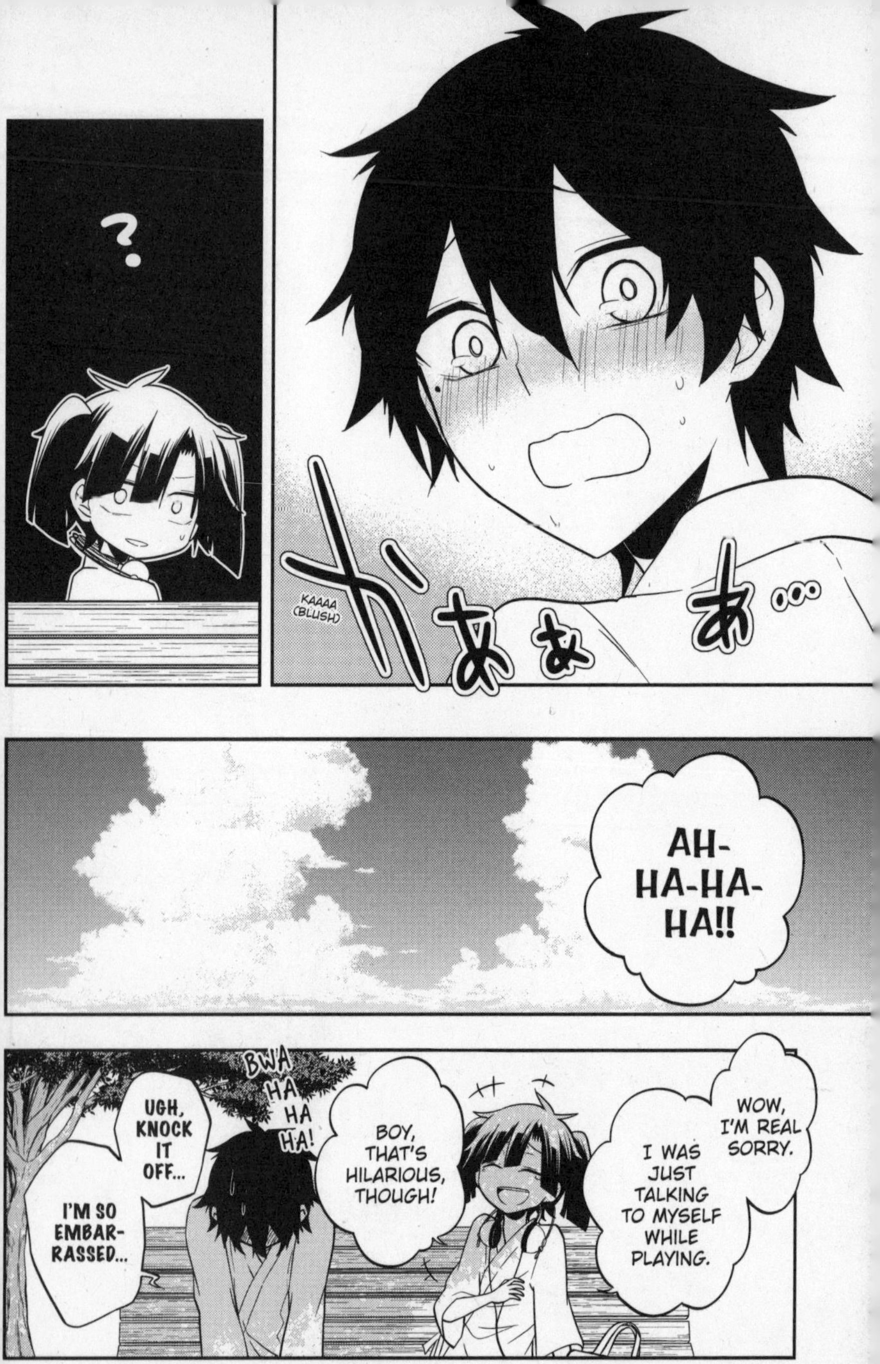

があぁあ…
KAAAA (BLUSH)
?
AH-HA-HA-HA!!
WOW, I'M REAL SORRY.
I WAS JUST TALKING TO MYSELF WHILE PLAYING.
BOY, THAT'S HILARIOUS, THOUGH!
BWA HA HA HA!
UGH, KNOCK IT OFF...
I'M SO EMBARRASSED...

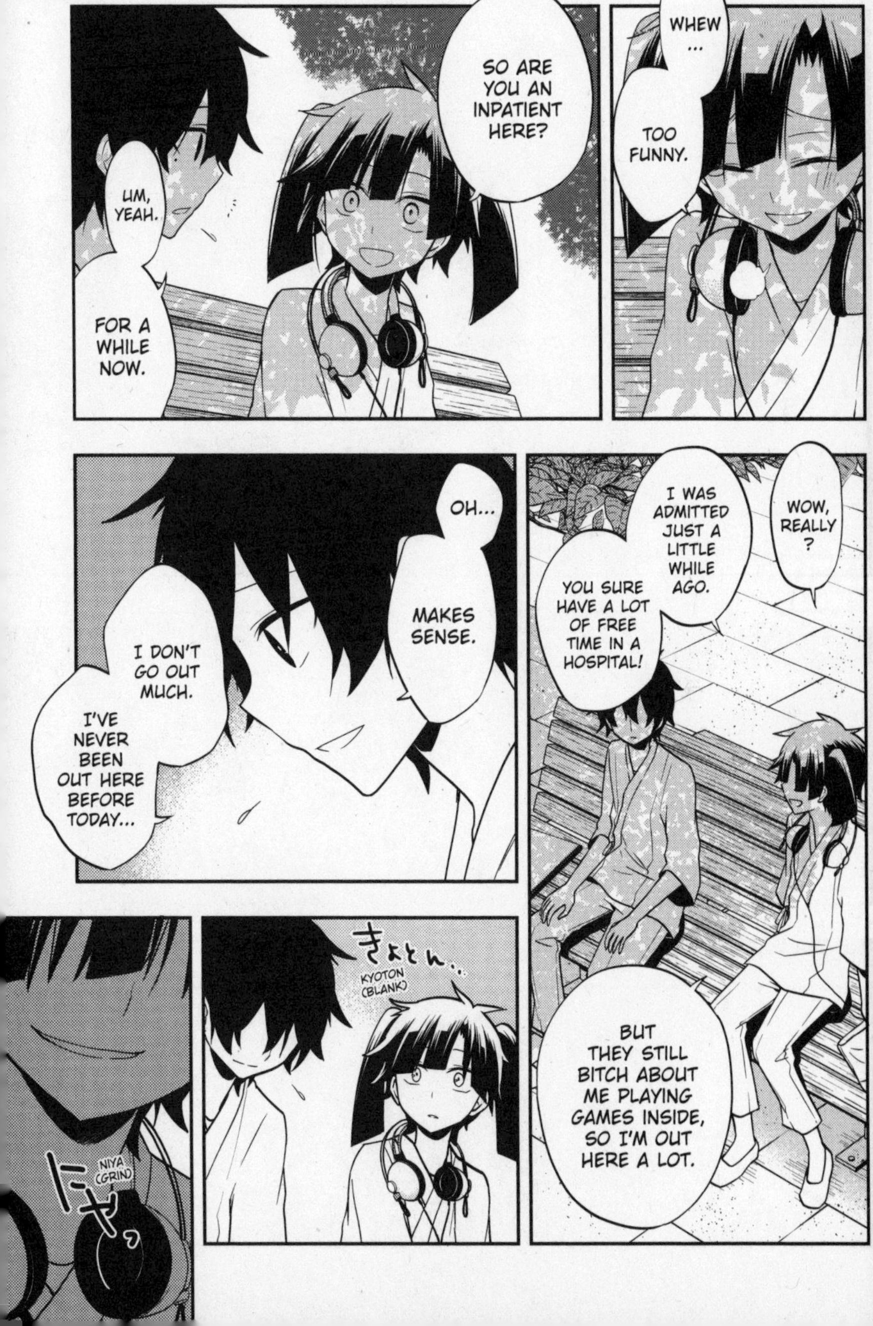
WHEW...
TOO FUNNY.
SO ARE YOU AN INPATIENT HERE?
UM, YEAH.
FOR A WHILE NOW.
WOW, REALLY?
I WAS ADMITTED JUST A LITTLE WHILE AGO.
YOU SURE HAVE A LOT OF FREE TIME IN A HOSPITAL!
BUT THEY STILL BITCH ABOUT ME PLAYING GAMES INSIDE, SO I'M OUT HERE A LOT.
OH...
MAKES SENSE.
I DON'T GO OUT MUCH.
I'VE NEVER BEEN OUT HERE BEFORE TODAY...
きょとん..
KYOTON (BLANK)
にやっ
NIYA (GRIN)

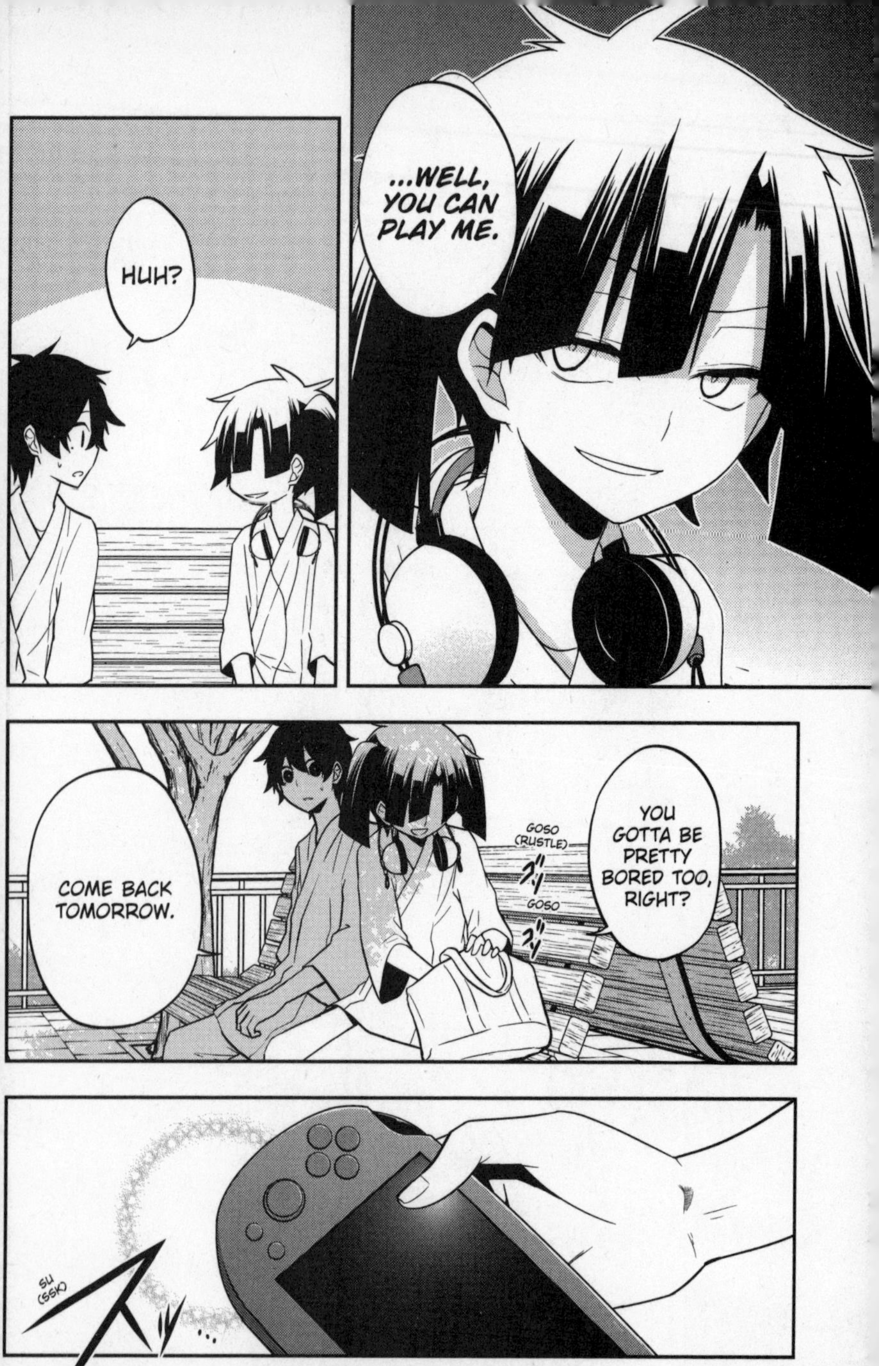
...WELL, YOU CAN PLAY ME.
HUH?
YOU GOTTA BE PRETTY BORED TOO, RIGHT?
GOSO (RUSTLE)
GOSO
COME BACK TOMORROW.
SU (SSK)

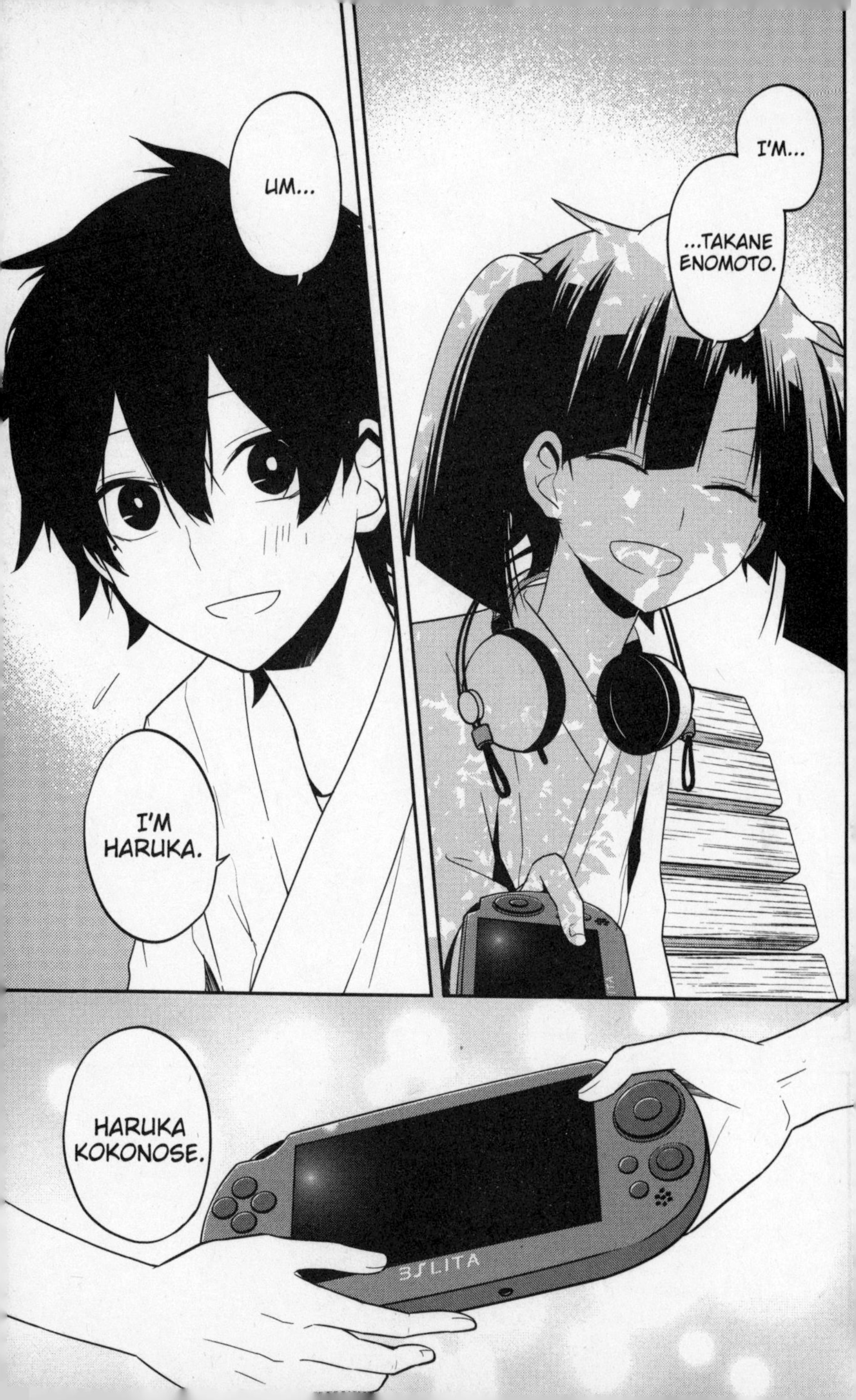
I'M...
...TAKANE ENOMOTO.
UM...
I'M HARUKA.
HARUKA KOKONOSE.

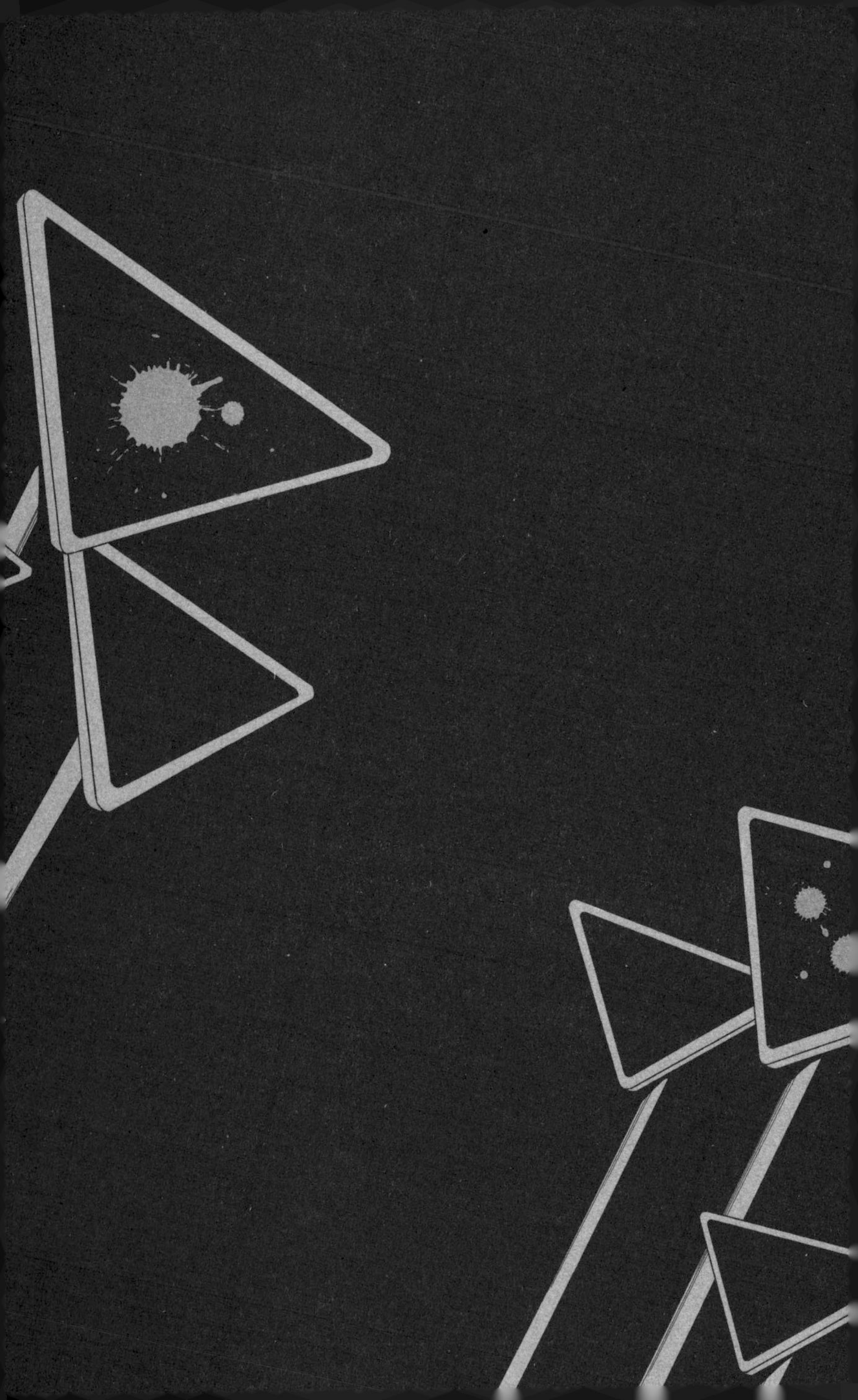

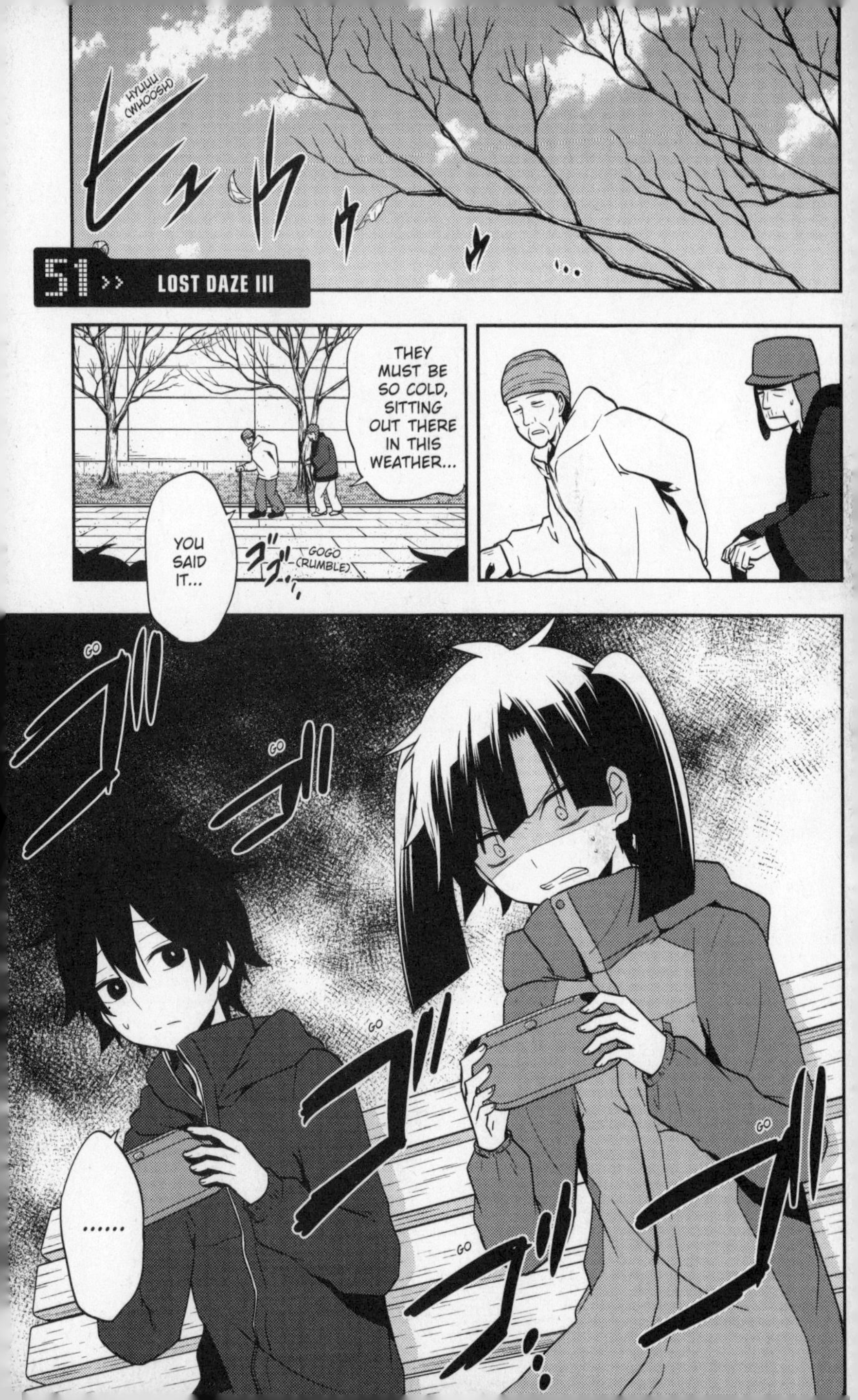
HYUUU (WHOOSH)
51 >> LOST DAZE III
THEY MUST BE SO COLD, SITTING OUT THERE IN THIS WEATHER...
YOU SAID IT...
GOGO (RUMBLE)
GO
GO
GO
GO
GO
......

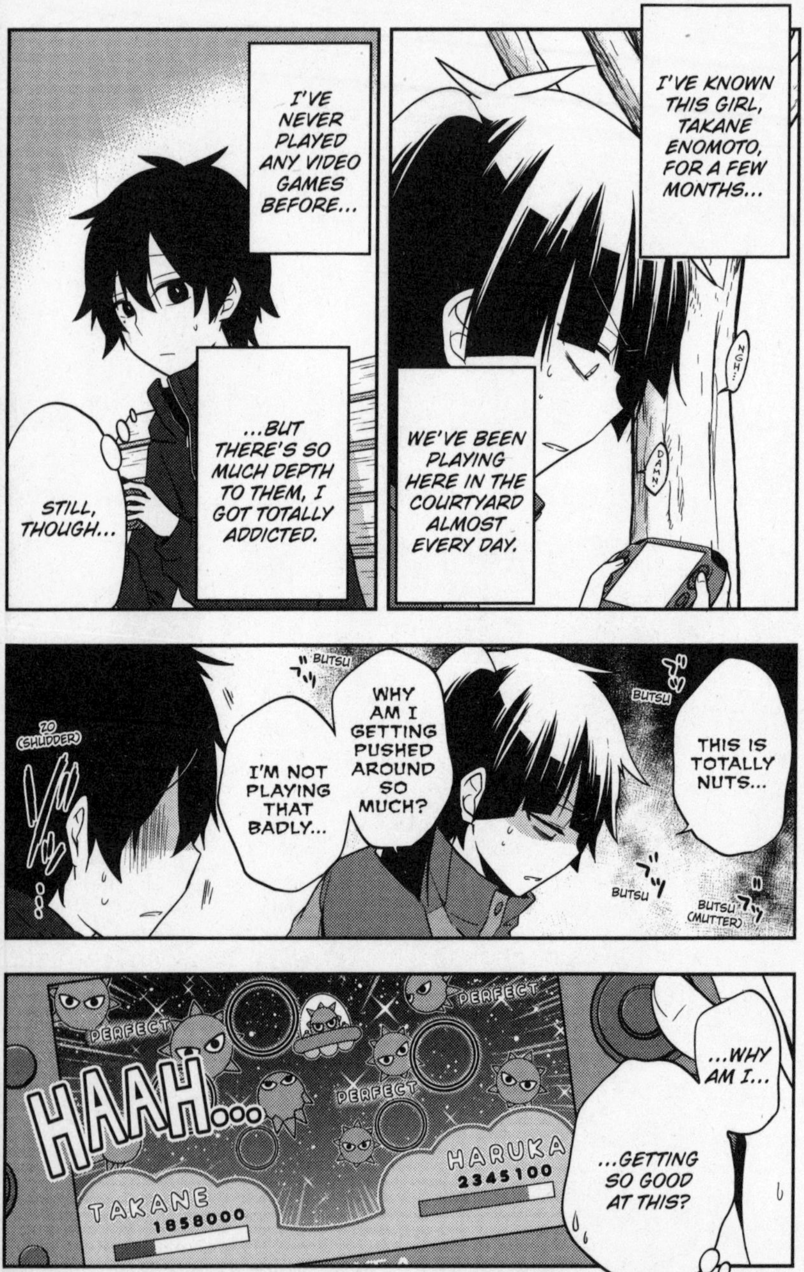
I'VE KNOWN THIS GIRL, TAKANE ENOMOTO, FOR A FEW MONTHS...
NGH...
DAMN.
WE'VE BEEN PLAYING HERE IN THE COURTYARD ALMOST EVERY DAY.
I'VE NEVER PLAYED ANY VIDEO GAMES BEFORE...
...BUT THERE'S SO MUCH DEPTH TO THEM, I GOT TOTALLY ADDICTED.
STILL, THOUGH...
BUTSU
THIS IS TOTALLY NUTS...
BUTSU (MUTTER)
BUTSU
WHY AM I GETTING PUSHED AROUND SO MUCH?
BUTSU
I'M NOT PLAYING THAT BADLY...
ZO (SHUDDER)
...WHY AM I...
...GETTING SO GOOD AT THIS?
PERFECT
PERFECT
PERFECT
HARUKA
2345100
HAAH...
TAKANE
1858000

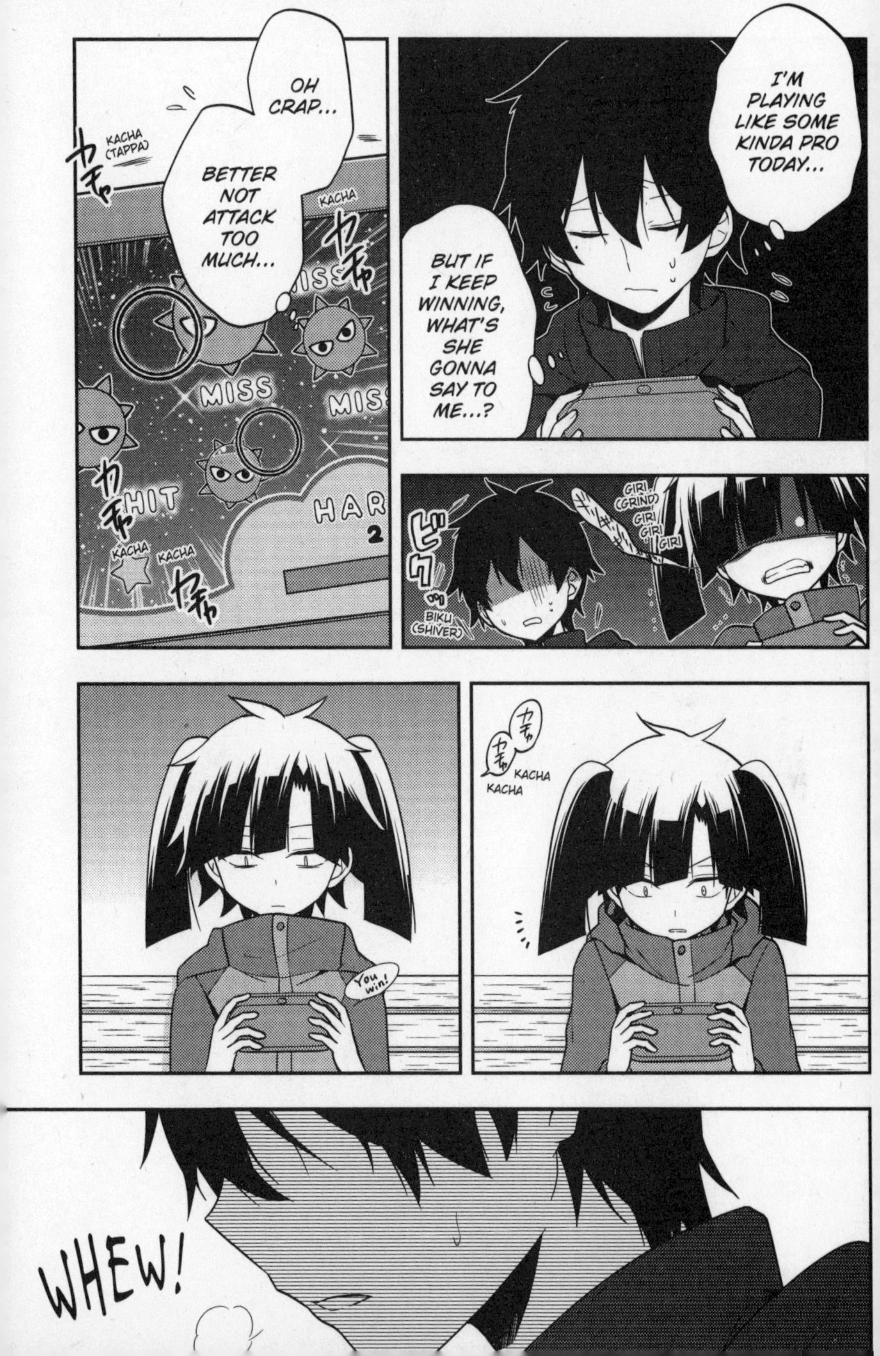
I'M PLAYING LIKE SOME KINDA PRO TODAY...
BUT IF I KEEP WINNING, WHAT'S SHE GONNA SAY TO ME...?
GIRI (GRIND) GIRI GIRI GIRI
BIKU (SHIVER)
OH CRAP...
BETTER NOT ATTACK TOO MUCH...
KACHA (TAPPA)
KACHA
MISS
MISS
MISS
HIT
HAR
2
KACHA
KACHA
KACHA KACHA
You win!
WHEW!

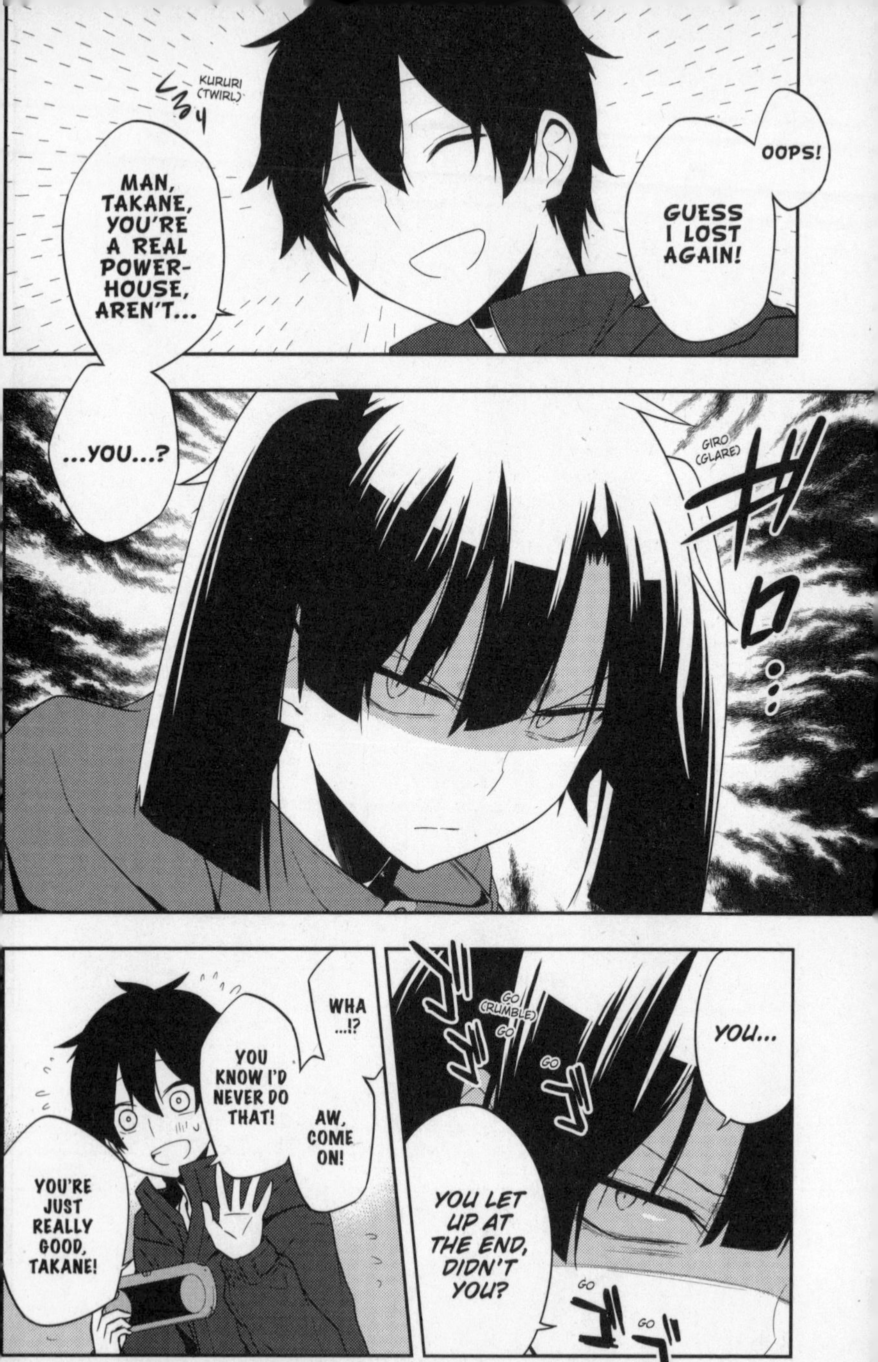
OOPS!
GUESS I LOST AGAIN!
KURURI (TWIRL)
MAN, TAKANE, YOU'RE A REAL POWER-HOUSE, AREN'T...
...YOU...?
GIRO (GLARE)
GO (RUMBLE) GO
GO
YOU...
YOU LET UP AT THE END, DIDN'T YOU?
GO
GO
WHA ...!?
AW, COME ON!
YOU KNOW I'D NEVER DO THAT!
YOU'RE JUST REALLY GOOD, TAKANE!

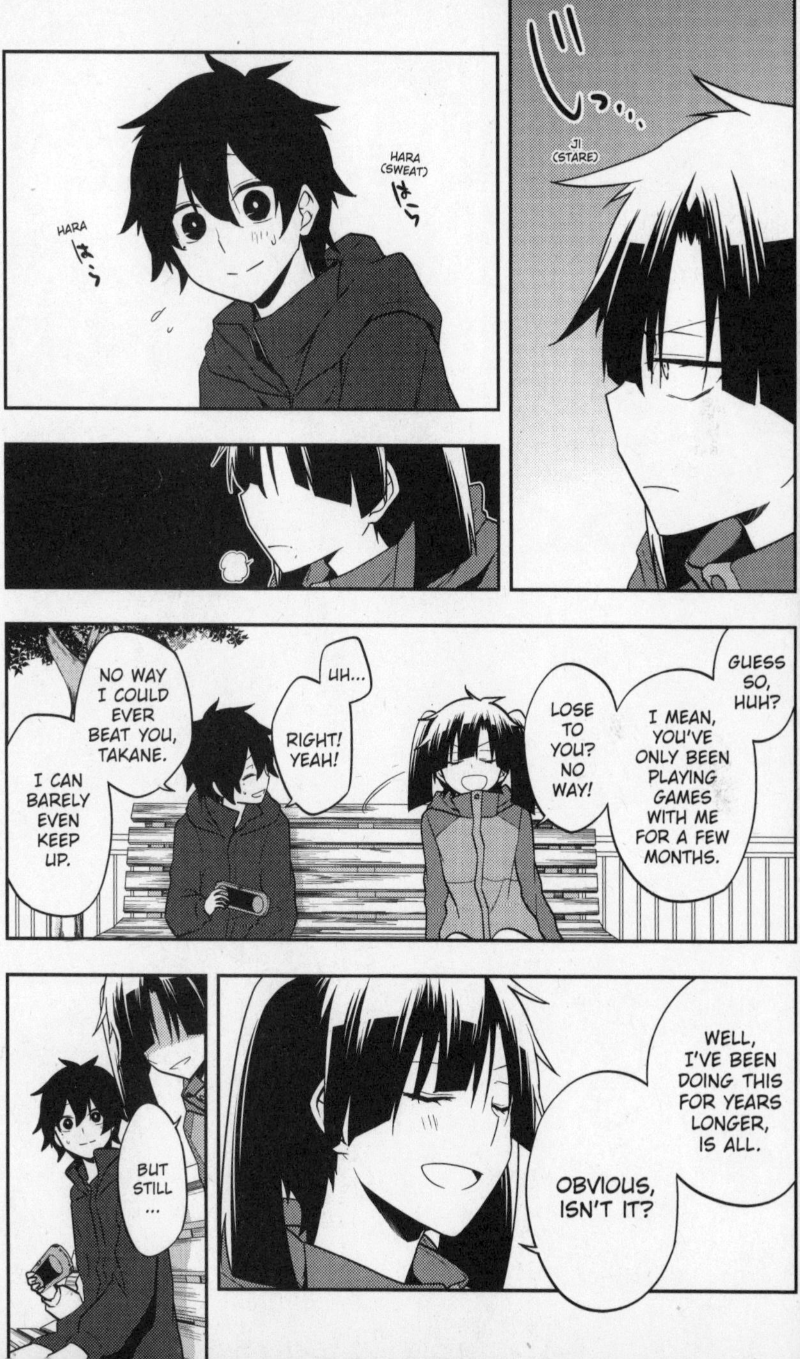
じっ...
JI (STARE)
はら
HARA (SWEAT)
はら
HARA
GUESS SO, HUH?
I MEAN, YOU'VE ONLY BEEN PLAYING GAMES WITH ME FOR A FEW MONTHS.
LOSE TO YOU? NO WAY!
UH...
RIGHT! YEAH!
NO WAY I COULD EVER BEAT YOU, TAKANE.
I CAN BARELY EVEN KEEP UP.
WELL, I'VE BEEN DOING THIS FOR YEARS LONGER, IS ALL.
OBVIOUS, ISN'T IT?
BUT STILL ...

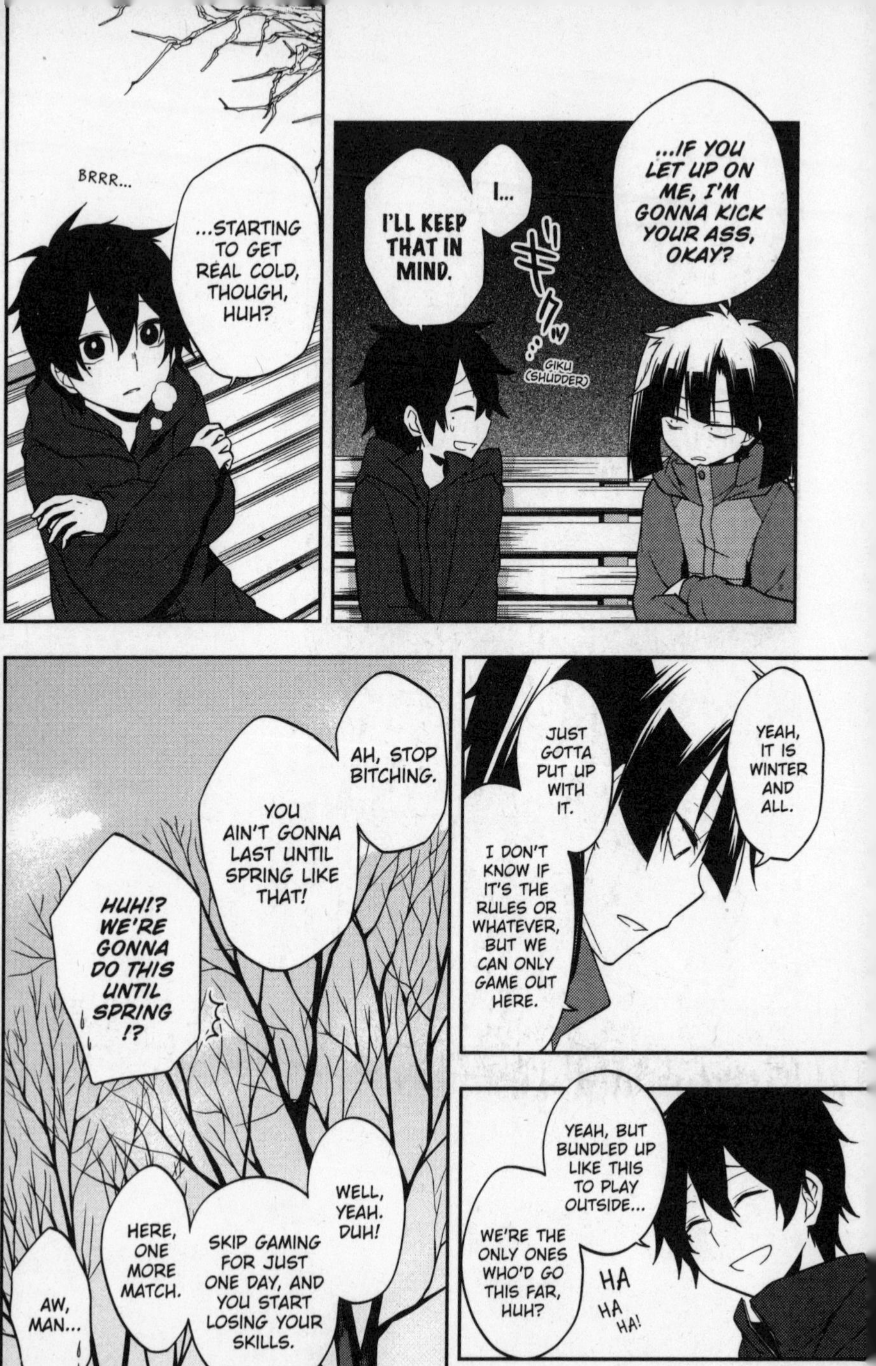
...IF YOU LET UP ON ME, I'M GONNA KICK YOUR ASS, OKAY?
I...
I'LL KEEP THAT IN MIND.
GIKU (SHUDDER)
BRRR...
...STARTING TO GET REAL COLD, THOUGH, HUH?
YEAH, IT IS WINTER AND ALL.
JUST GOTTA PUT UP WITH IT.
I DON'T KNOW IF IT'S THE RULES OR WHATEVER, BUT WE CAN ONLY GAME OUT HERE.
YEAH, BUT BUNDLED UP LIKE THIS TO PLAY OUTSIDE...
WE'RE THE ONLY ONES WHO'D GO THIS FAR, HUH?
HA HA HA!
AH, STOP BITCHING.
YOU AIN'T GONNA LAST UNTIL SPRING LIKE THAT!
HUH!? WE'RE GONNA DO THIS UNTIL SPRING!?
WELL, YEAH. DUH!
SKIP GAMING FOR JUST ONE DAY, AND YOU START LOSING YOUR SKILLS.
HERE, ONE MORE MATCH.
AW, MAN...

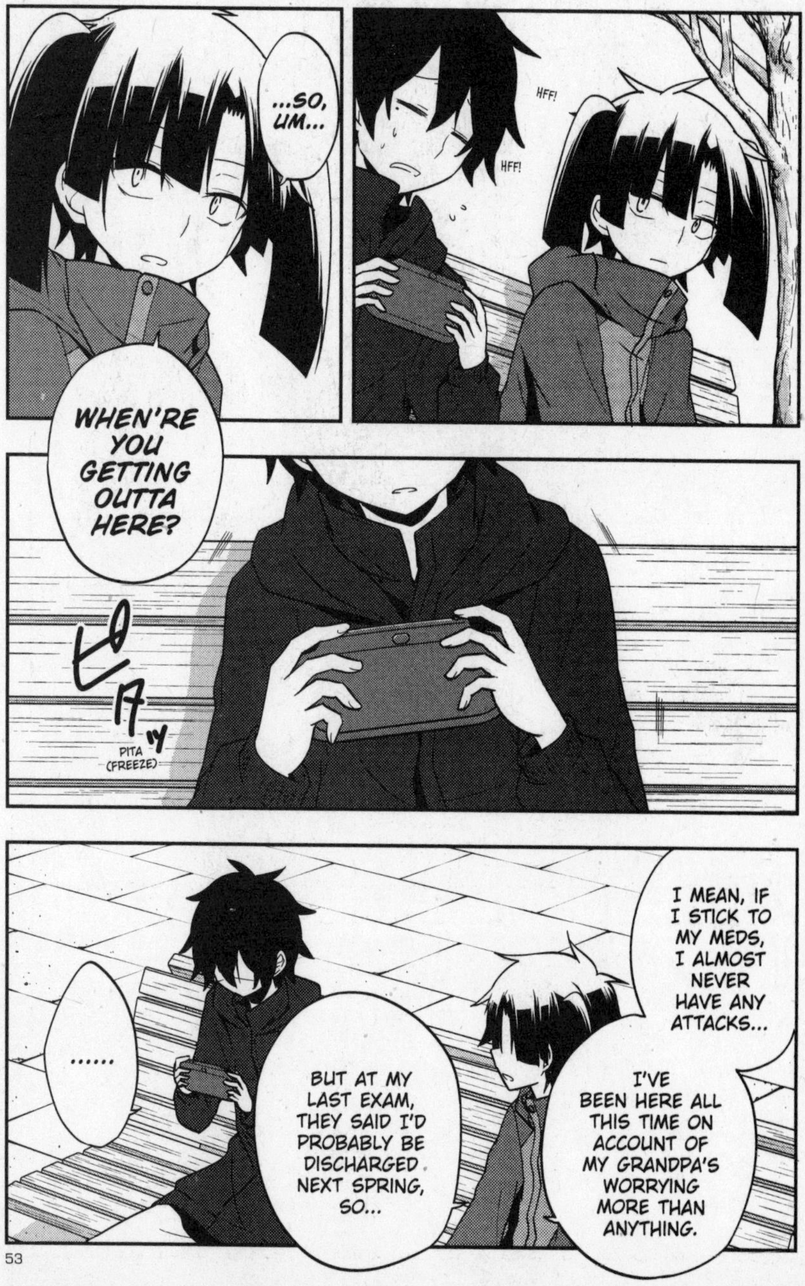
HFF!
HFF!
...SO, UM...
WHEN'RE YOU GETTING OUTTA HERE?
PITA (FREEZE)
I MEAN, IF I STICK TO MY MEDS, I ALMOST NEVER HAVE ANY ATTACKS...
I'VE BEEN HERE ALL THIS TIME ON ACCOUNT OF MY GRANDPA'S WORRYING MORE THAN ANYTHING.
BUT AT MY LAST EXAM, THEY SAID I'D PROBABLY BE DISCHARGED NEXT SPRING, SO...
......

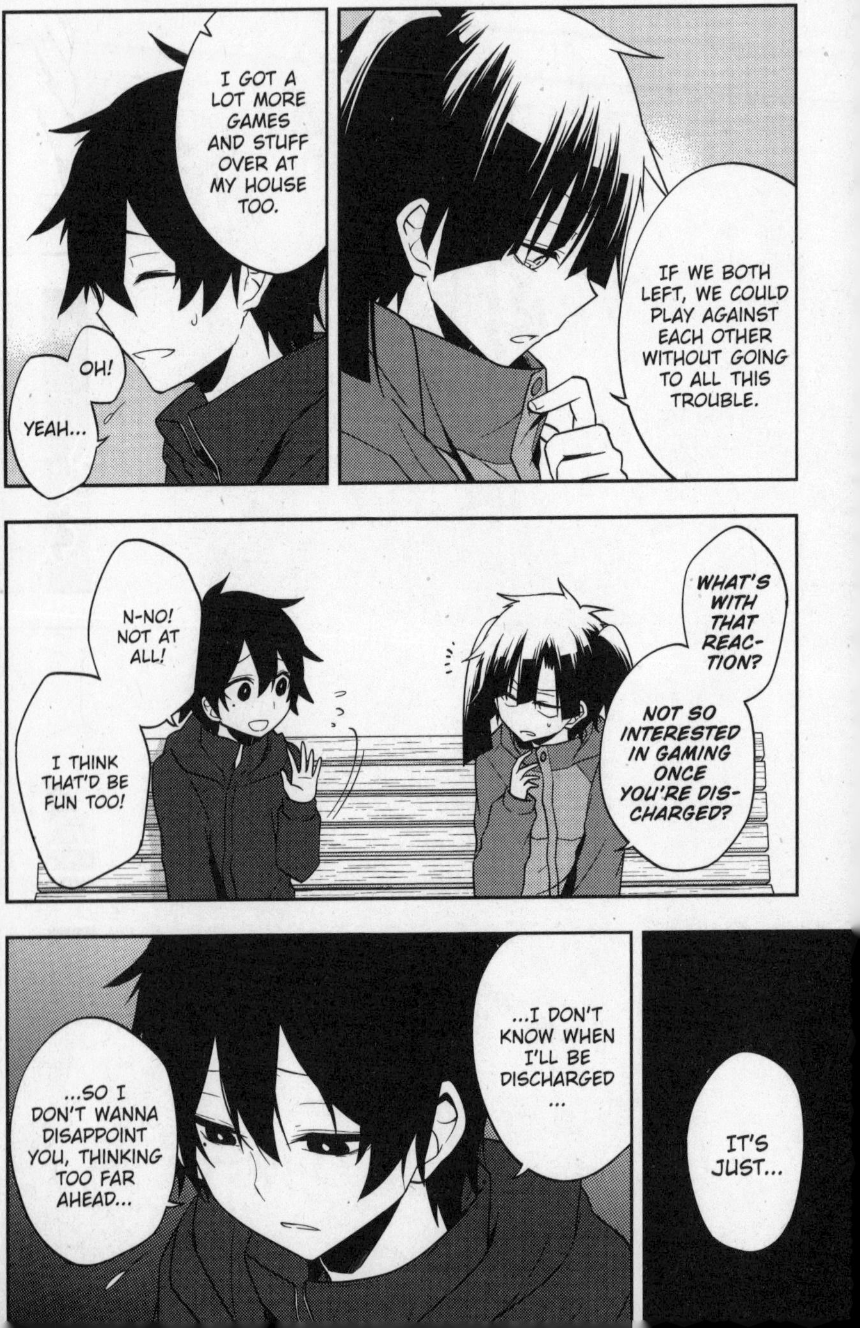
IF WE BOTH LEFT, WE COULD PLAY AGAINST EACH OTHER WITHOUT GOING TO ALL THIS TROUBLE.
I GOT A LOT MORE GAMES AND STUFF OVER AT MY HOUSE TOO.
OH!
YEAH...
WHAT'S WITH THAT REAC-TION?
NOT SO INTERESTED IN GAMING ONCE YOU'RE DIS-CHARGED?
N-NO! NOT AT ALL!
I THINK THAT'D BE FUN TOO!
IT'S JUST...
...I DON'T KNOW WHEN I'LL BE DISCHARGED...
...SO I DON'T WANNA DISAPPOINT YOU, THINKING TOO FAR AHEAD...

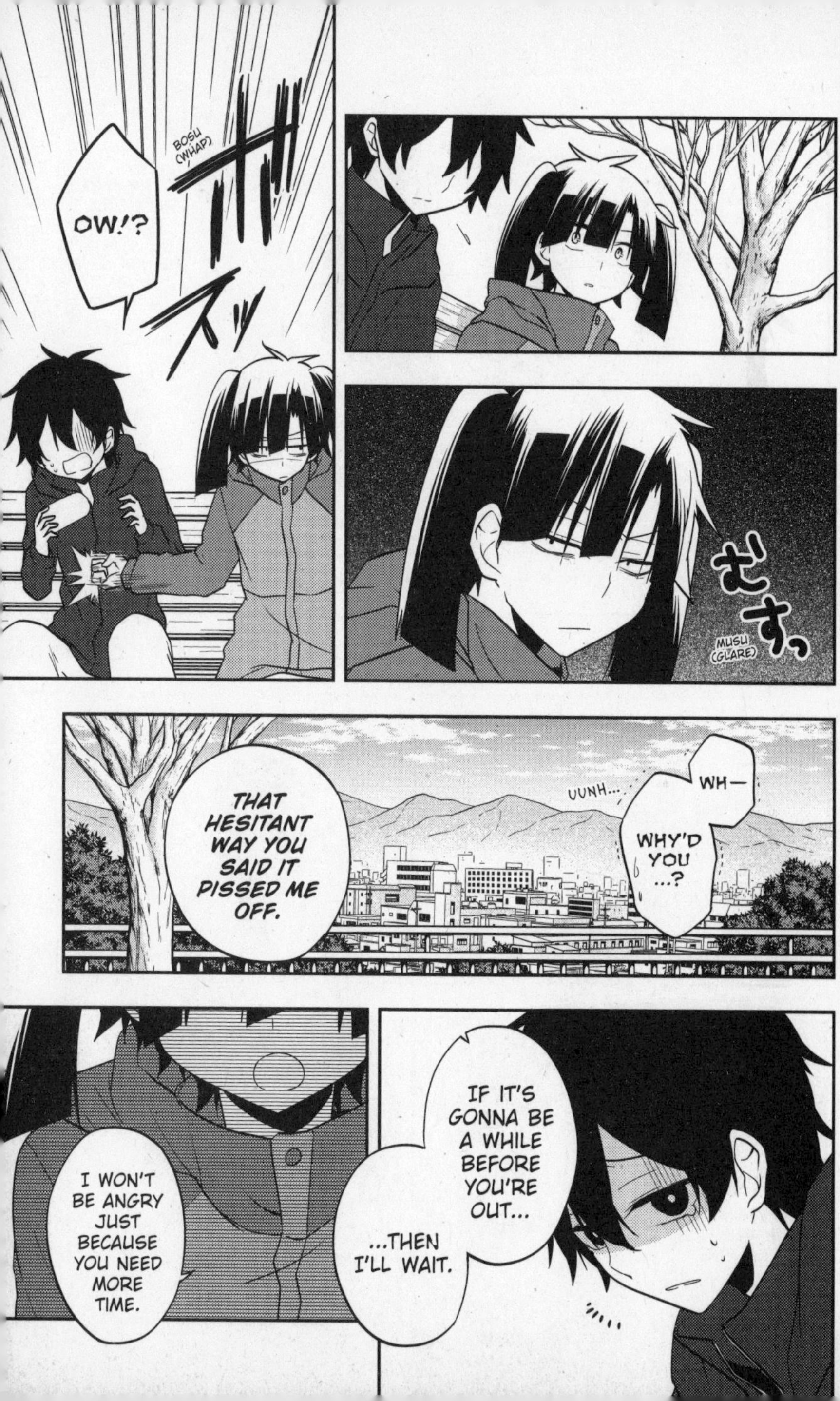
むすっ
MUSU (GLARE)
BOSU (WHAP)
OW!?
WH—
WHY'D YOU ...?
UUNH...
THAT HESITANT WAY YOU SAID IT PISSED ME OFF.
IF IT'S GONNA BE A WHILE BEFORE YOU'RE OUT...
...THEN I'LL WAIT.
I WON'T BE ANGRY JUST BECAUSE YOU NEED MORE TIME.

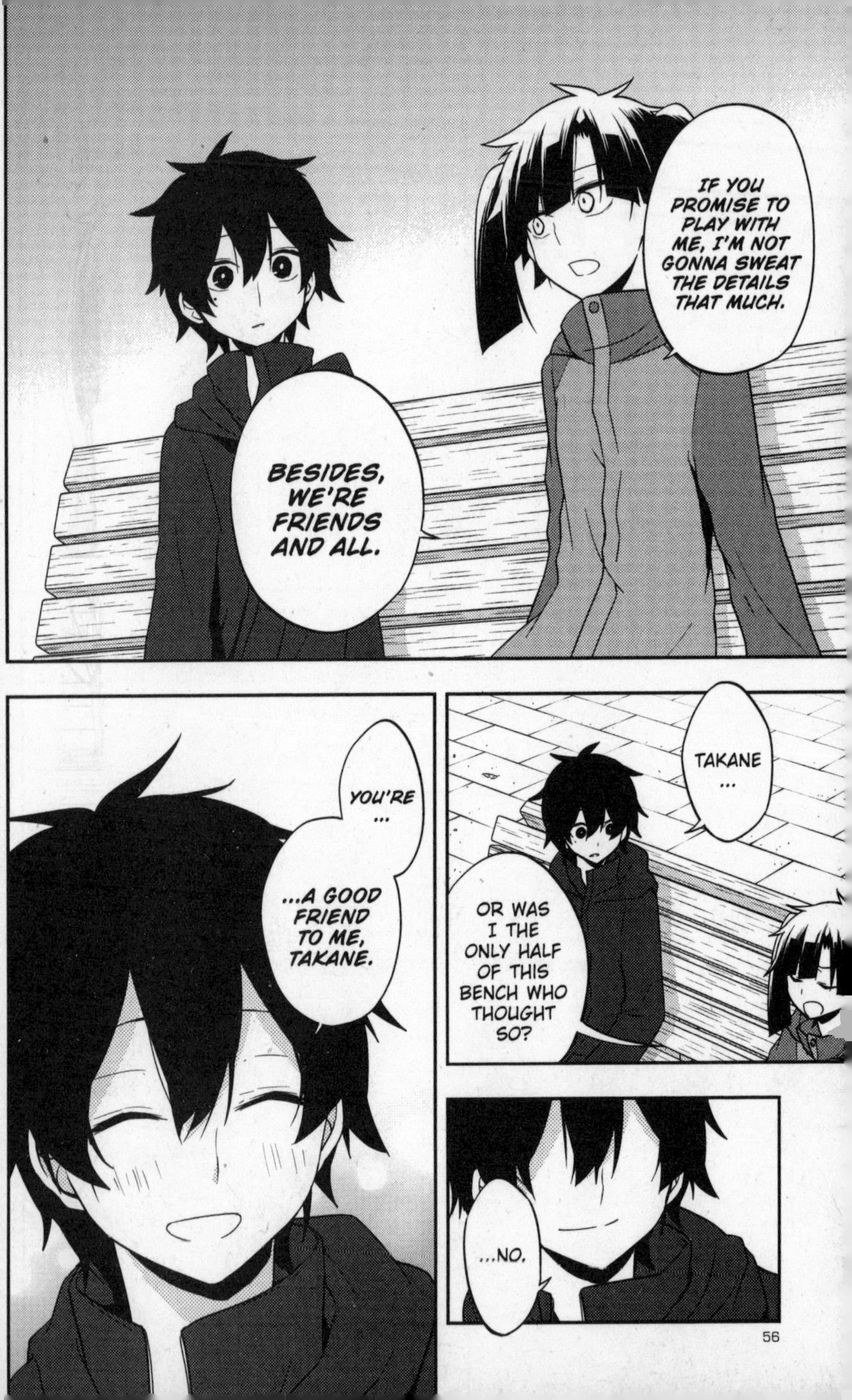
IF YOU PROMISE TO PLAY WITH ME, I'M NOT GONNA SWEAT THE DETAILS THAT MUCH.
BESIDES, WE'RE FRIENDS AND ALL.
TAKANE ...
OR WAS I THE ONLY HALF OF THIS BENCH WHO THOUGHT SO?
...NO.
YOU'RE ...
...A GOOD FRIEND TO ME, TAKANE.

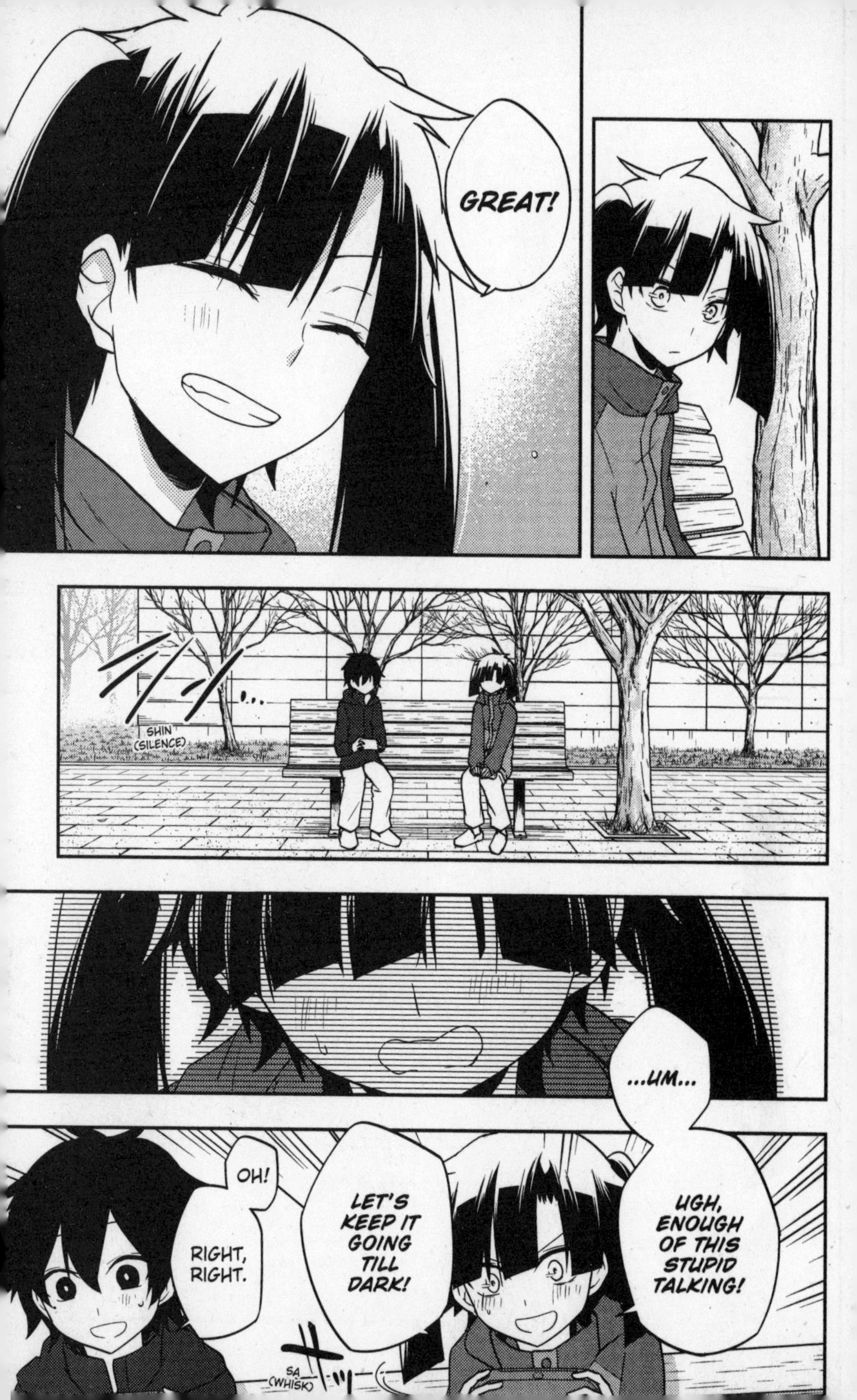
GREAT!
...
SHIN (SILENCE)
...UM...
UGH, ENOUGH OF THIS STUPID TALKING!
LET'S KEEP IT GOING TILL DARK!
SA (WHISK)
OH!
RIGHT, RIGHT.

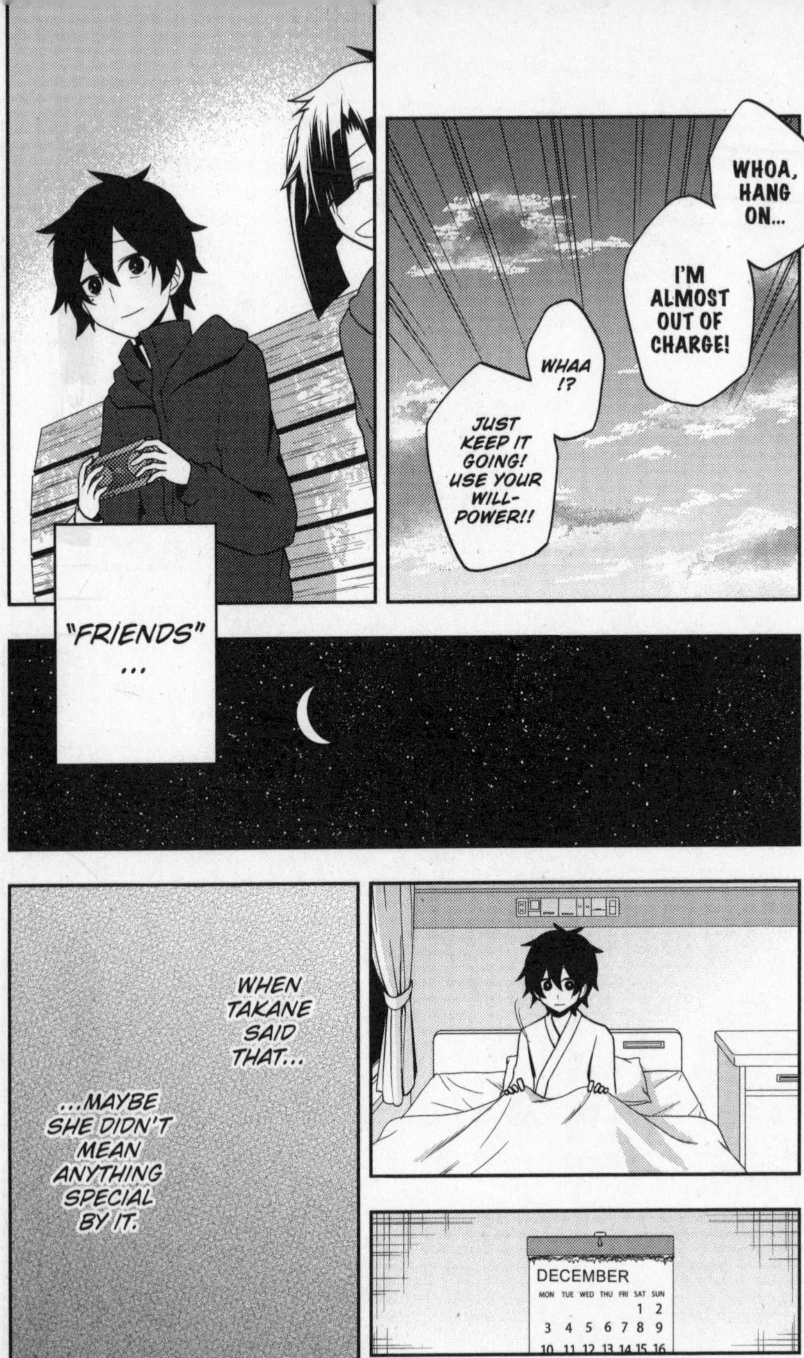
WHOA, HANG ON...
I'M ALMOST OUT OF CHARGE!
WHAA!?
JUST KEEP IT GOING! USE YOUR WILL-POWER!!
"FRIENDS"...
WHEN TAKANE SAID THAT...
...MAYBE SHE DIDN'T MEAN ANYTHING SPECIAL BY IT.
DECEMBER
MON TUE WED THU FRI SAT SUN
1 2
3 4 5 6 7 8 9
10 11 12 13 14 15 16

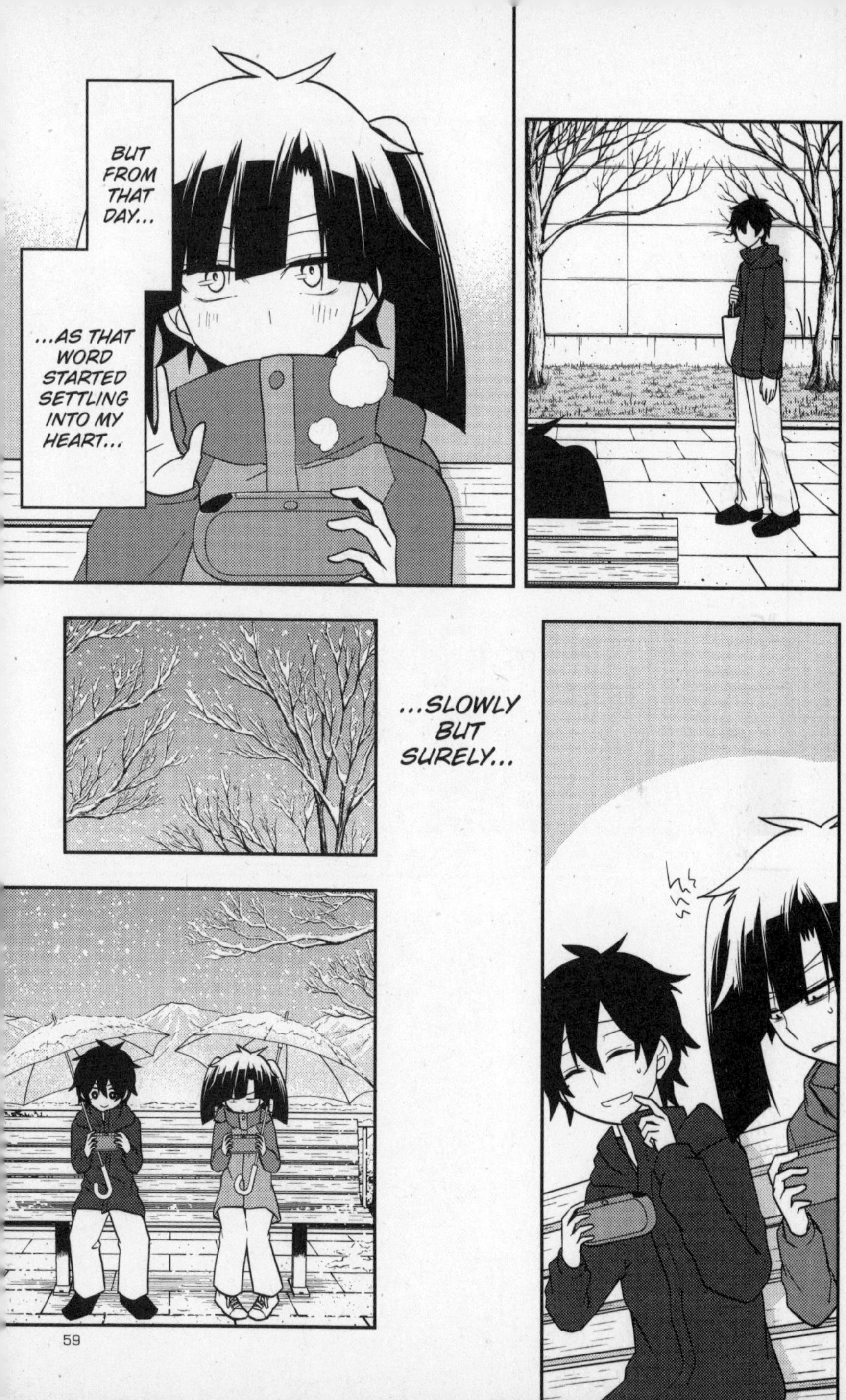
BUT FROM THAT DAY...
...AS THAT WORD STARTED SETTLING INTO MY HEART...
...SLOWLY BUT SURELY...

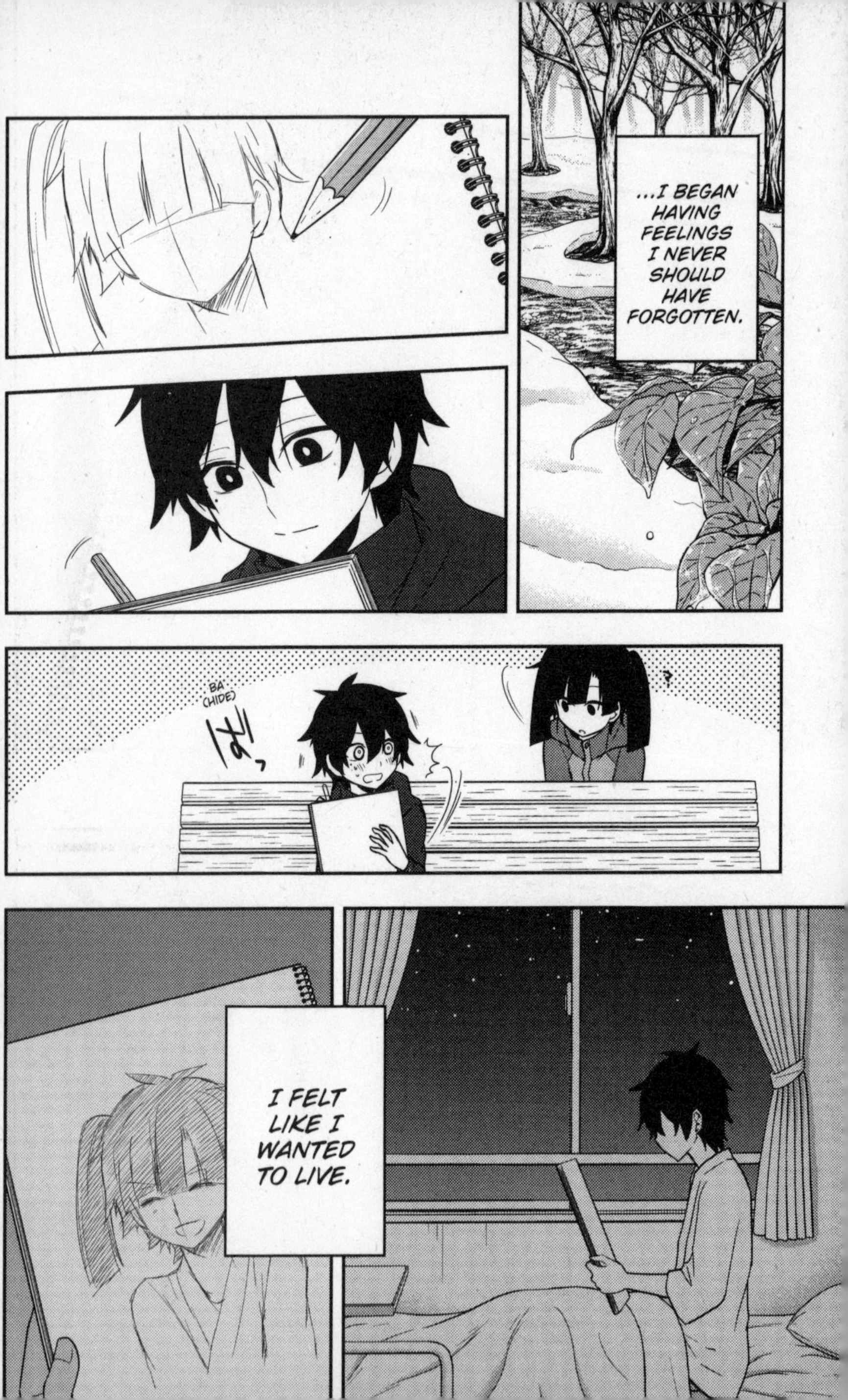
...I BEGAN HAVING FEELINGS I NEVER SHOULD HAVE FORGOTTEN.
BA (HIDE)
I FELT LIKE I WANTED TO LIVE.

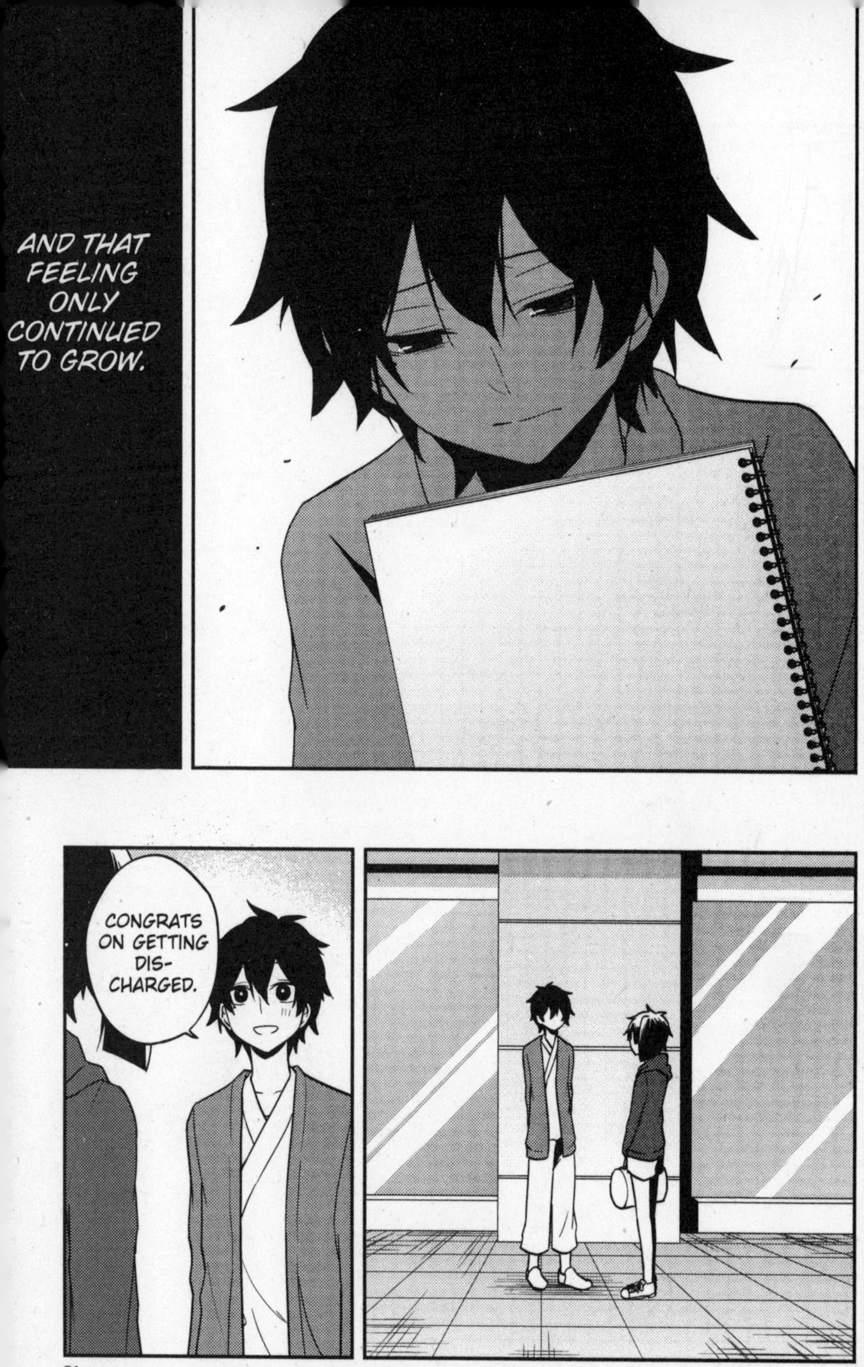
AND THAT FEELING ONLY CONTINUED TO GROW.
CONGRATS ON GETTING DIS-CHARGED.

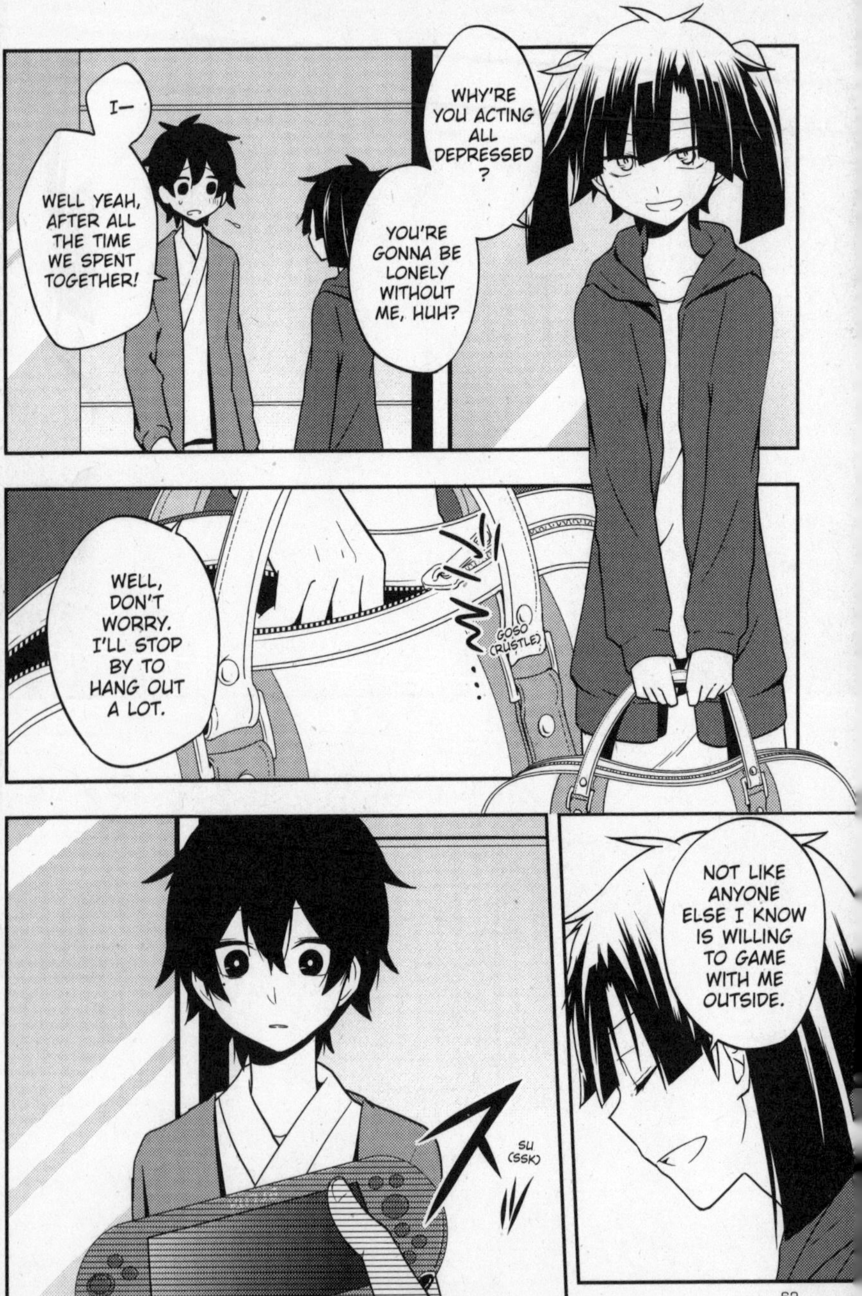
WHY'RE YOU ACTING ALL DEPRESSED?
YOU'RE GONNA BE LONELY WITHOUT ME, HUH?
I—
WELL YEAH, AFTER ALL THE TIME WE SPENT TOGETHER!
GOSO (RUSTLE)
...
WELL, DON'T WORRY. I'LL STOP BY TO HANG OUT A LOT.
NOT LIKE ANYONE ELSE I KNOW IS WILLING TO GAME WITH ME OUTSIDE.
SU (SSK)

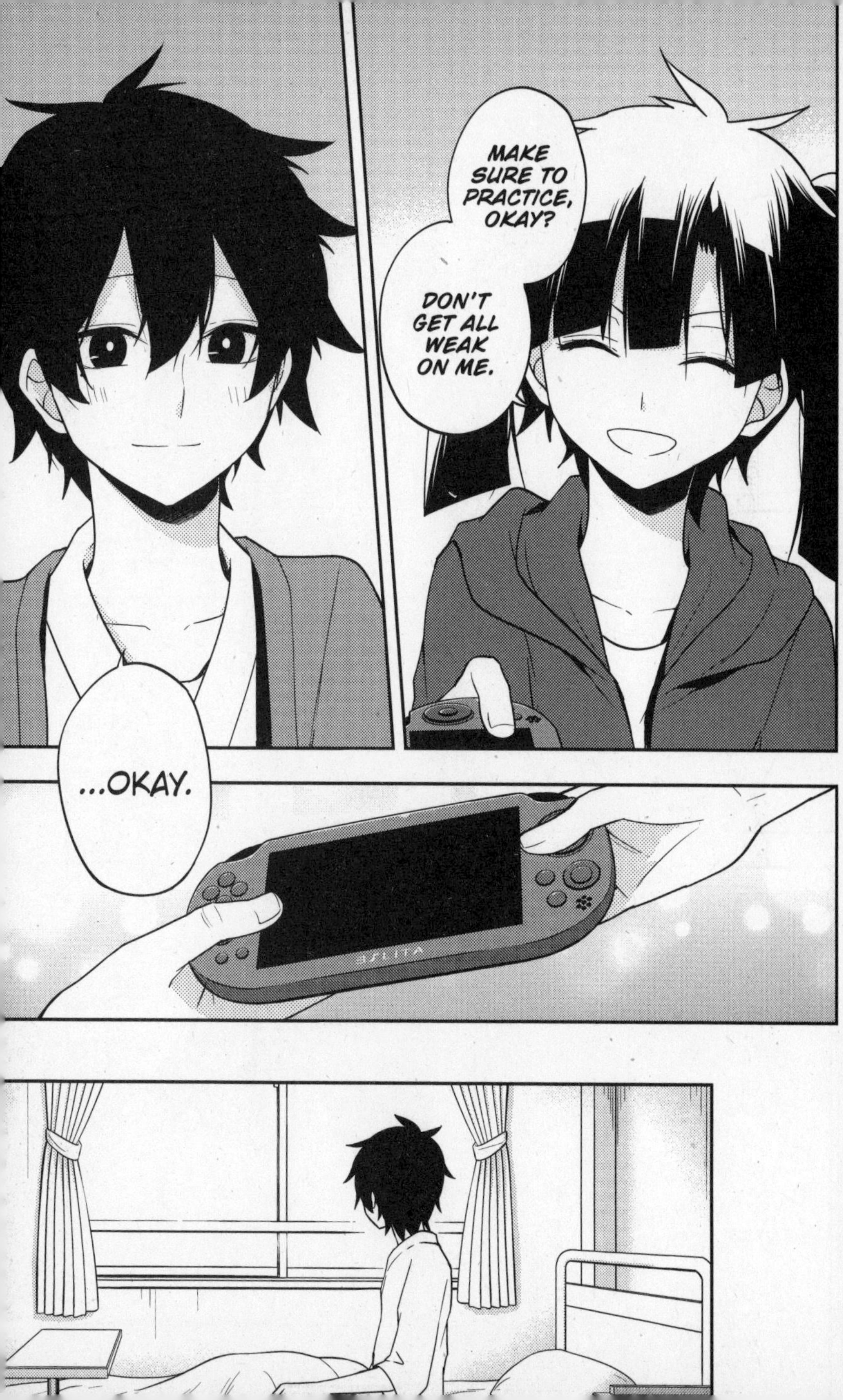
MAKE SURE TO PRACTICE, OKAY?
DON'T GET ALL WEAK ON ME.
...OKAY.

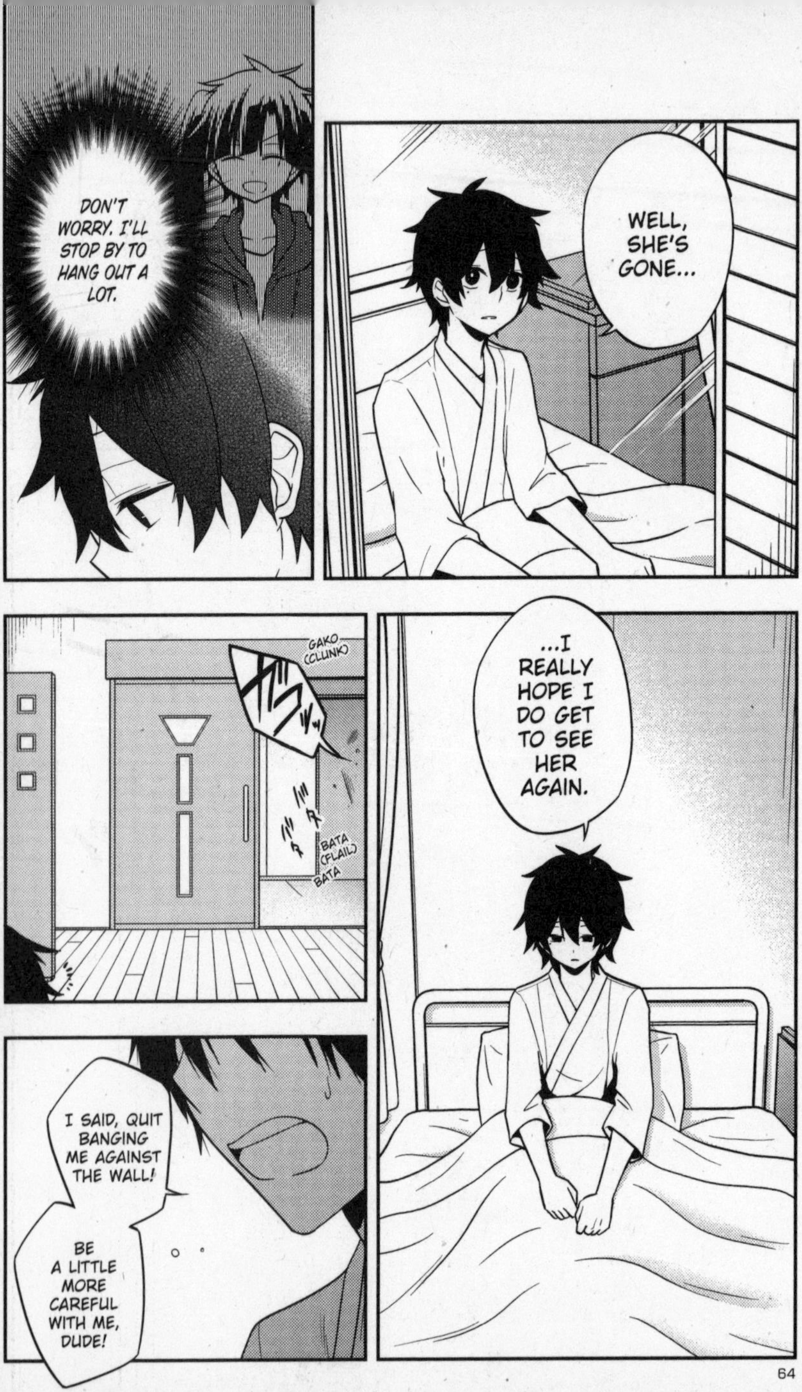
WELL, SHE'S GONE...
DON'T WORRY. I'LL STOP BY TO HANG OUT A LOT.
...I REALLY HOPE I DO GET TO SEE HER AGAIN.
GAKO (CLUNK)
BATA (FLAIL) BATA
I SAID, QUIT BANGING ME AGAINST THE WALL!
BE A LITTLE MORE CAREFUL WITH ME, DUDE!

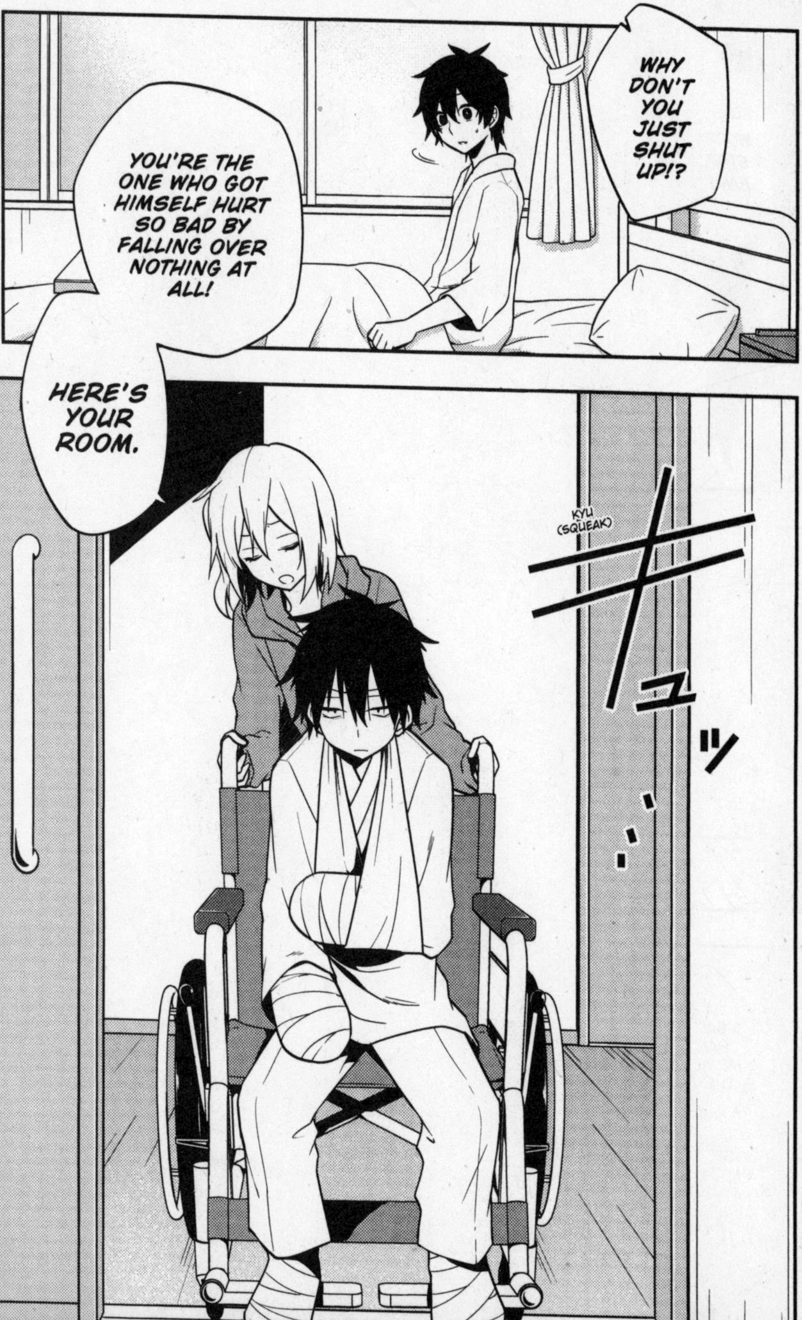
WHY DON'T YOU JUST SHUT UP!?
YOU'RE THE ONE WHO GOT HIMSELF HURT SO BAD BY FALLING OVER NOTHING AT ALL!
HERE'S YOUR ROOM.
KYU (SQUEAK)

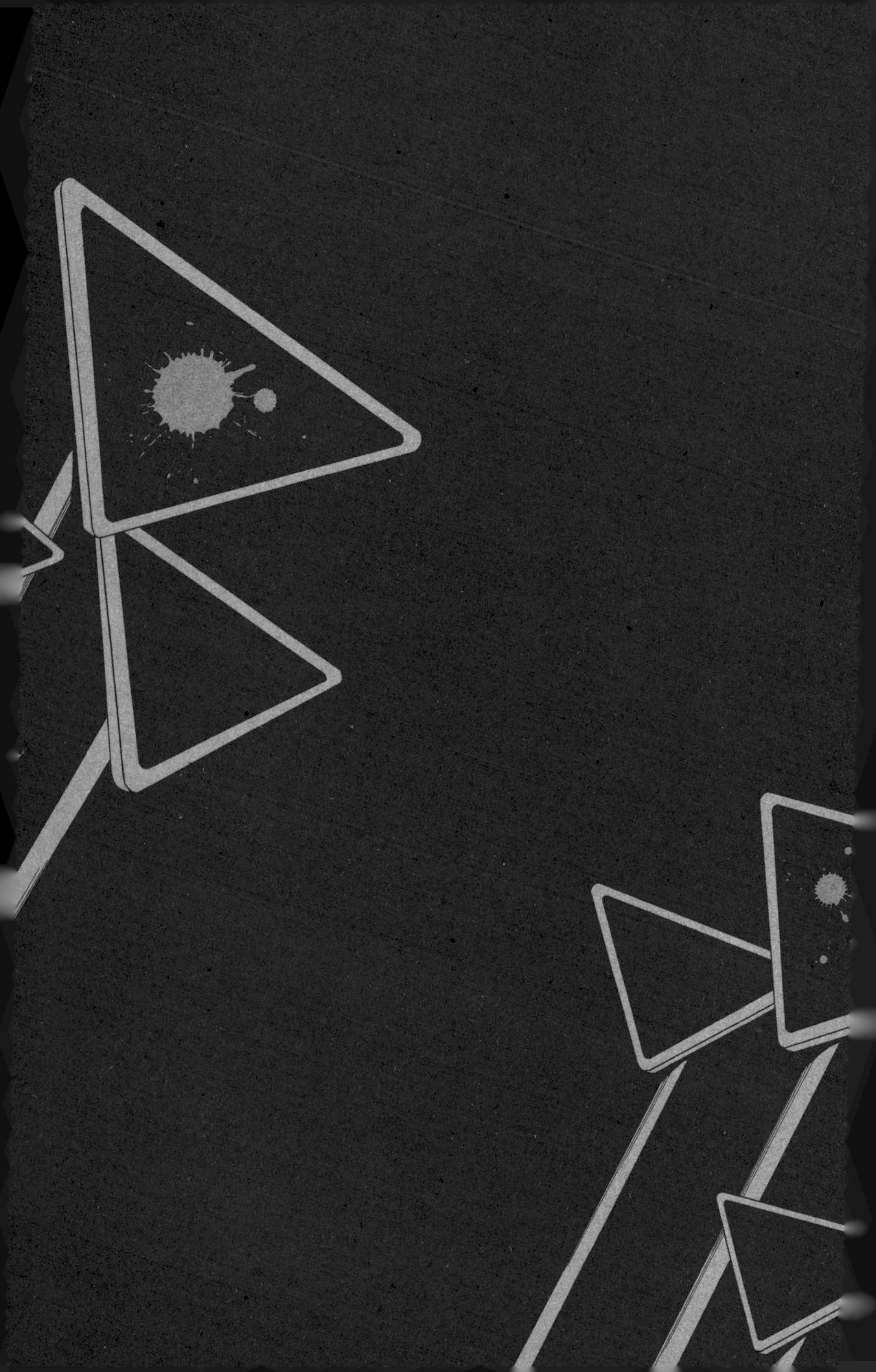

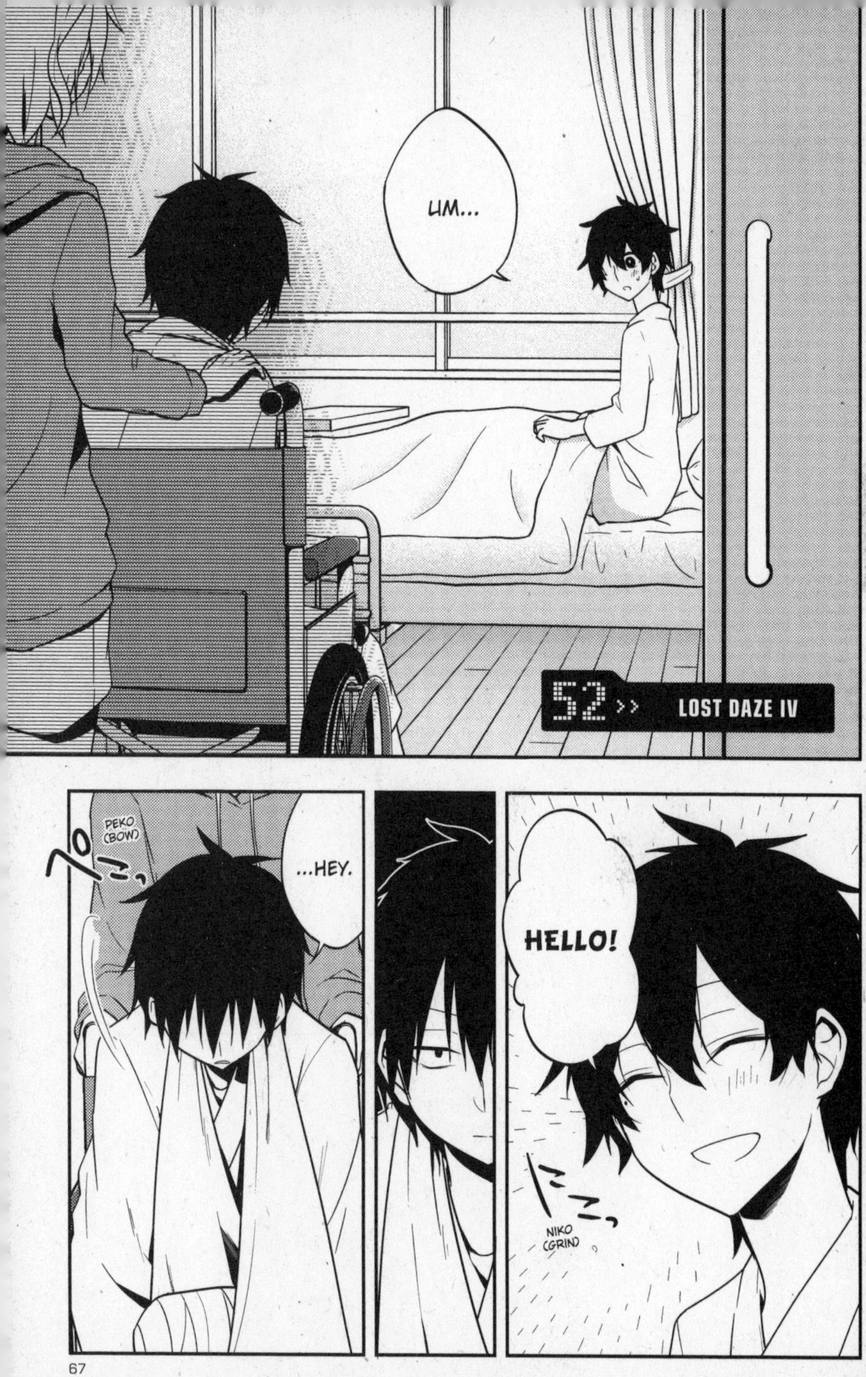
UM...
52 >> LOST DAZE IV
HELLO!
NIKO (GRIN)
...HEY.
PEKO (BOW)

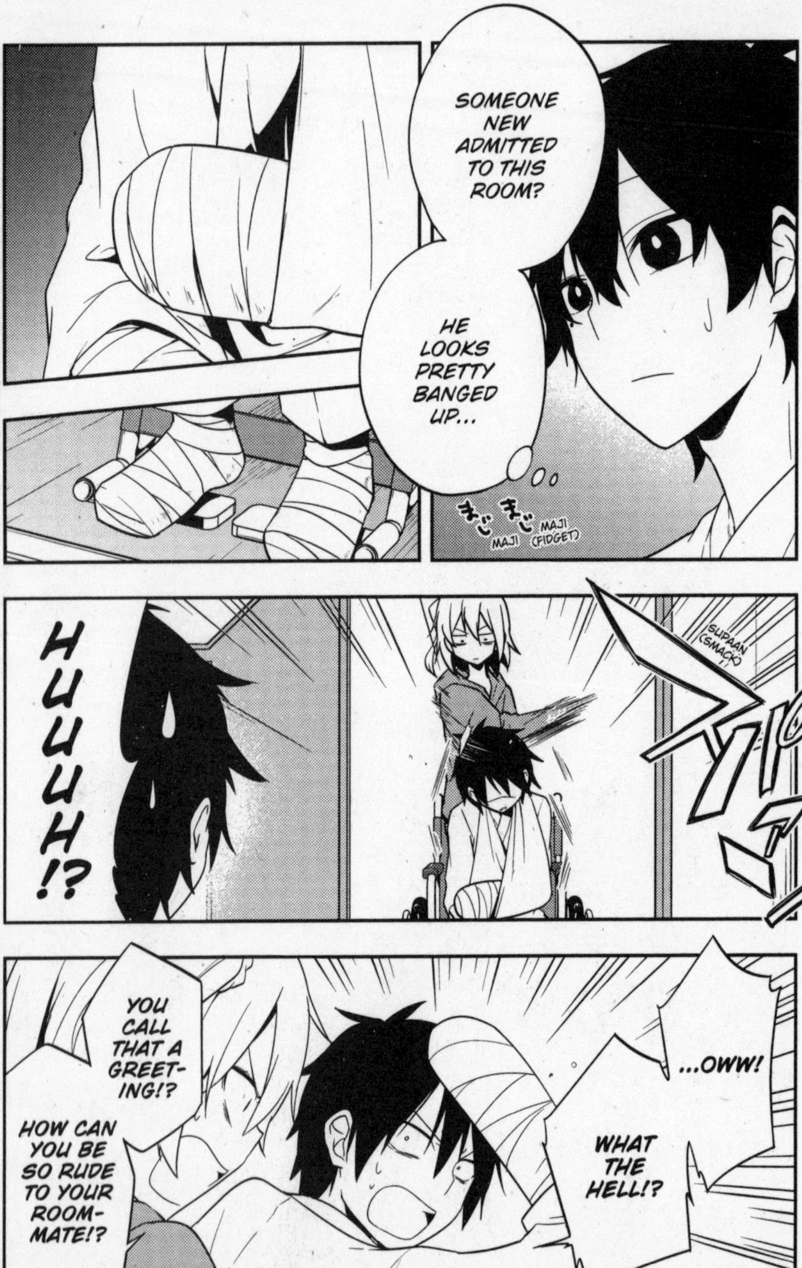
SOMEONE NEW ADMITTED TO THIS ROOM?
HE LOOKS PRETTY BANGED UP...
まじ まじ
MAJI MAJI (FIDGET)
スパァ
SUPAAN (SMACK)
HUUUH!?
...OWW!
WHAT THE HELL!?
YOU CALL THAT A GREET-ING!?
HOW CAN YOU BE SO RUDE TO YOUR ROOM-MATE!?

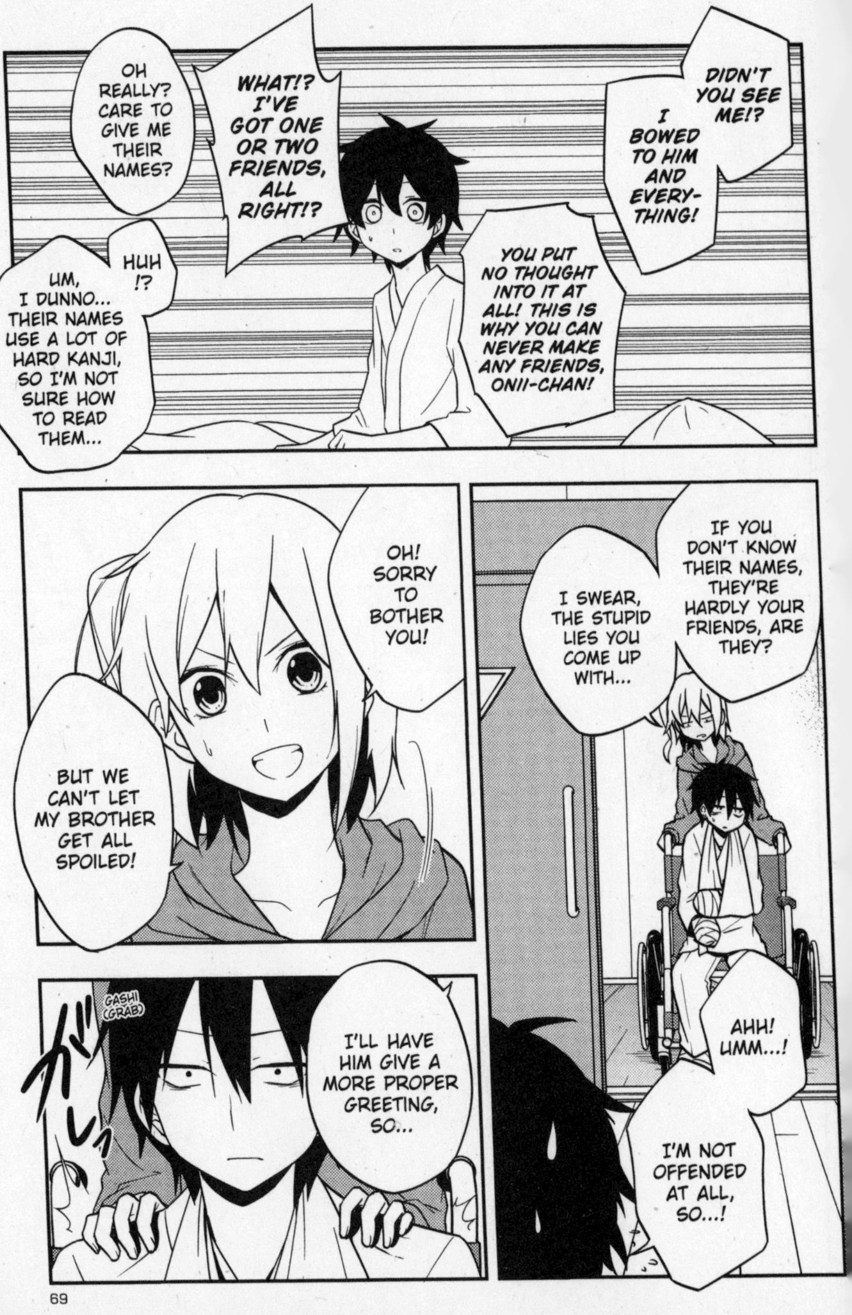
DIDN'T YOU SEE ME!?
I BOWED TO HIM AND EVERY-THING!
YOU PUT NO THOUGHT INTO IT AT ALL! THIS IS WHY YOU CAN NEVER MAKE ANY FRIENDS, ONII-CHAN!
WHAT!? I'VE GOT ONE OR TWO FRIENDS, ALL RIGHT!?
OH REALLY? CARE TO GIVE ME THEIR NAMES?
HUH !?
UM, I DUNNO... THEIR NAMES USE A LOT OF HARD KANJI, SO I'M NOT SURE HOW TO READ THEM...
IF YOU DON'T KNOW THEIR NAMES, THEY'RE HARDLY YOUR FRIENDS, ARE THEY?
I SWEAR, THE STUPID LIES YOU COME UP WITH...
AHH! UMM...!
I'M NOT OFFENDED AT ALL, SO...!
OH! SORRY TO BOTHER YOU!
BUT WE CAN'T LET MY BROTHER GET ALL SPOILED!
I'LL HAVE HIM GIVE A MORE PROPER GREETING, SO...
GASHI (GRAB)

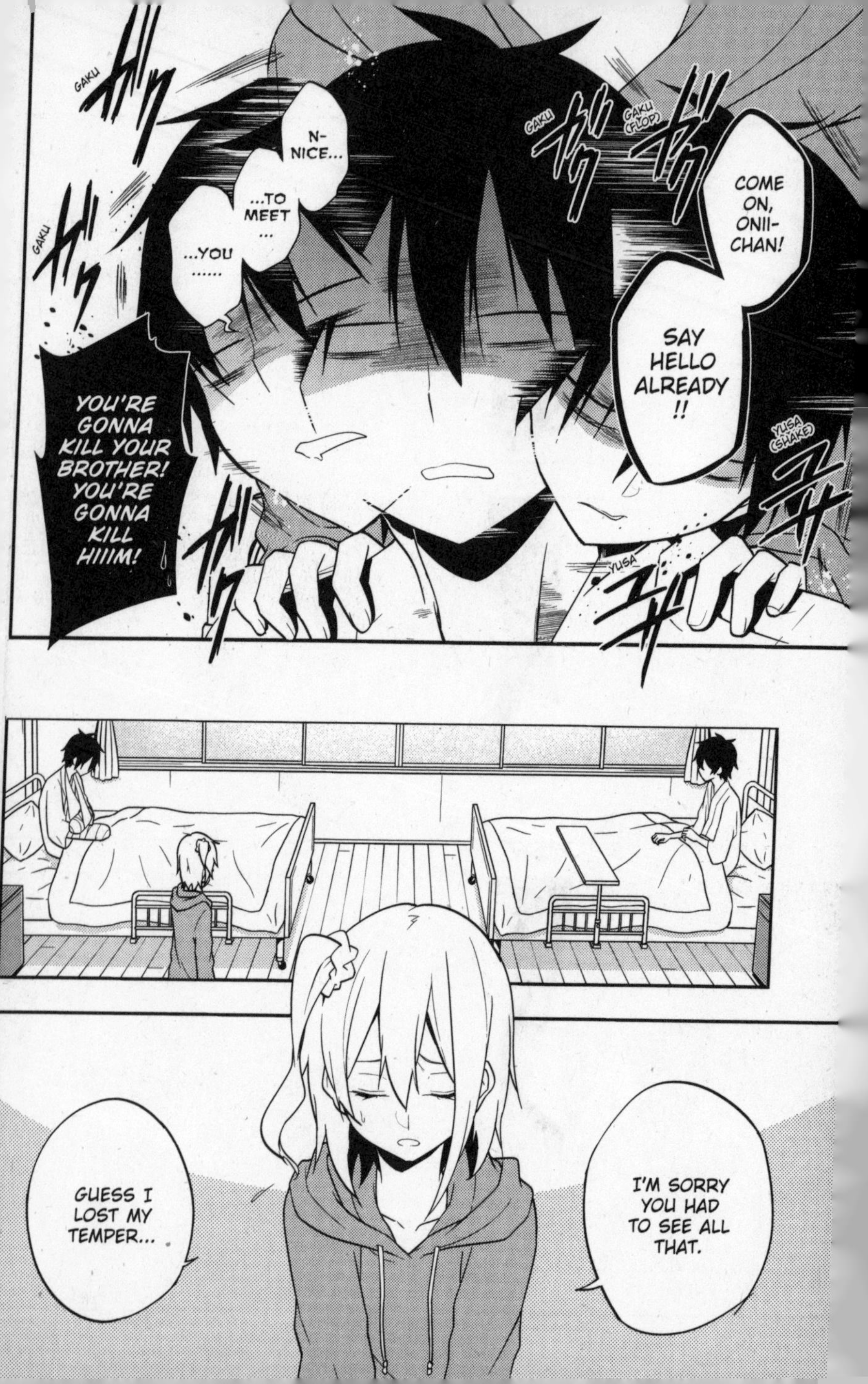
YUSA (SHAKE)
YUSA
COME ON, ONII-CHAN!
SAY HELLO ALREADY!!
GAKU (FLOP)
GAKU
N-NICE...
...TO MEET...
...YOU......
GAKU
GAKU
YOU'RE GONNA KILL YOUR BROTHER! YOU'RE GONNA KILL HIIIM!
I'M SORRY YOU HAD TO SEE ALL THAT.
GUESS I LOST MY TEMPER...

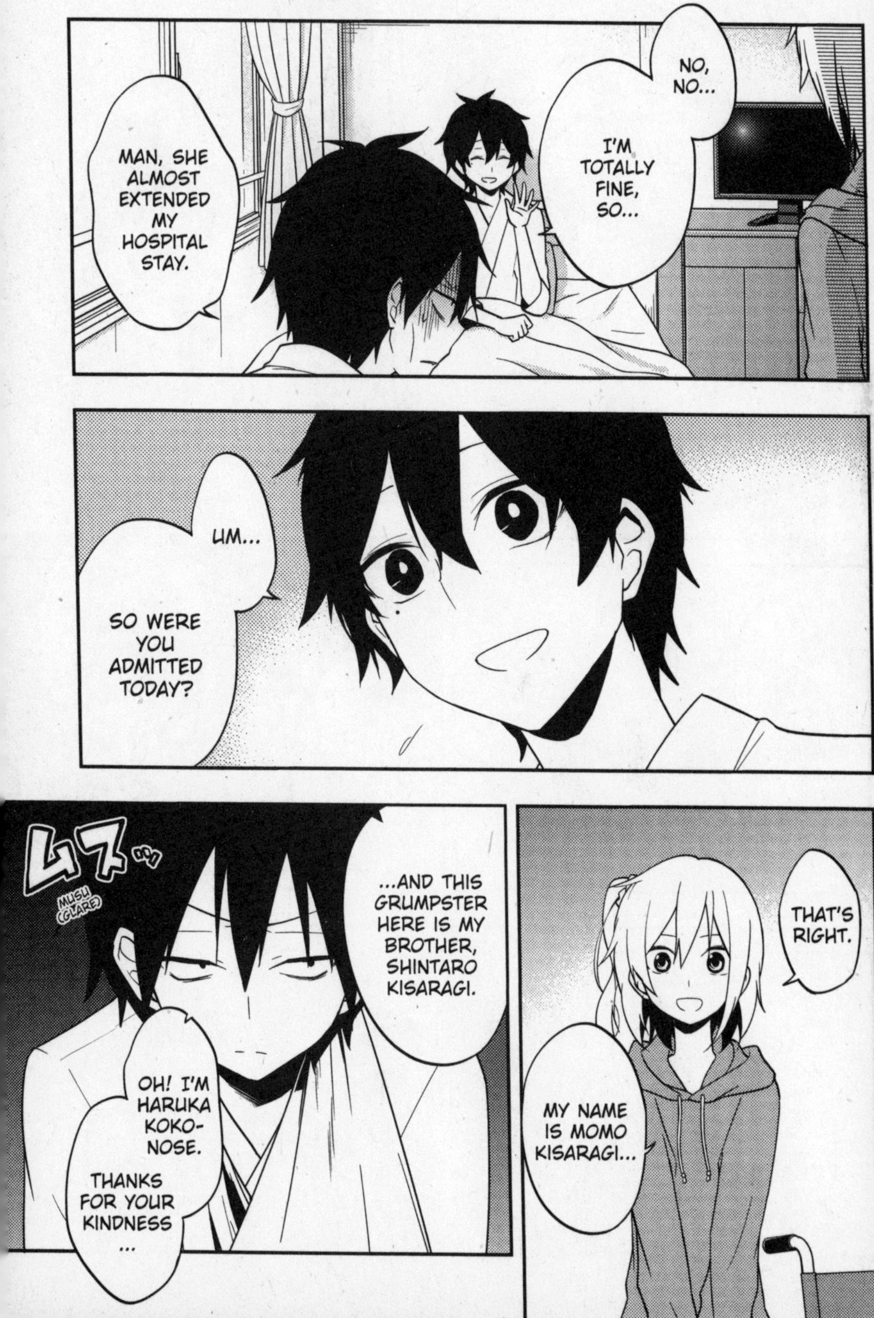
NO, NO... I'M TOTALLY FINE, SO...
MAN, SHE ALMOST EXTENDED MY HOSPITAL STAY.
UM... SO WERE YOU ADMITTED TODAY?
THAT'S RIGHT.
MY NAME IS MOMO KISARAGI...
...AND THIS GRUMPSTER HERE IS MY BROTHER, SHINTARO KISARAGI.
MUSU (GLARE)
OH! I'M HARUKA KOKO-NOSE. THANKS FOR YOUR KINDNESS...

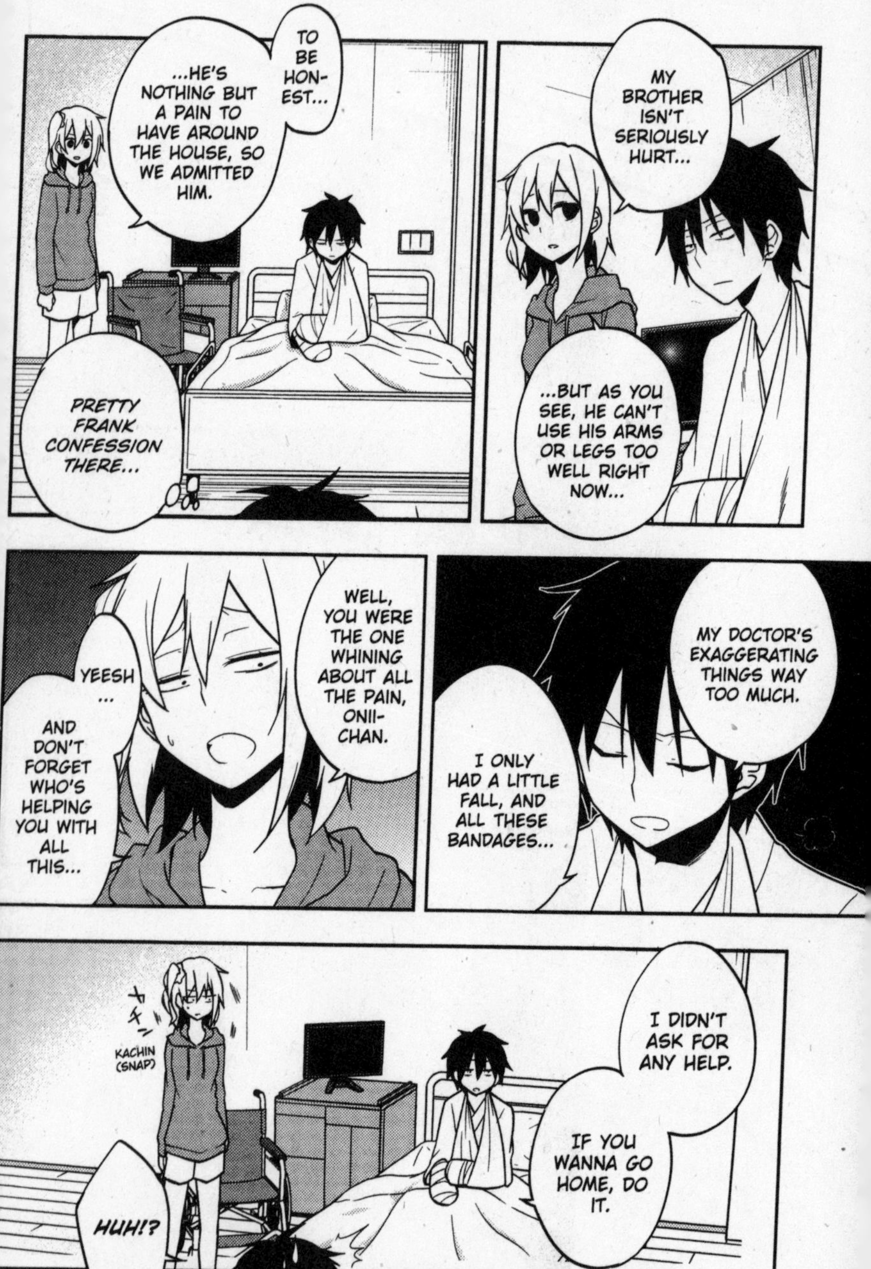
MY BROTHER ISN'T SERIOUSLY HURT...
...BUT AS YOU SEE, HE CAN'T USE HIS ARMS OR LEGS TOO WELL RIGHT NOW...
TO BE HON-EST...
...HE'S NOTHING BUT A PAIN TO HAVE AROUND THE HOUSE, SO WE ADMITTED HIM.
PRETTY FRANK CONFESSION THERE...
MY DOCTOR'S EXAGGERATING THINGS WAY TOO MUCH.
I ONLY HAD A LITTLE FALL, AND ALL THESE BANDAGES...
WELL, YOU WERE THE ONE WHINING ABOUT ALL THE PAIN, ONII-CHAN.
YEESH ...
AND DON'T FORGET WHO'S HELPING YOU WITH ALL THIS...
I DIDN'T ASK FOR ANY HELP.
IF YOU WANNA GO HOME, DO IT.
KACHIN (SNAP)
HUH!?

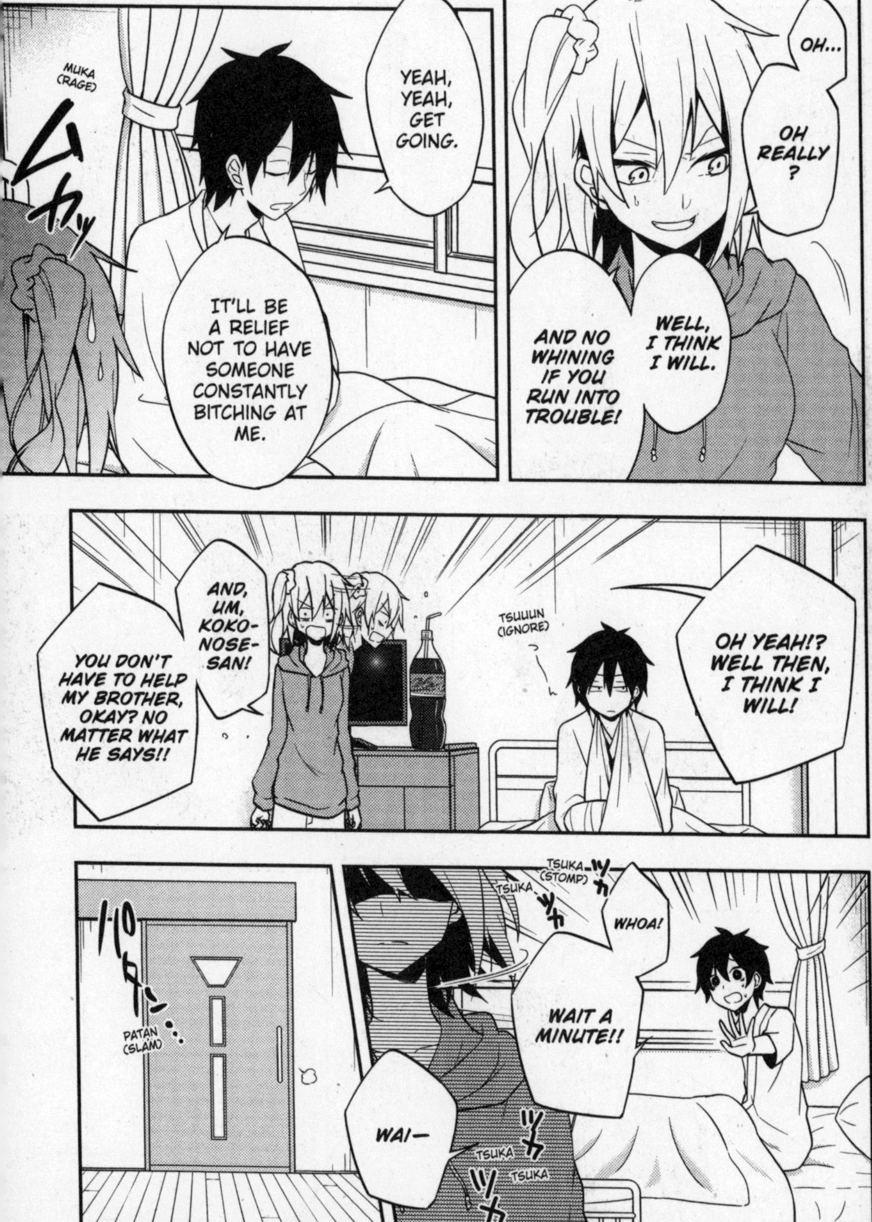
OH...
OH REALLY?
WELL, I THINK I WILL.
AND NO WHINING IF YOU RUN INTO TROUBLE!
YEAH, YEAH, GET GOING.
MUKA (RAGE)
IT'LL BE A RELIEF NOT TO HAVE SOMEONE CONSTANTLY BITCHING AT ME.
OH YEAH!? WELL THEN, I THINK I WILL!
TSUUUN (IGNORE)
AND, UM, KOKONOSE-SAN!
YOU DON'T HAVE TO HELP MY BROTHER, OKAY? NO MATTER WHAT HE SAYS!!
TSUKA (STOMP)
TSUKA
WHOA!
WAIT A MINUTE!!
WAI—
TSUKA
TSUKA
PATAN (SLAM)

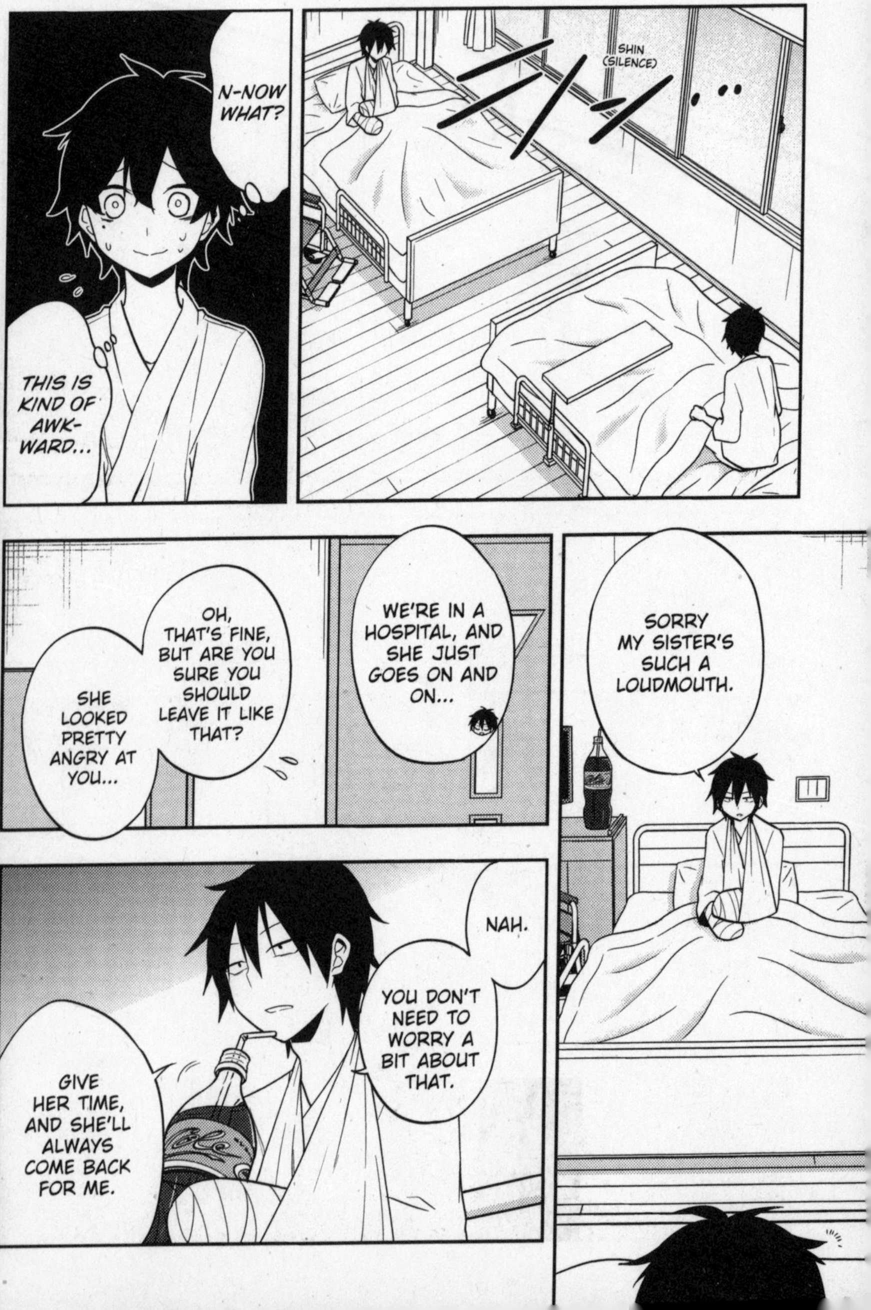
SHIN (SILENCE)
...
N-NOW WHAT?
THIS IS KIND OF AWK-WARD...
SORRY MY SISTER'S SUCH A LOUDMOUTH.
WE'RE IN A HOSPITAL, AND SHE JUST GOES ON AND ON...
OH, THAT'S FINE, BUT ARE YOU SURE YOU SHOULD LEAVE IT LIKE THAT?
SHE LOOKED PRETTY ANGRY AT YOU...
NAH.
YOU DON'T NEED TO WORRY A BIT ABOUT THAT.
GIVE HER TIME, AND SHE'LL ALWAYS COME BACK FOR ME.

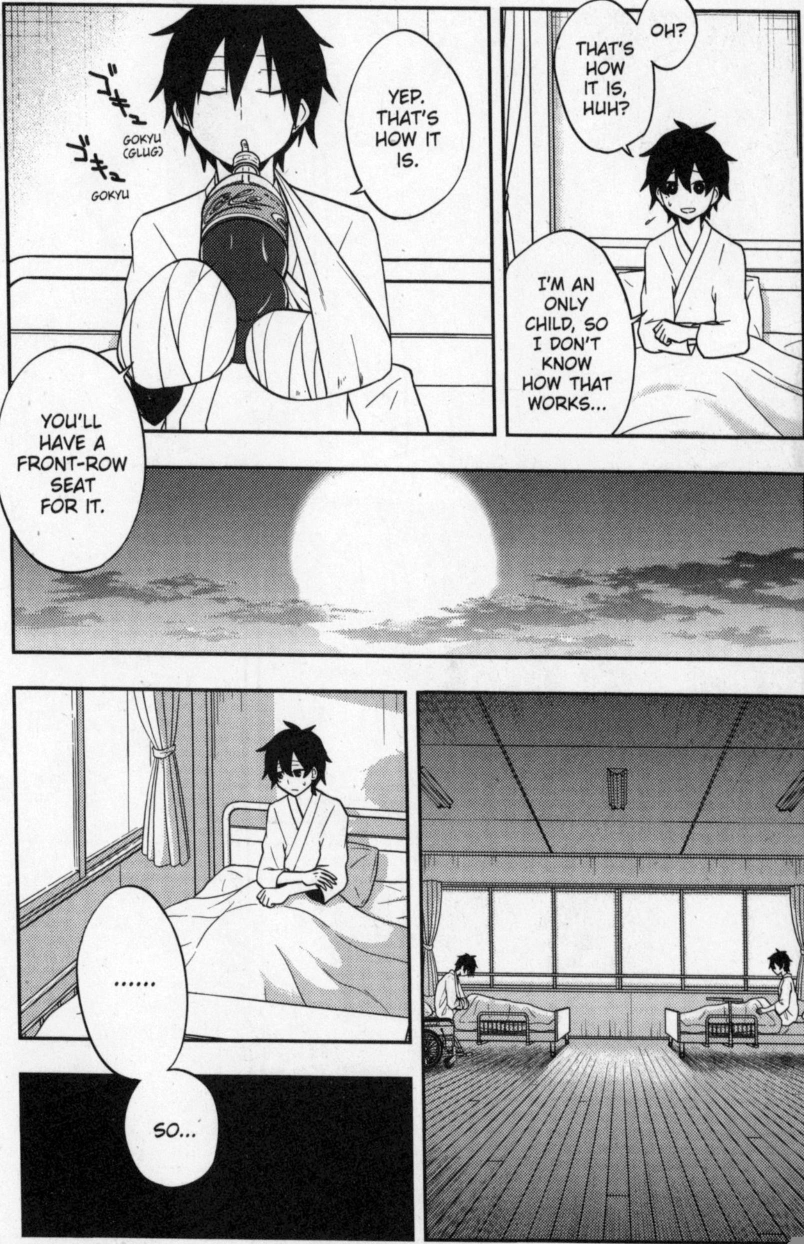
OH?
THAT'S HOW IT IS, HUH?
I'M AN ONLY CHILD, SO I DON'T KNOW HOW THAT WORKS...
YEP. THAT'S HOW IT IS.
ゴキュ
GOKYU (GLUG)
ゴキュ
GOKYU
YOU'LL HAVE A FRONT-ROW SEAT FOR IT.
......
SO...

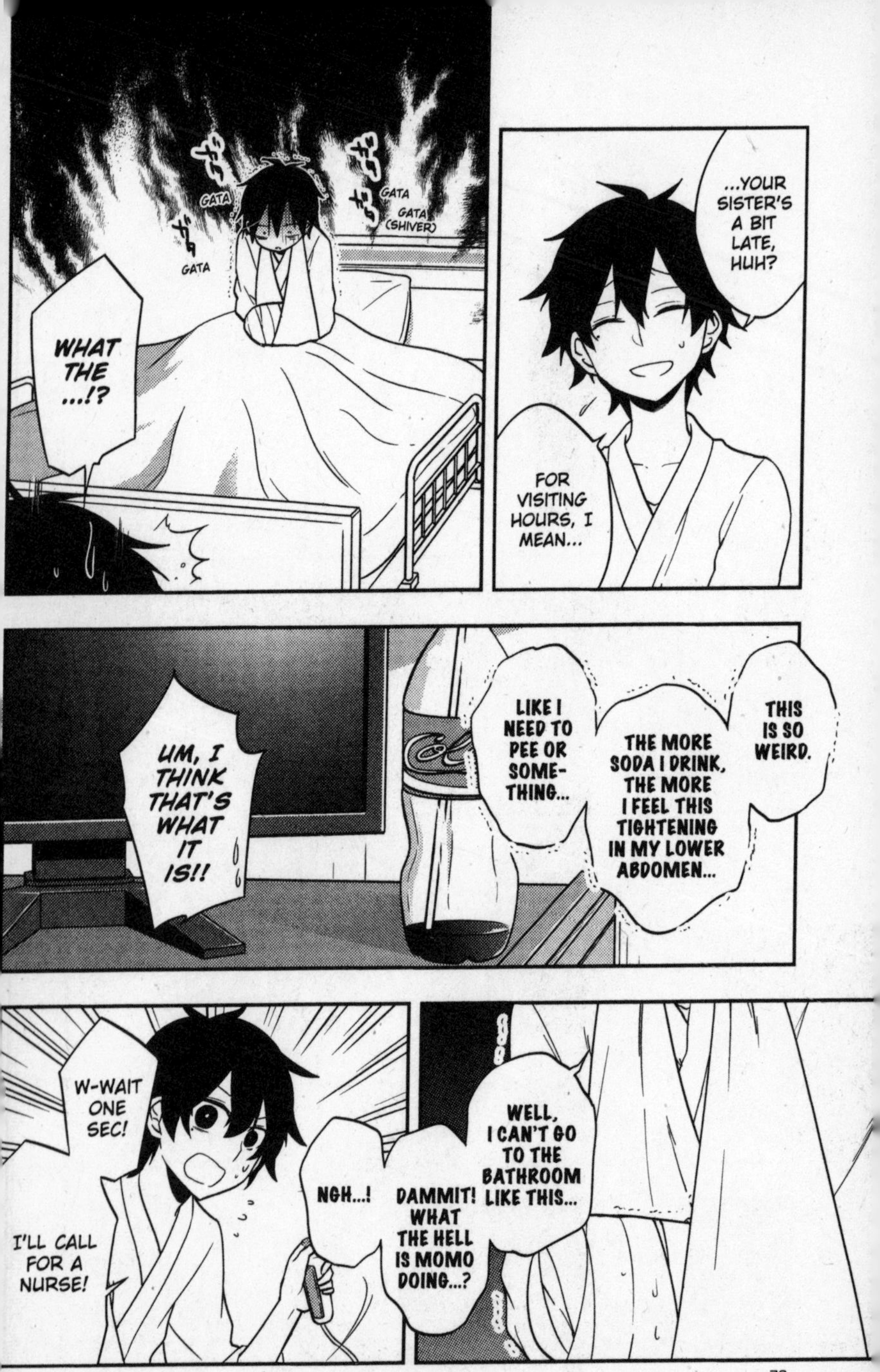

...YOUR SISTER'S A BIT LATE, HUH?
FOR VISITING HOURS, I MEAN...
GATA GATA (SHIVER)
GATA
GATA
WHAT THE ...!?
THIS IS SO WEIRD.
THE MORE SODA I DRINK, THE MORE I FEEL THIS TIGHTENING IN MY LOWER ABDOMEN...
LIKE I NEED TO PEE OR SOME-THING...
UM, I THINK THAT'S WHAT IT IS!!
WELL, I CAN'T GO TO THE BATHROOM LIKE THIS...
DAMMIT! WHAT THE HELL IS MOMO DOING...?
NGH...!
W-WAIT ONE SEC!
I'LL CALL FOR A NURSE!

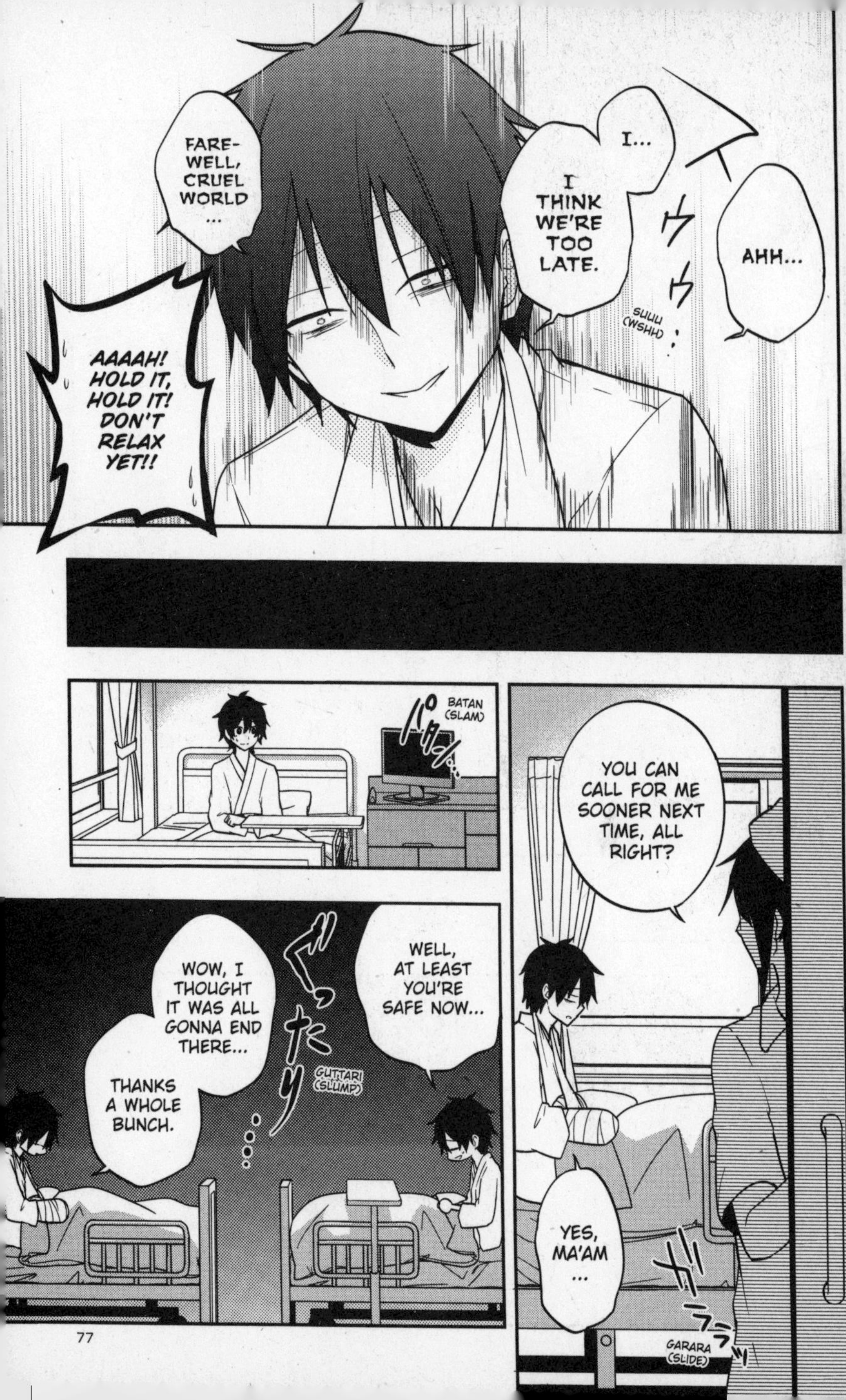
AHH...
I...
I THINK WE'RE TOO LATE.
SUUU (WSHH)
FARE-WELL, CRUEL WORLD...
AAAAH! HOLD IT, HOLD IT! DON'T RELAX YET!!
YOU CAN CALL FOR ME SOONER NEXT TIME, ALL RIGHT?
YES, MA'AM...
GARARA (SLIDE)
BATAN (SLAM)
WELL, AT LEAST YOU'RE SAFE NOW...
GUTTARI (SLUMP)
WOW, I THOUGHT IT WAS ALL GONNA END THERE...
THANKS A WHOLE BUNCH.

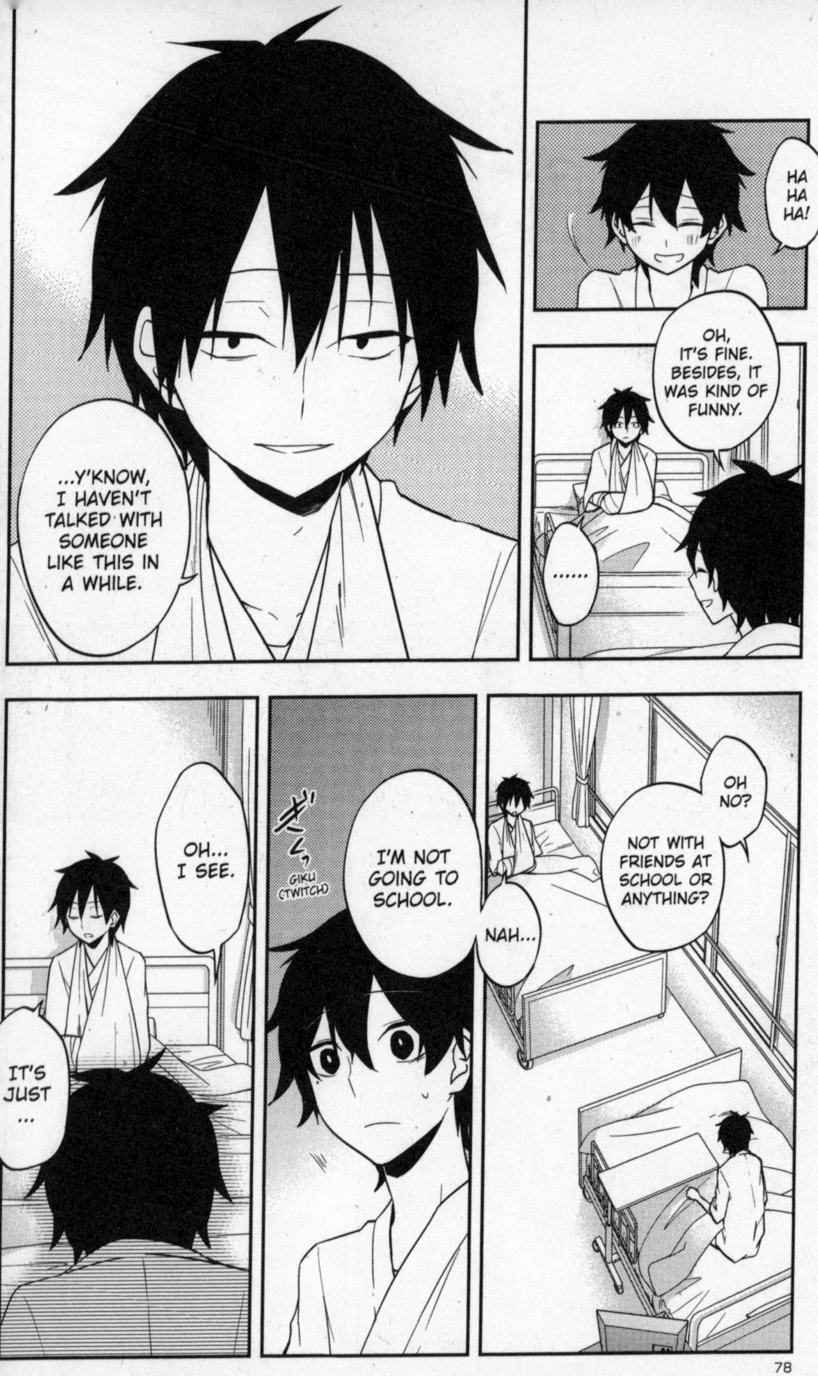

HA HA HA!
OH, IT'S FINE. BESIDES, IT WAS KIND OF FUNNY.
......
...Y'KNOW, I HAVEN'T TALKED WITH SOMEONE LIKE THIS IN A WHILE.
OH NO?
NOT WITH FRIENDS AT SCHOOL OR ANYTHING?
NAH...
ぎくっ
GIKU (TWITCH)
I'M NOT GOING TO SCHOOL.
OH... I SEE.
IT'S JUST ...

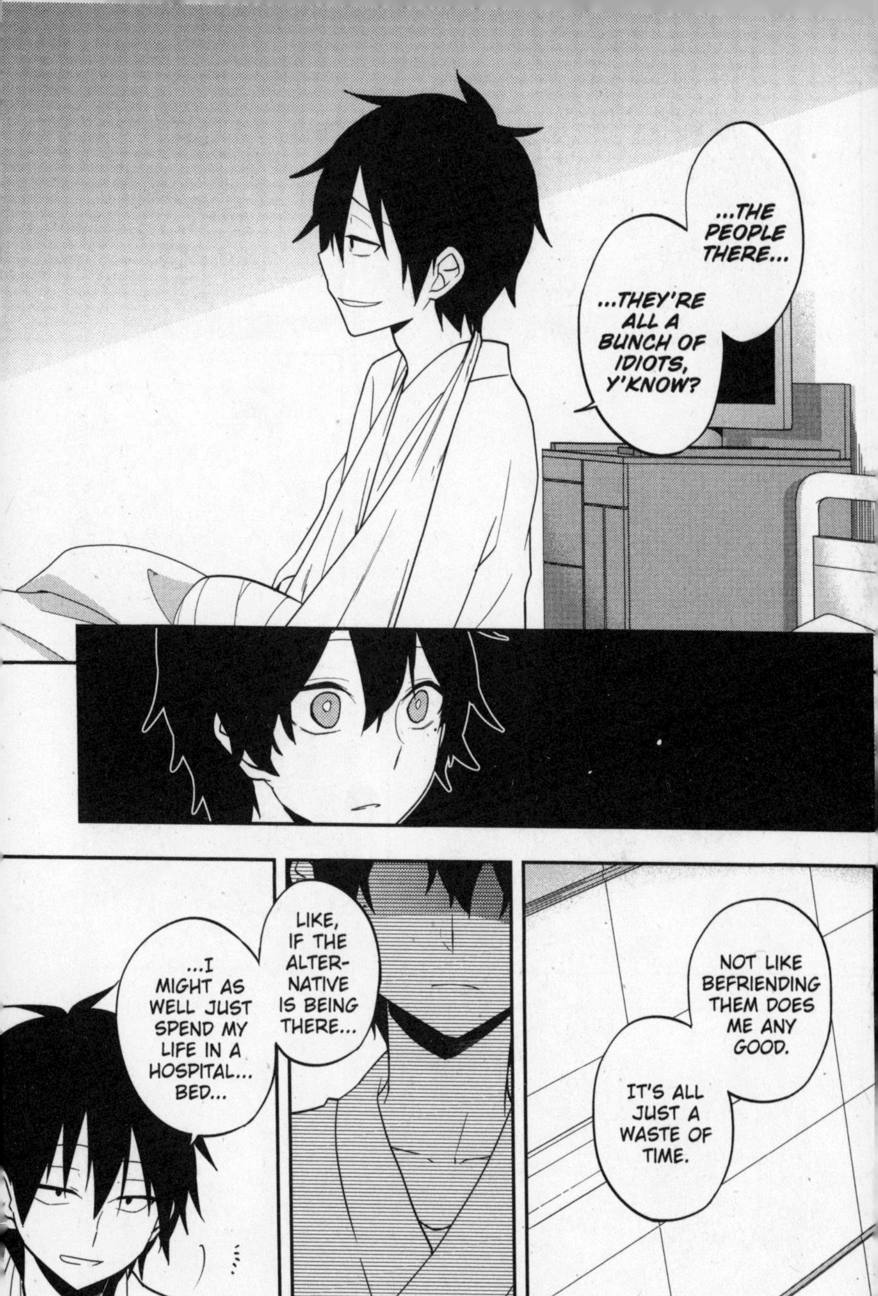
...THE PEOPLE THERE...
...THEY'RE ALL A BUNCH OF IDIOTS, Y'KNOW?
NOT LIKE BEFRIENDING THEM DOES ME ANY GOOD.
IT'S ALL JUST A WASTE OF TIME.
LIKE, IF THE ALTER-NATIVE IS BEING THERE...
...I MIGHT AS WELL JUST SPEND MY LIFE IN A HOSPITAL... BED...
...

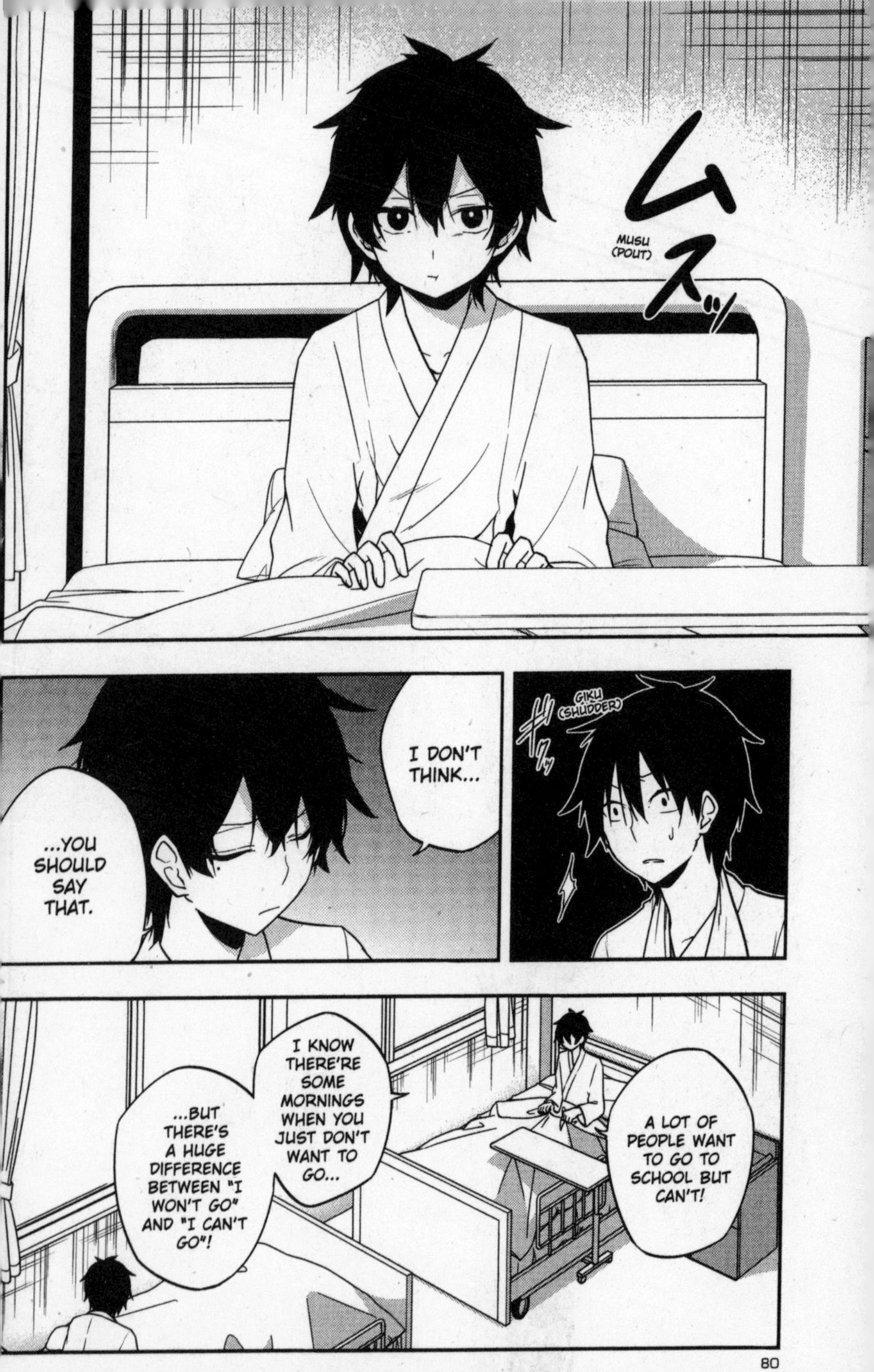
ムスッ
MUSU (POUT)
ギクッ
GIKU (SHUDDER)
I DON'T THINK...
...YOU SHOULD SAY THAT.
A LOT OF PEOPLE WANT TO GO TO SCHOOL BUT CAN'T!
I KNOW THERE'RE SOME MORNINGS WHEN YOU JUST DON'T WANT TO GO...
...BUT THERE'S A HUGE DIFFERENCE BETWEEN "I WON'T GO" AND "I CAN'T GO"!

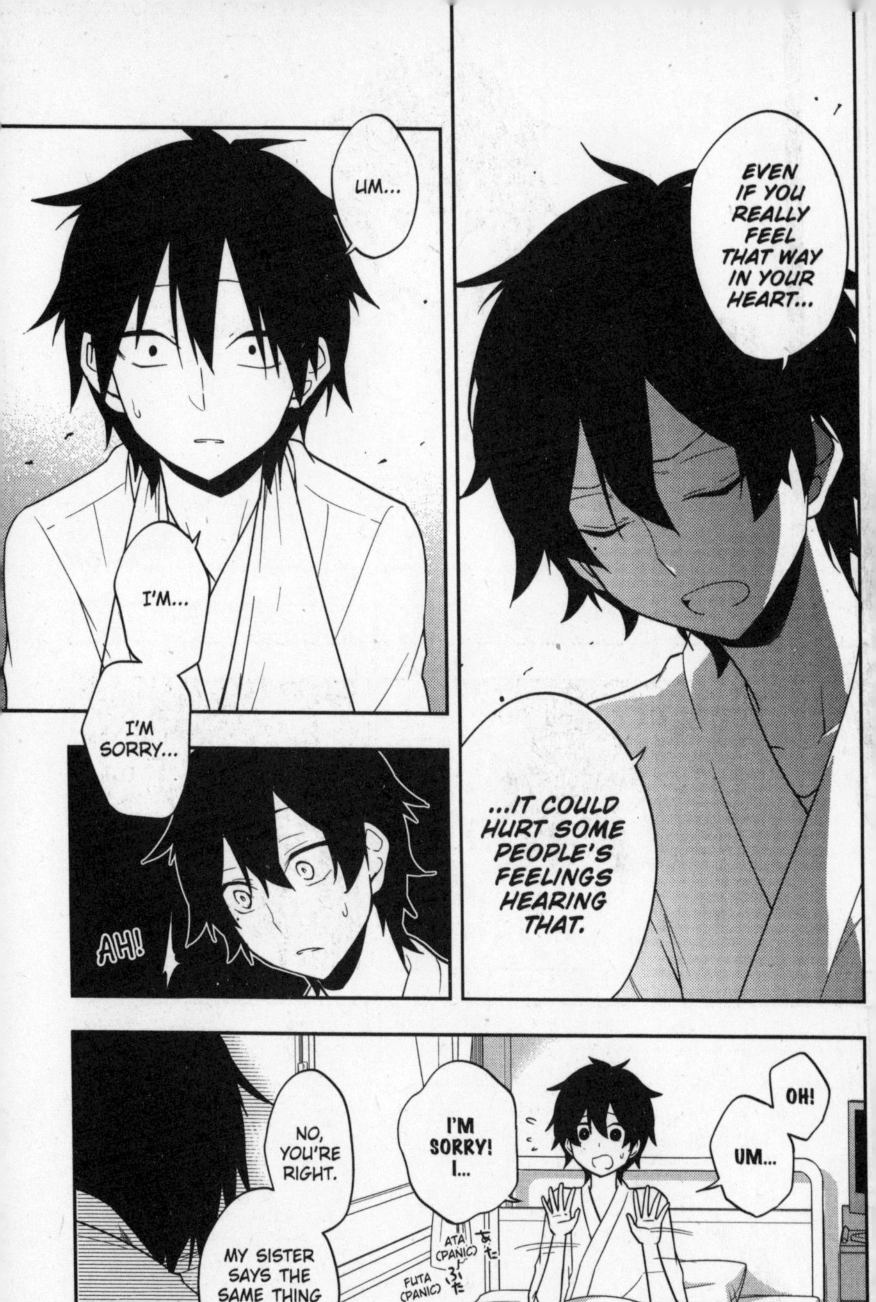
EVEN IF YOU REALLY FEEL THAT WAY IN YOUR HEART...
...IT COULD HURT SOME PEOPLE'S FEELINGS HEARING THAT.
UM...
I'M...
I'M SORRY...
AH!
OH!
UM...
I'M SORRY! I...
ATA (PANIC)
あた
FUTA (PANIC)
ふた
NO, YOU'RE RIGHT.
MY SISTER SAYS THE SAME THING ALL THE TIME...

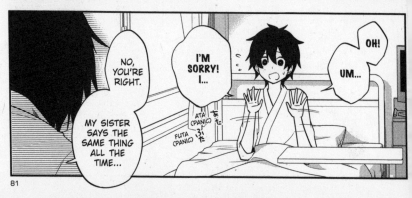

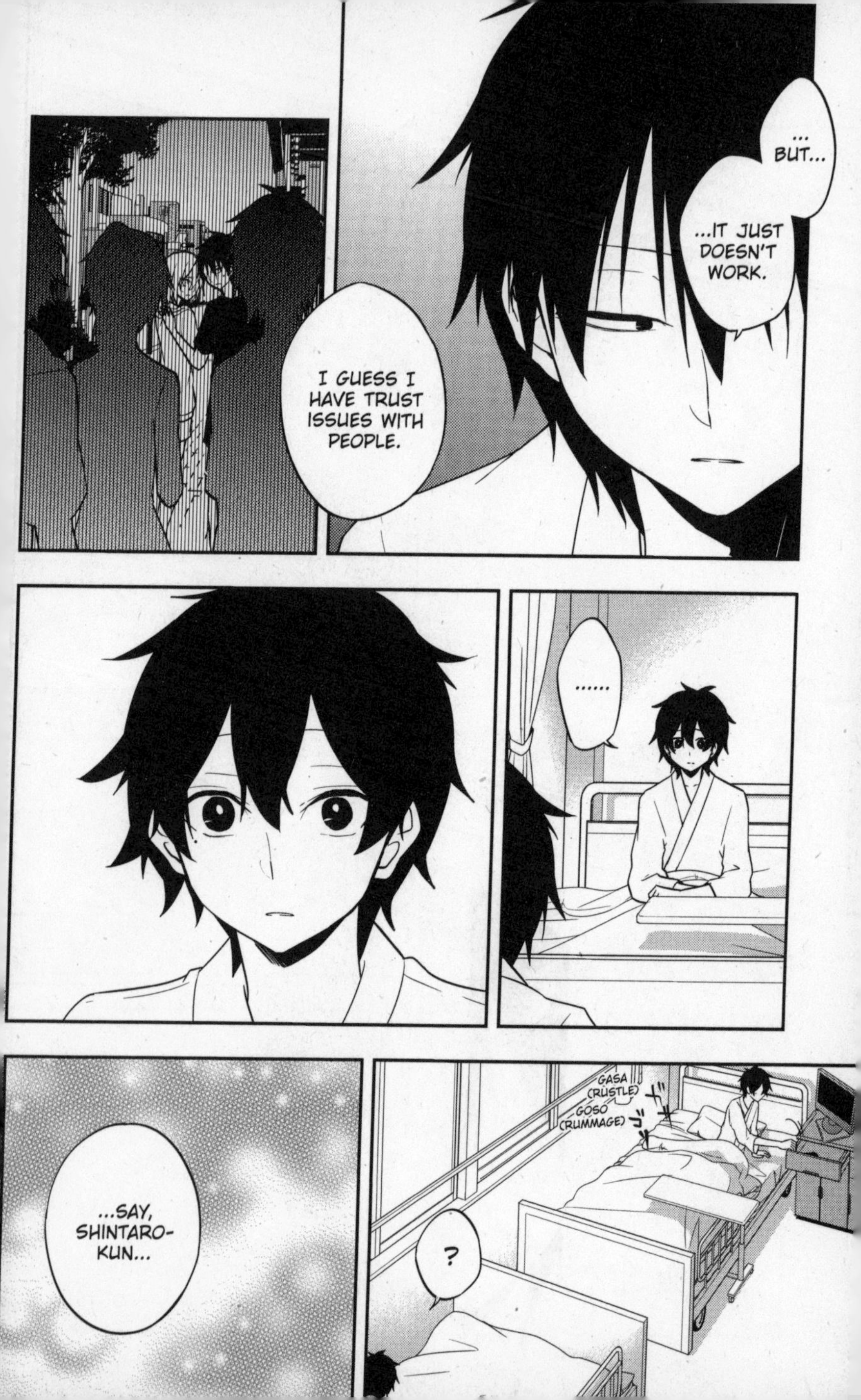
... BUT...
...IT JUST DOESN'T WORK.
I GUESS I HAVE TRUST ISSUES WITH PEOPLE.
......
GASA (RUSTLE)
GOSO (RUMMAGE)
?
...SAY, SHINTARO-KUN...

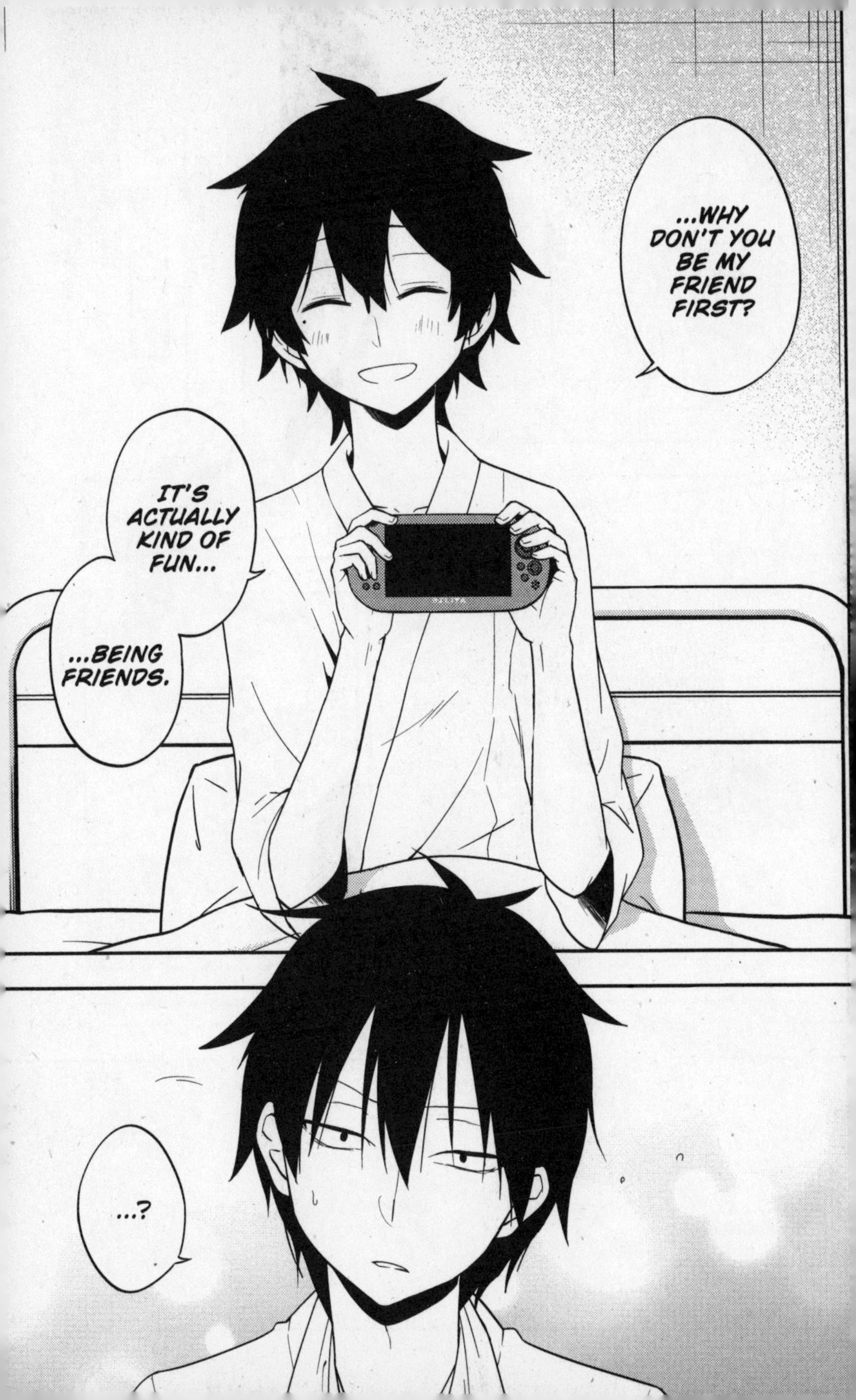
...WHY DON'T YOU BE MY FRIEND FIRST?
IT'S ACTUALLY KIND OF FUN...
...BEING FRIENDS.
...?

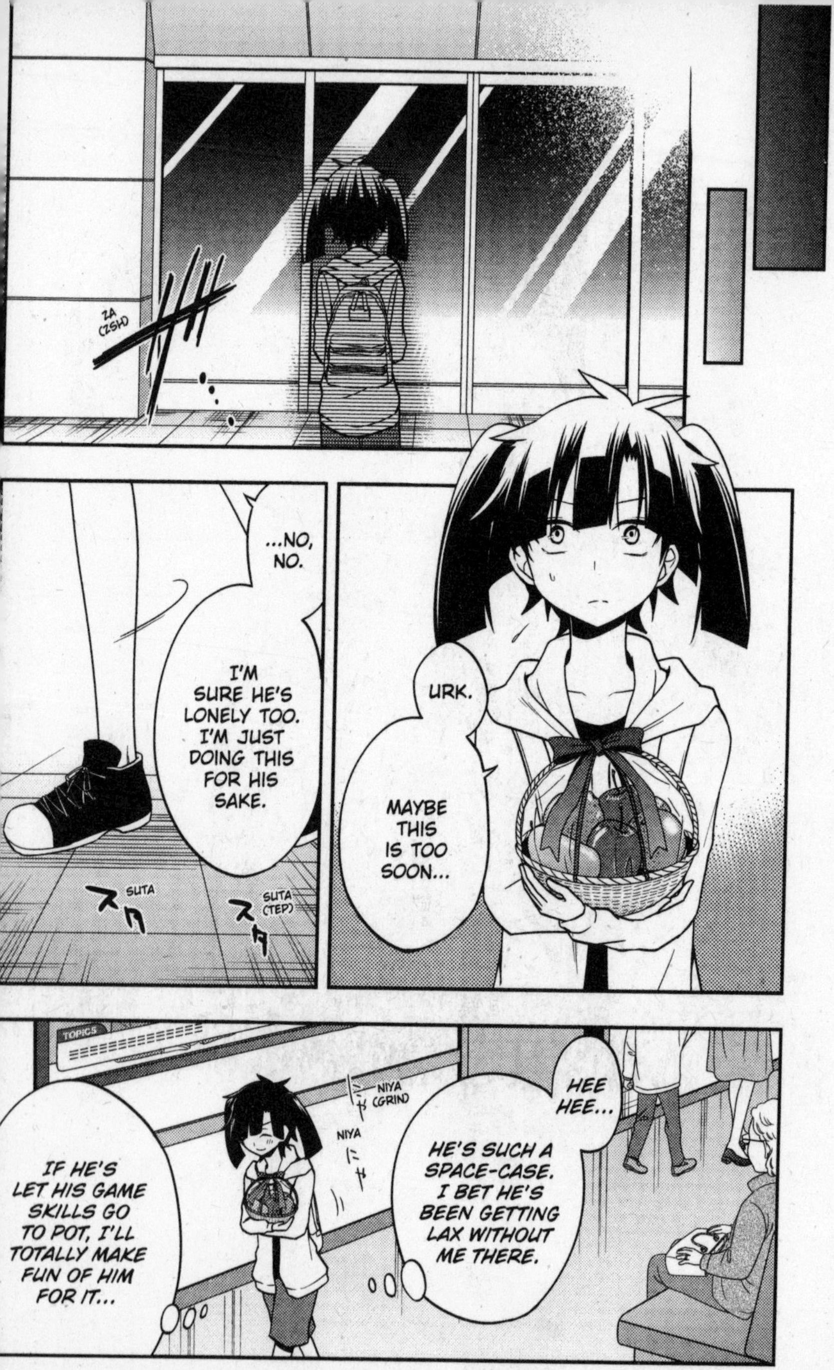

ZA (ZSH)
URK.
MAYBE THIS IS TOO SOON...
...NO, NO.
I'M SURE HE'S LONELY TOO. I'M JUST DOING THIS FOR HIS SAKE.
SUTA
SUTA (TEP)
TOPICS
HEE HEE...
HE'S SUCH A SPACE-CASE. I BET HE'S BEEN GETTING LAX WITHOUT ME THERE.
NIYA (GRIND)
NIYA
IF HE'S LET HIS GAME SKILLS GO TO POT, I'LL TOTALLY MAKE FUN OF HIM FOR IT...

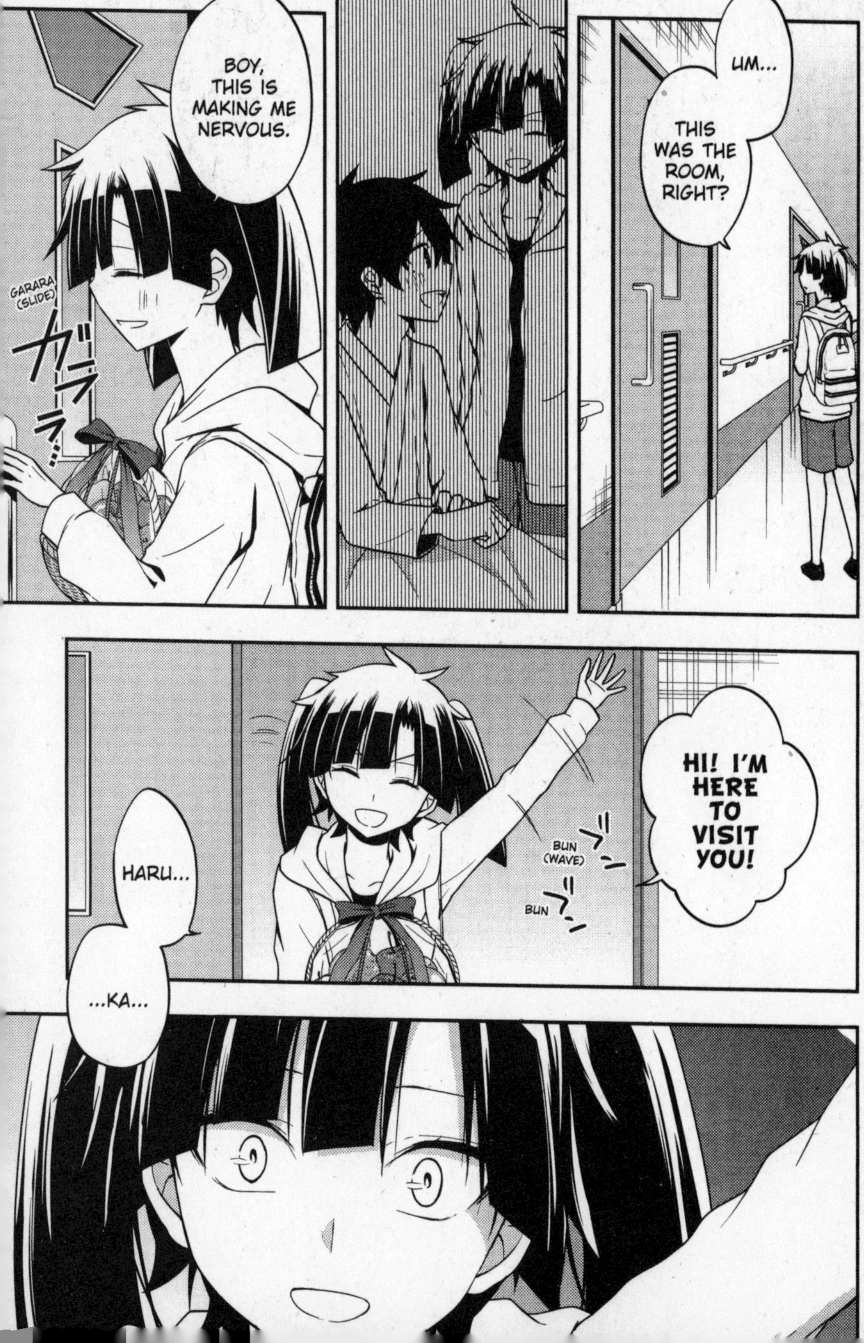
UM...
THIS WAS THE ROOM, RIGHT?
BOY, THIS IS MAKING ME NERVOUS.
GARARA (SLIDE)
ガララ…
HI! I'M HERE TO VISIT YOU!
BUN (WAVE)
BUN
HARU...
...KA...

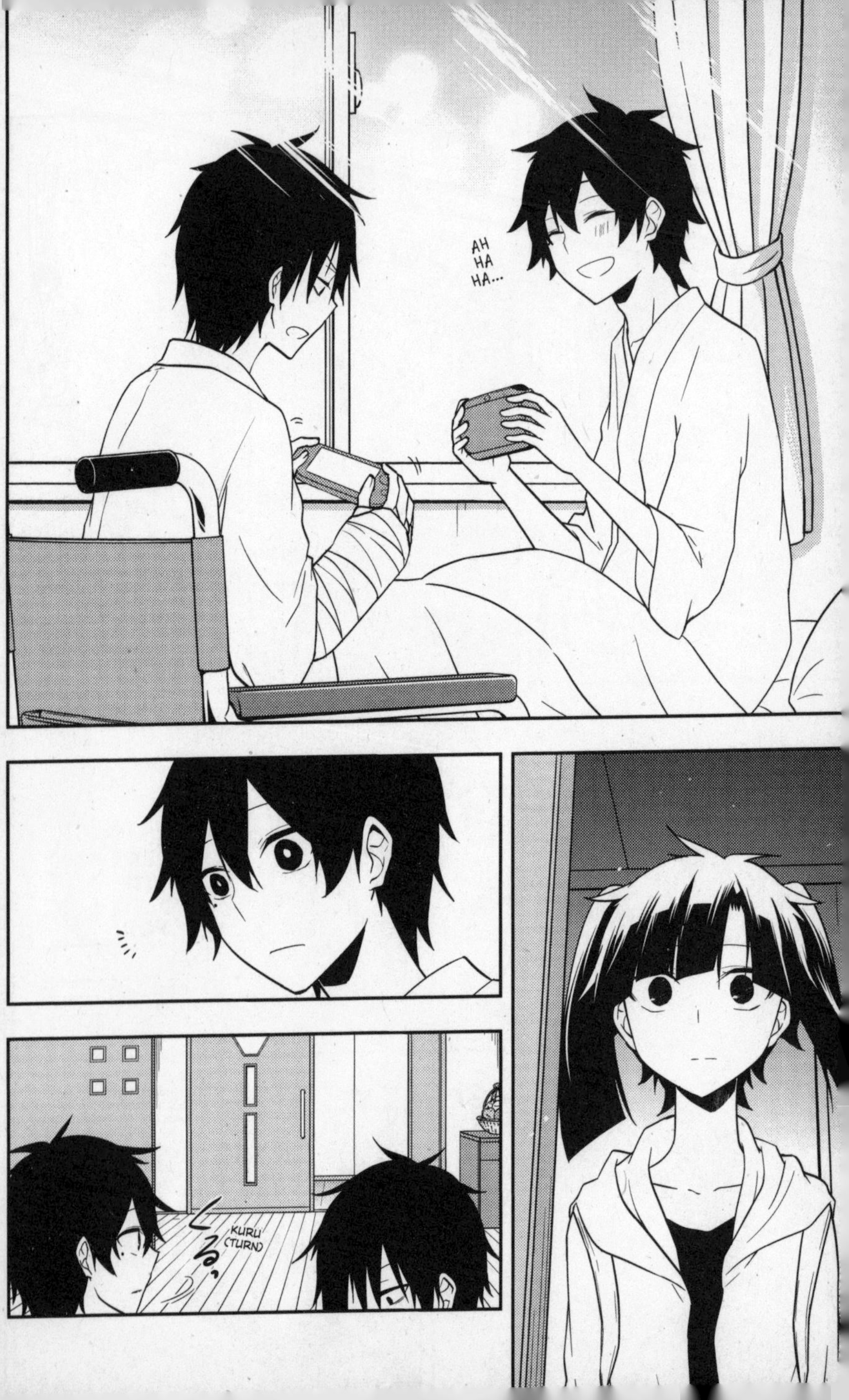
AH HA HA...
KURU (TURN)

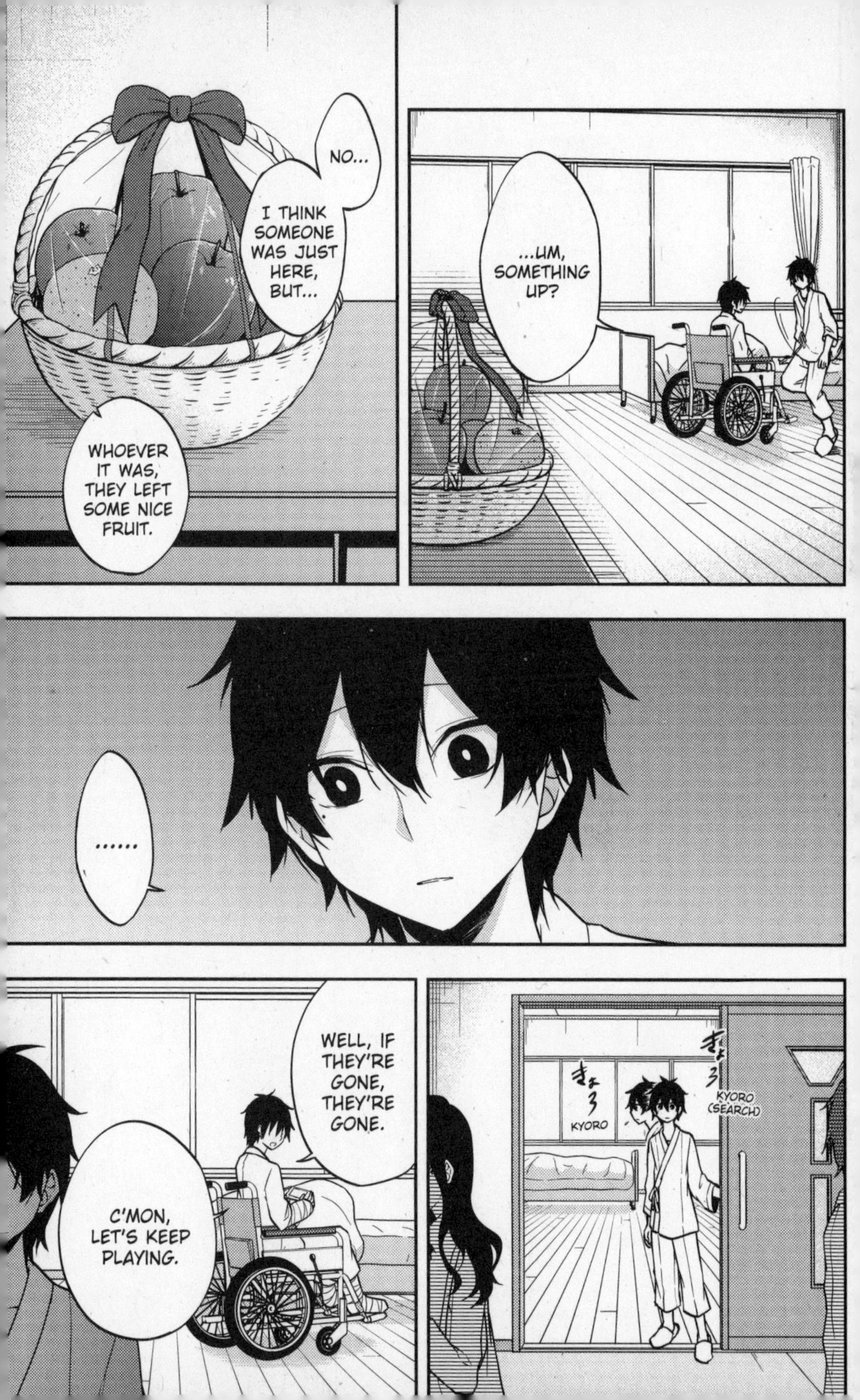
...UM, SOMETHING UP?
NO...
I THINK SOMEONE WAS JUST HERE, BUT...
WHOEVER IT WAS, THEY LEFT SOME NICE FRUIT.
......
きょろ
KYORO (SEARCH)
きょろ
KYORO
WELL, IF THEY'RE GONE, THEY'RE GONE.
C'MON, LET'S KEEP PLAYING.

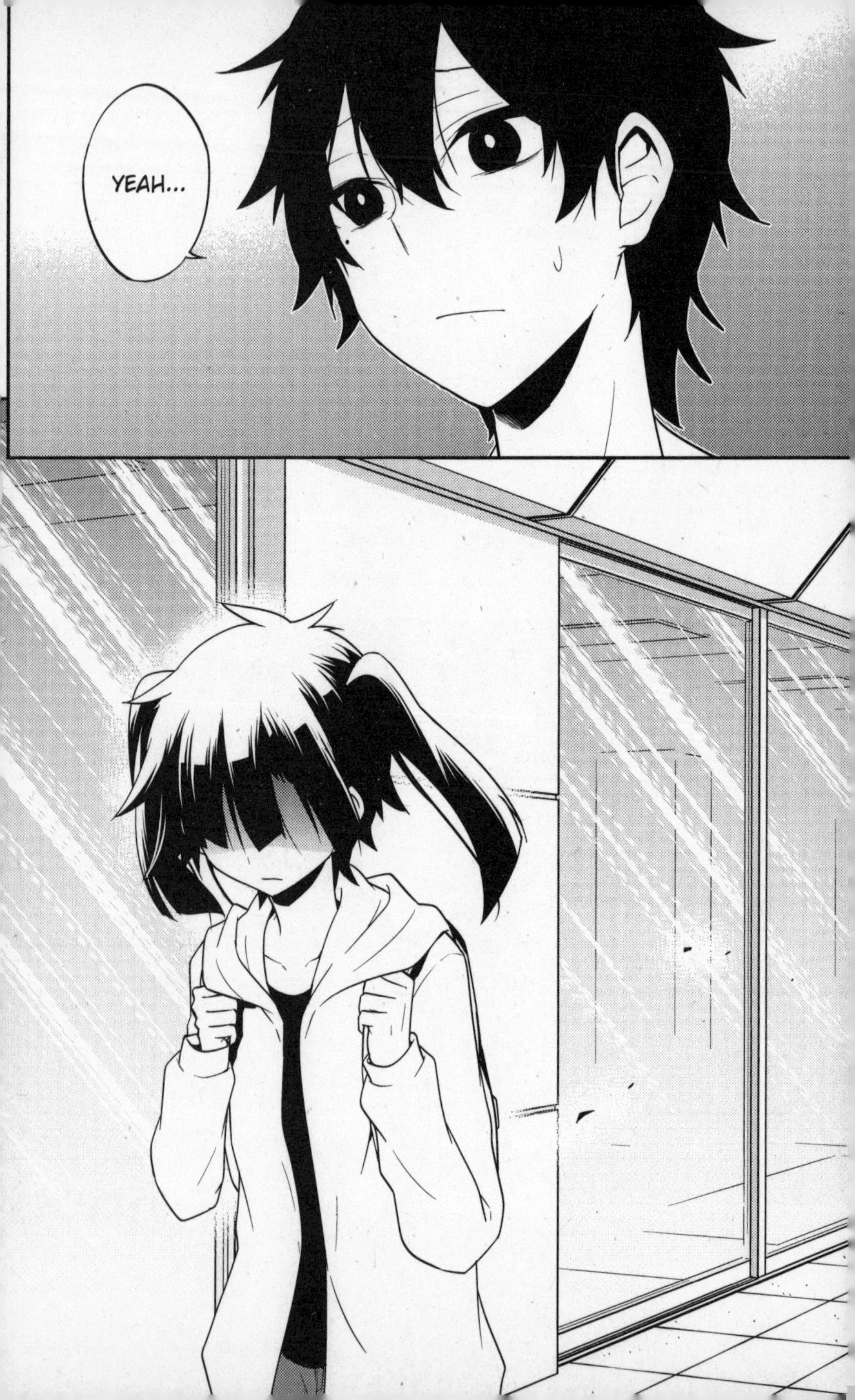
YEAH...

KAGEROU DAZE

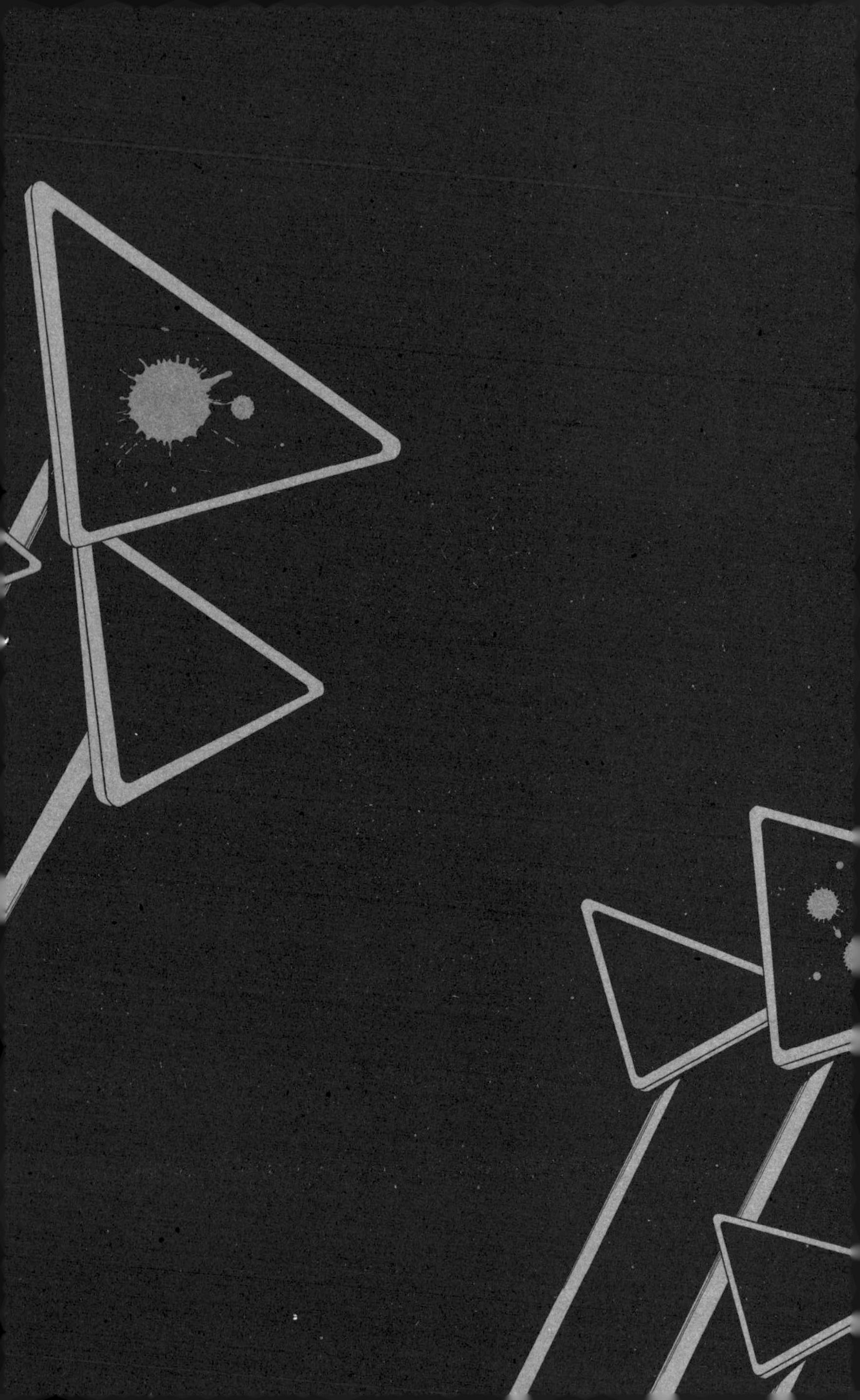

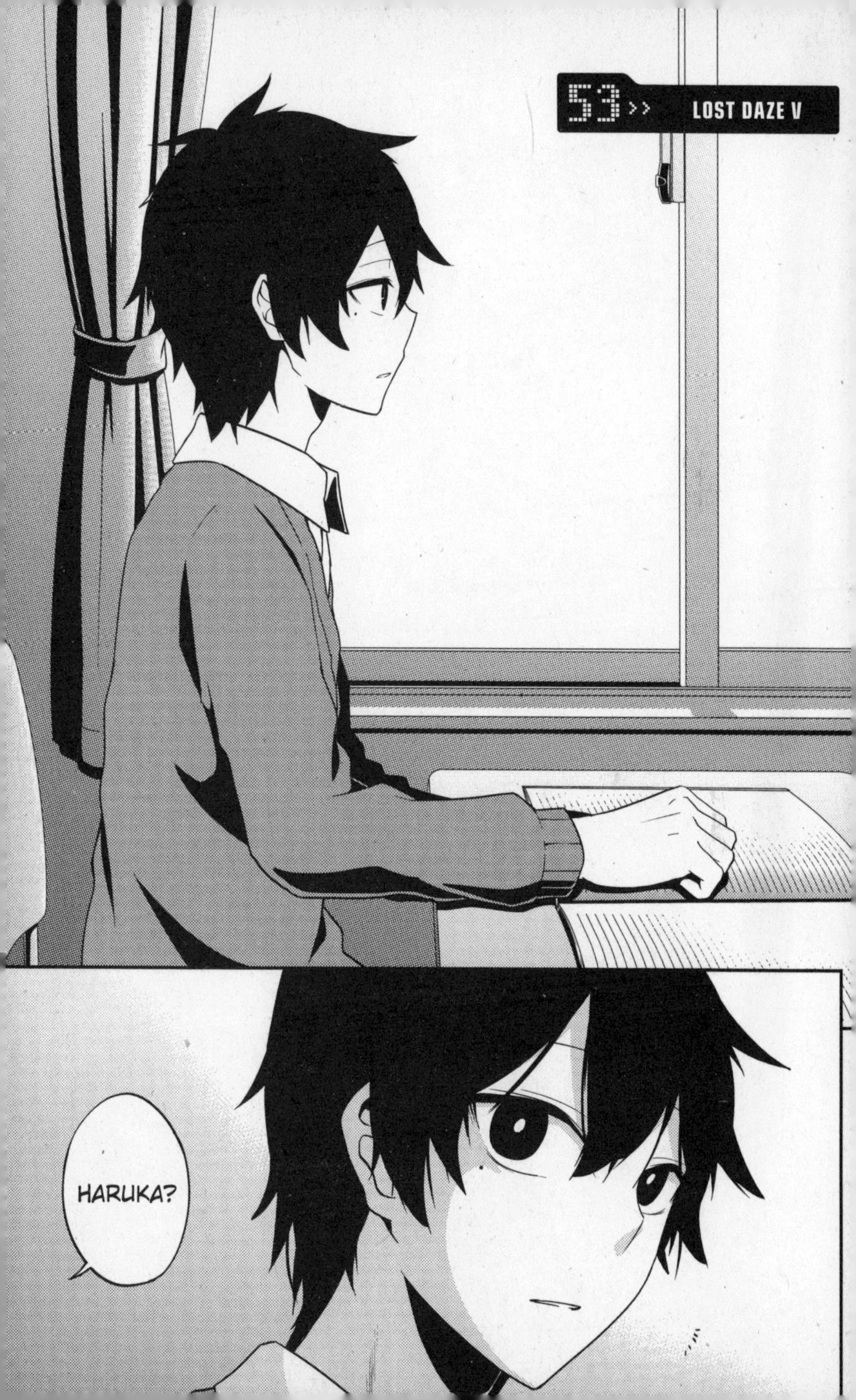
53 >> LOST DAZE V
HARUKA?

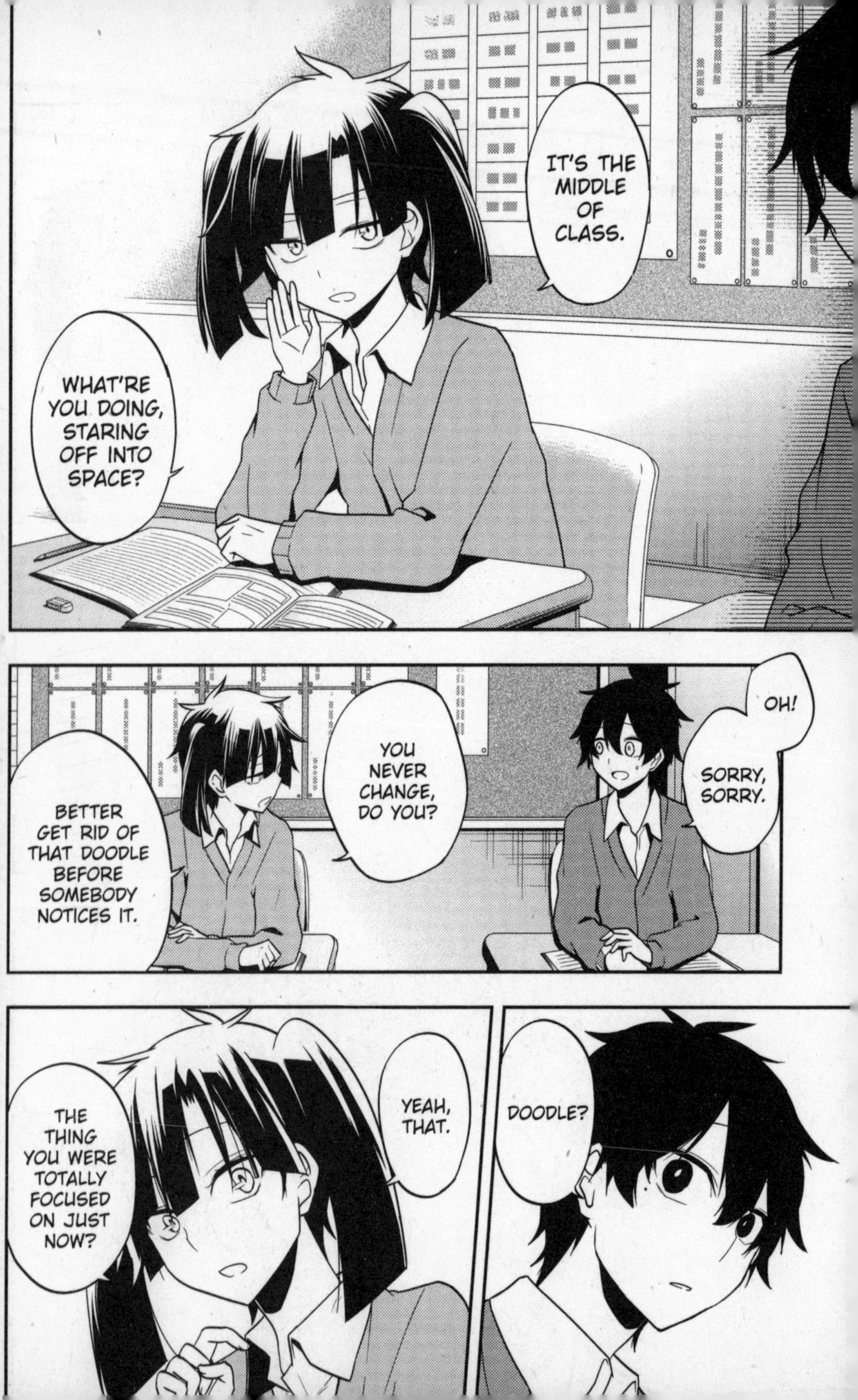
IT'S THE MIDDLE OF CLASS.
WHAT'RE YOU DOING, STARING OFF INTO SPACE?
OH!
SORRY, SORRY.
YOU NEVER CHANGE, DO YOU?
BETTER GET RID OF THAT DOODLE BEFORE SOMEBODY NOTICES IT.
DOODLE?
YEAH, THAT.
THE THING YOU WERE TOTALLY FOCUSED ON JUST NOW?

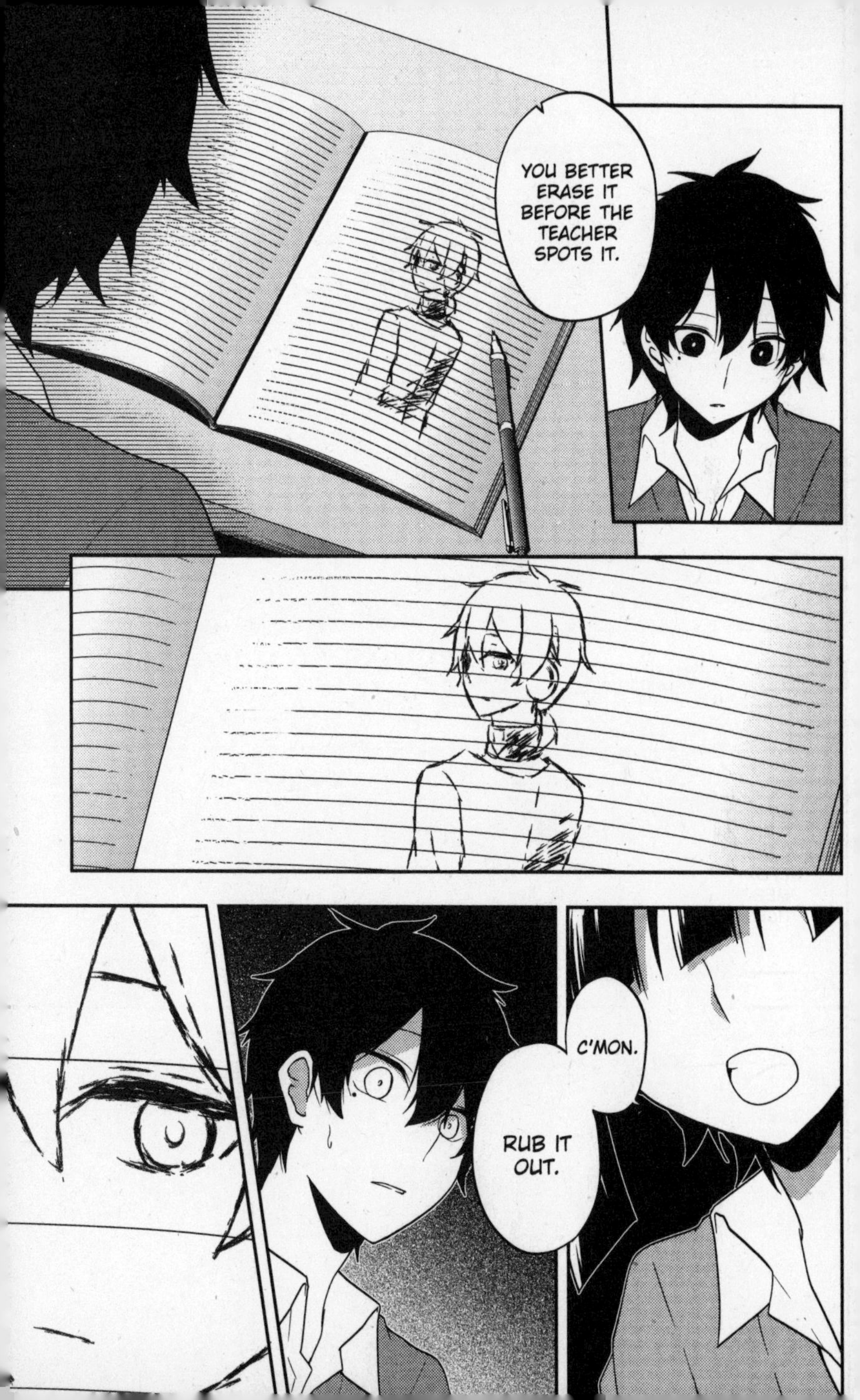
YOU BETTER ERASE IT BEFORE THE TEACHER SPOTS IT.
C'MON.
RUB IT OUT.

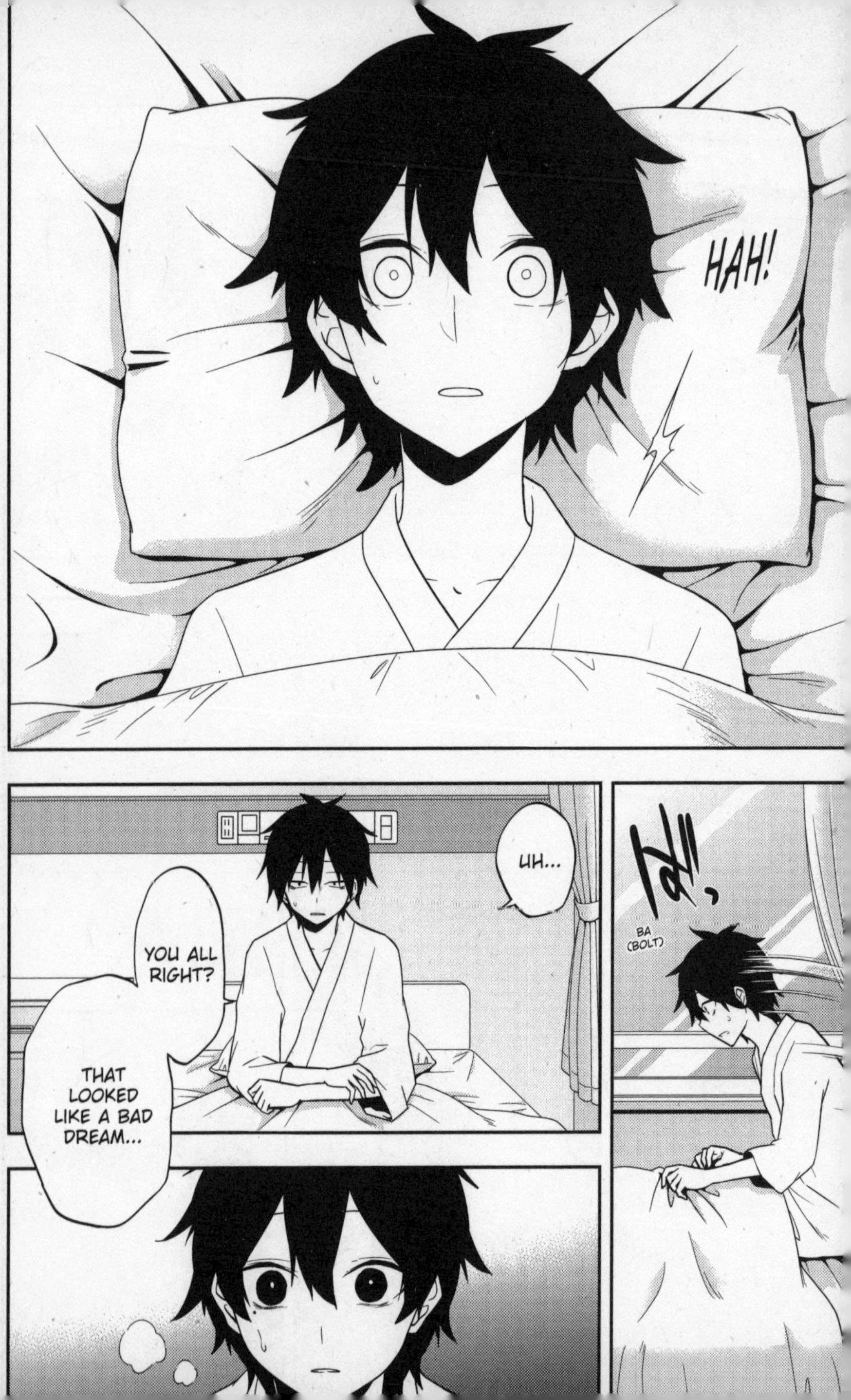
HAH!
BA
(BOLT)
UH...
YOU ALL RIGHT?
THAT LOOKED LIKE A BAD DREAM...

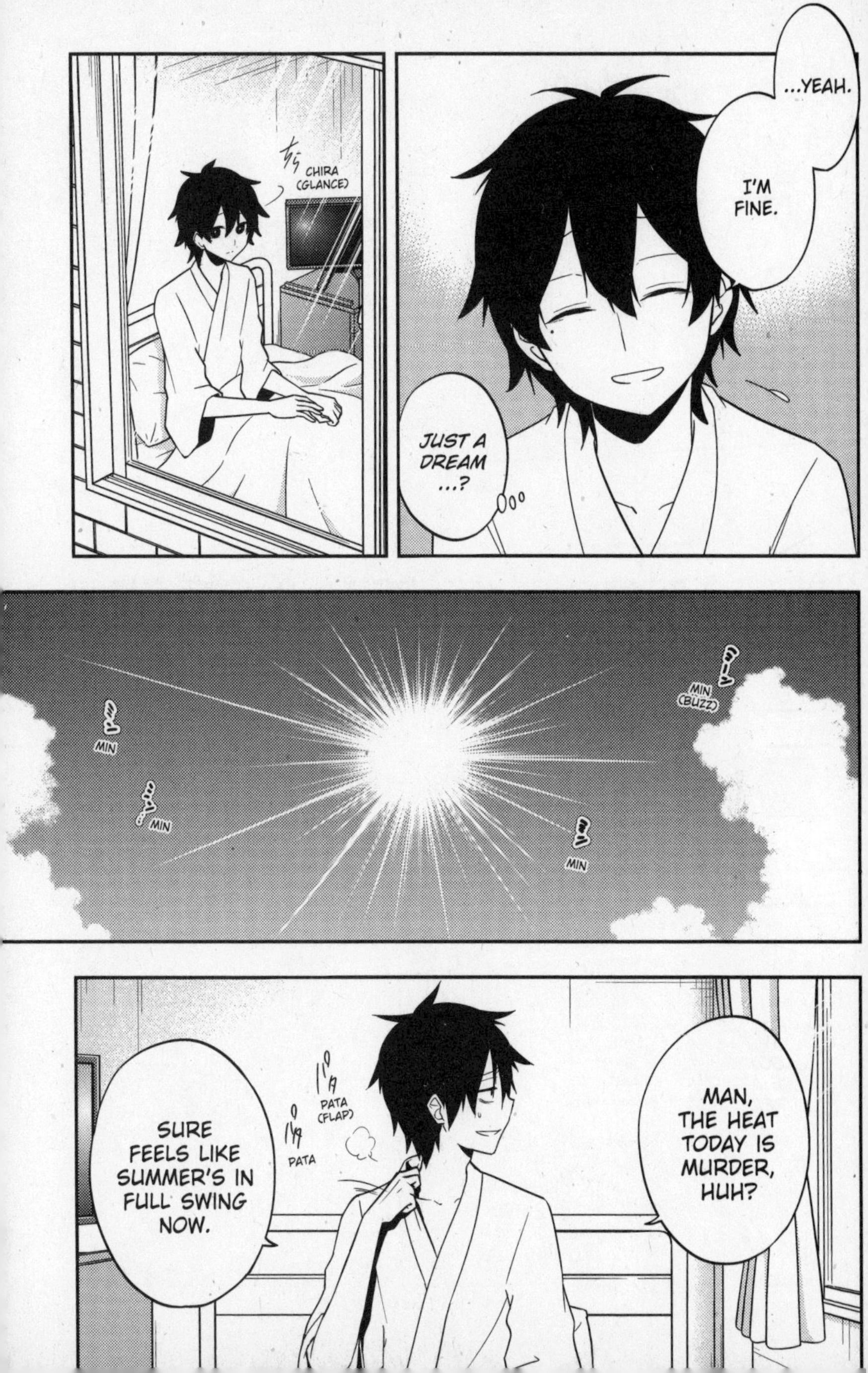
...YEAH.
I'M FINE.
JUST A DREAM ...?
CHIRA (GLANCE)
MIN (BUZZ)
MIN
MIN
MIN
MAN, THE HEAT TODAY IS MURDER, HUH?
PATA (FLAP)
PATA
SURE FEELS LIKE SUMMER'S IN FULL SWING NOW.

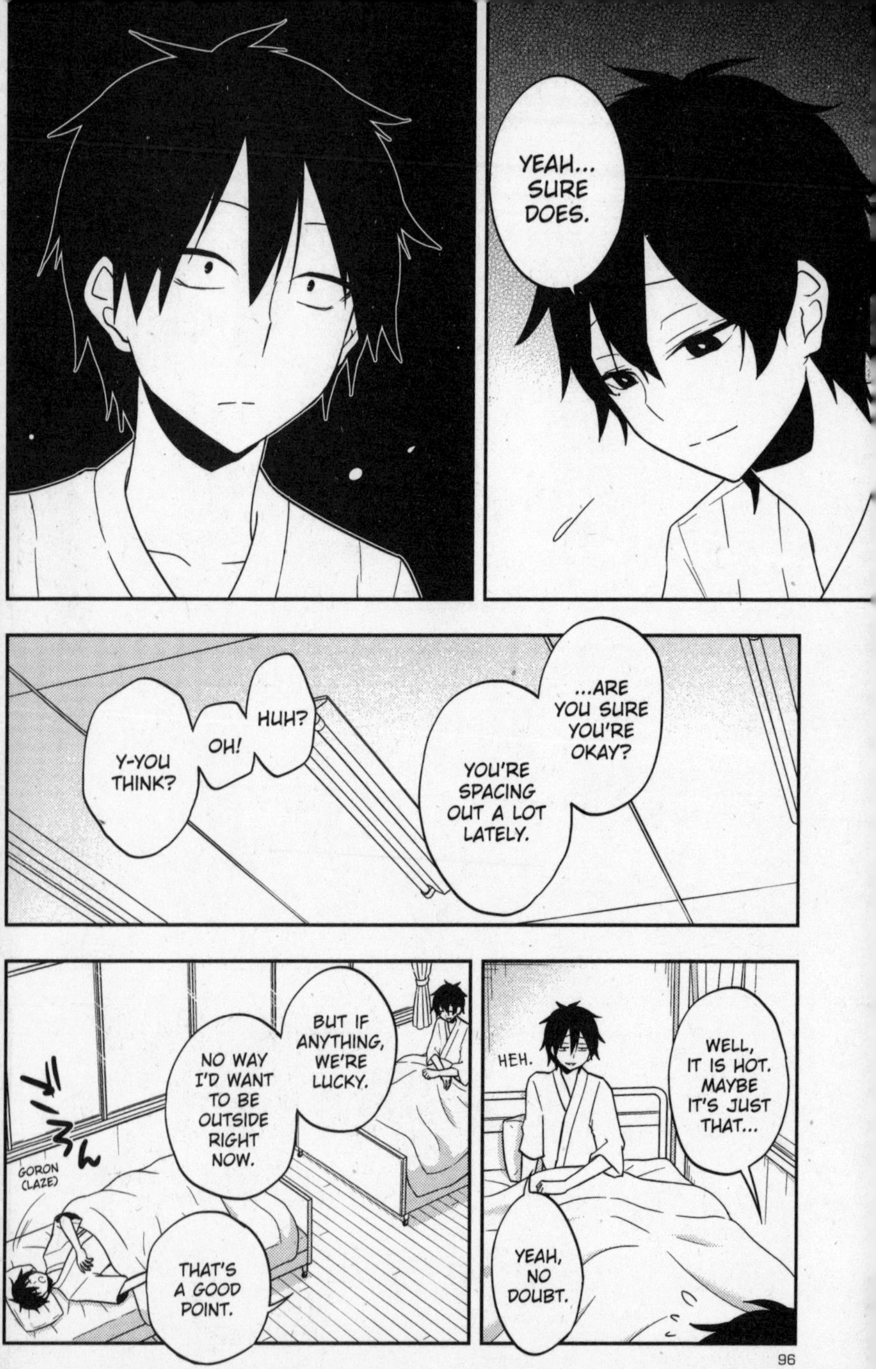
YEAH... SURE DOES.
...ARE YOU SURE YOU'RE OKAY?
YOU'RE SPACING OUT A LOT LATELY.
HUH?
OH!
Y-YOU THINK?
WELL, IT IS HOT. MAYBE IT'S JUST THAT...
HEH.
YEAH, NO DOUBT.
BUT IF ANYTHING, WE'RE LUCKY.
NO WAY I'D WANT TO BE OUTSIDE RIGHT NOW.
GORON (LAZE)
THAT'S A GOOD POINT.

EVEN I'D HESITATE A BIT IN THIS HEAT...

......

MM? WHAT?

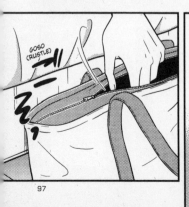

GOSO (RUSTLE)

NO, UM...

IT'S NOTHING.

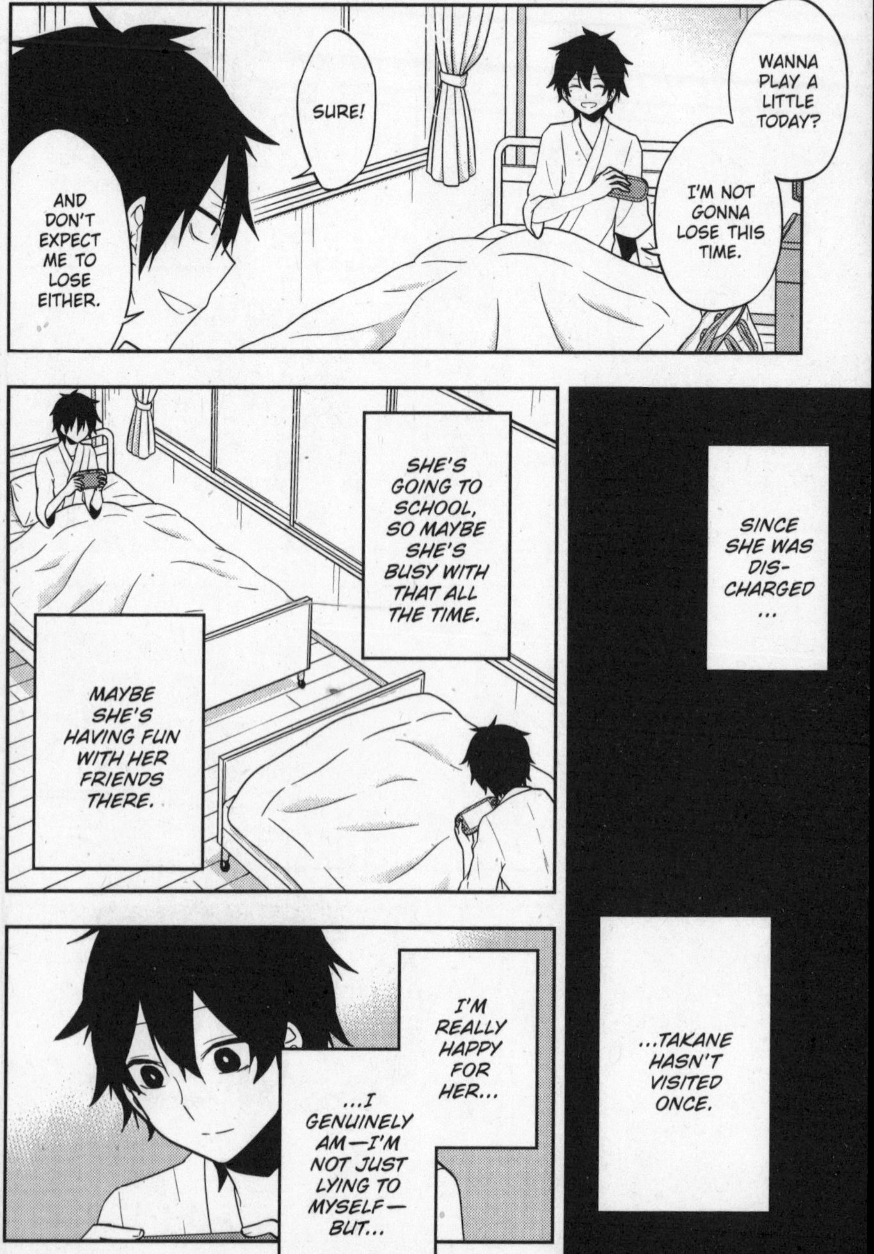
WANNA PLAY A LITTLE TODAY?
I'M NOT GONNA LOSE THIS TIME.
SURE!
AND DON'T EXPECT ME TO LOSE EITHER.
SINCE SHE WAS DIS-CHARGED...
...TAKANE HASN'T VISITED ONCE.
SHE'S GOING TO SCHOOL, SO MAYBE SHE'S BUSY WITH THAT ALL THE TIME.
MAYBE SHE'S HAVING FUN WITH HER FRIENDS THERE.
I'M REALLY HAPPY FOR HER...
...I GENUINELY AM—I'M NOT JUST LYING TO MYSELF—BUT...

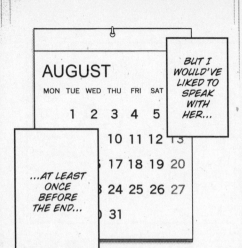

AUGUST

MON	TUE	WED	THU	FRI	SAT
1	2	3	4	5	
	10	11	12	13	
5	17	18	19	20	
8	24	25	26	27	
0	31				

BUT I WOULD'VE LIKED TO SPEAK WITH HER...

...AT LEAST ONCE BEFORE THE END...

CHIRA
(GLANCE)

UGH!

PLAYING GAMES AGAIN, ONII-CHAN?

UH, YEAH?

WHAT'S THE BIG DEAL?

BUT YOU'RE DOING THAT EVERY TIME I VISIT!

NOT LIKE I'M BOTHERING YOU.

YOU COULD AT LEAST LET ME JOIN IN SOMETIMES.

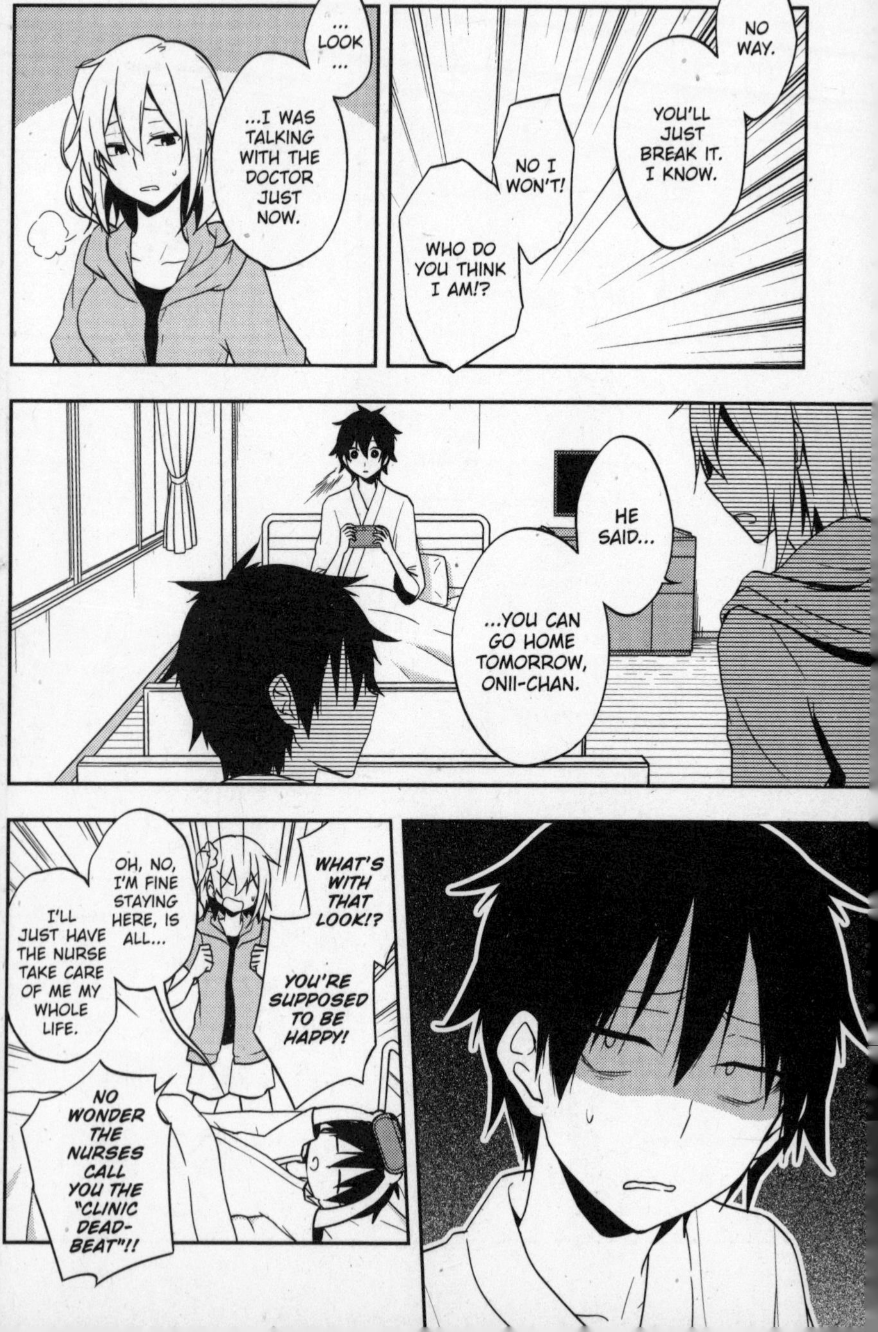
NO WAY.
YOU'LL JUST BREAK IT. I KNOW.
NO I WON'T!
WHO DO YOU THINK I AM!?
...LOOK...
...I WAS TALKING WITH THE DOCTOR JUST NOW.
HE SAID...
...YOU CAN GO HOME TOMORROW, ONII-CHAN.
WHAT'S WITH THAT LOOK!?
YOU'RE SUPPOSED TO BE HAPPY!
OH, NO, I'M FINE STAYING HERE, IS ALL...
I'LL JUST HAVE THE NURSE TAKE CARE OF ME MY WHOLE LIFE.
NO WONDER THE NURSES CALL YOU THE "CLINIC DEAD-BEAT"!!

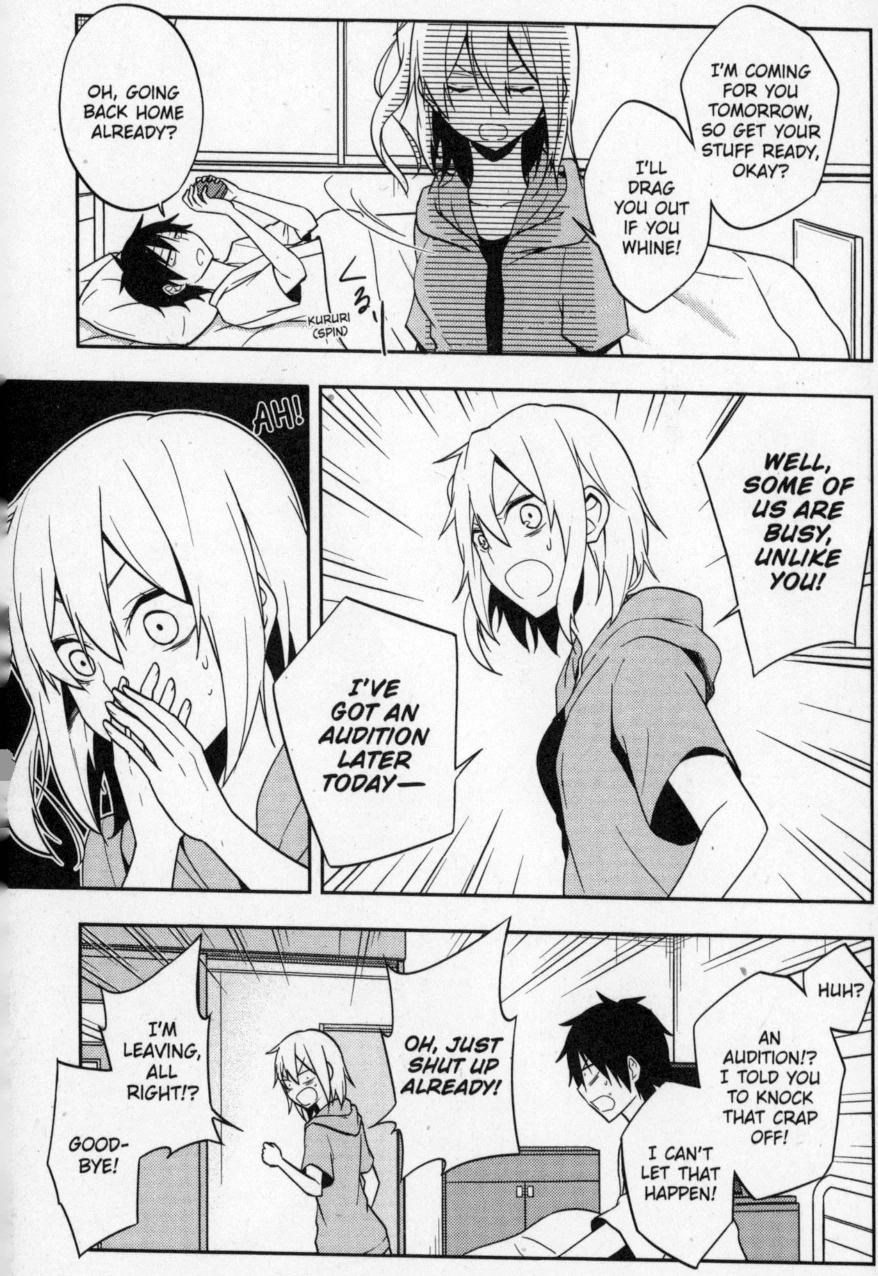
I'M COMING FOR YOU TOMORROW, SO GET YOUR STUFF READY, OKAY?
I'LL DRAG YOU OUT IF YOU WHINE!
KURURI (SPIN)
OH, GOING BACK HOME ALREADY?
WELL, SOME OF US ARE BUSY, UNLIKE YOU!
I'VE GOT AN AUDITION LATER TODAY—
AH!
HUH?
AN AUDITION!? I TOLD YOU TO KNOCK THAT CRAP OFF!
I CAN'T LET THAT HAPPEN!
OH, JUST SHUT UP ALREADY!
I'M LEAVING, ALL RIGHT!?
GOOD-BYE!

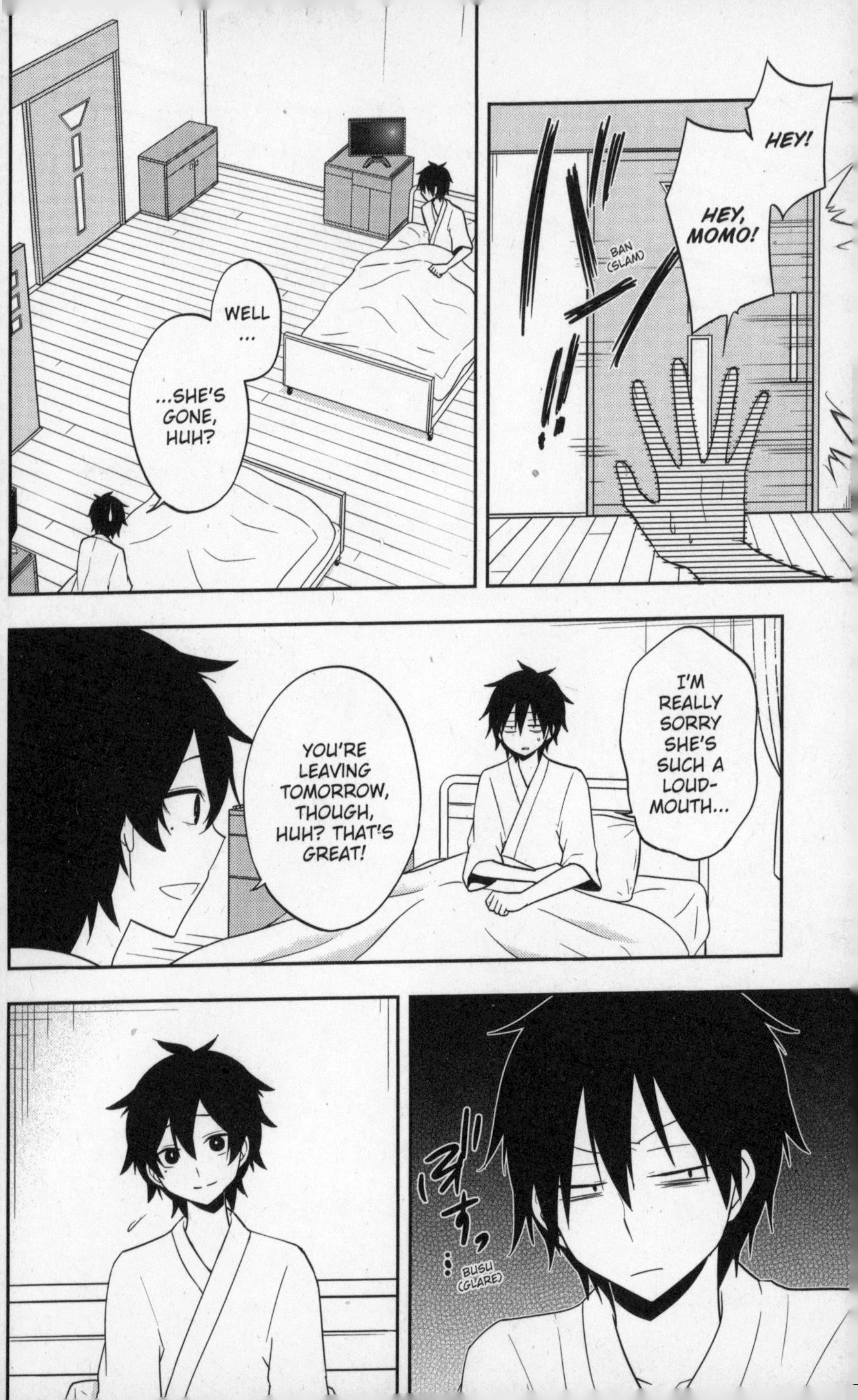
HEY!
HEY, MOMO!
BAN (SLAM)
WELL ...
...SHE'S GONE, HUH?
I'M REALLY SORRY SHE'S SUCH A LOUD-MOUTH...
YOU'RE LEAVING TOMORROW, THOUGH, HUH? THAT'S GREAT!
BUSU (GLARE)

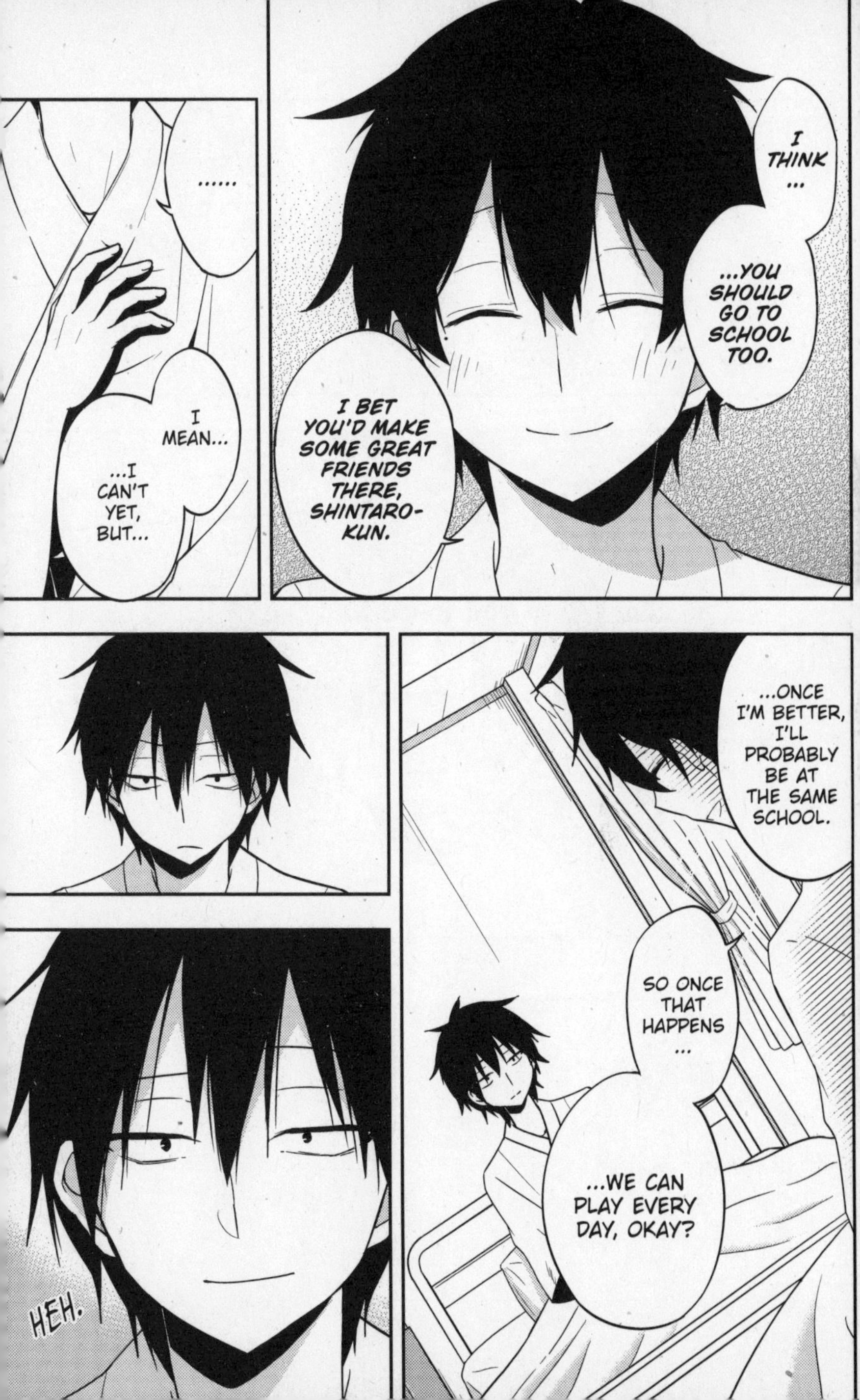
I THINK...
...YOU SHOULD GO TO SCHOOL TOO.
I BET YOU'D MAKE SOME GREAT FRIENDS THERE, SHINTARO-KUN.
......
I MEAN...
...I CAN'T YET, BUT...
...ONCE I'M BETTER, I'LL PROBABLY BE AT THE SAME SCHOOL.
SO ONCE THAT HAPPENS...
...WE CAN PLAY EVERY DAY, OKAY?
HEH.

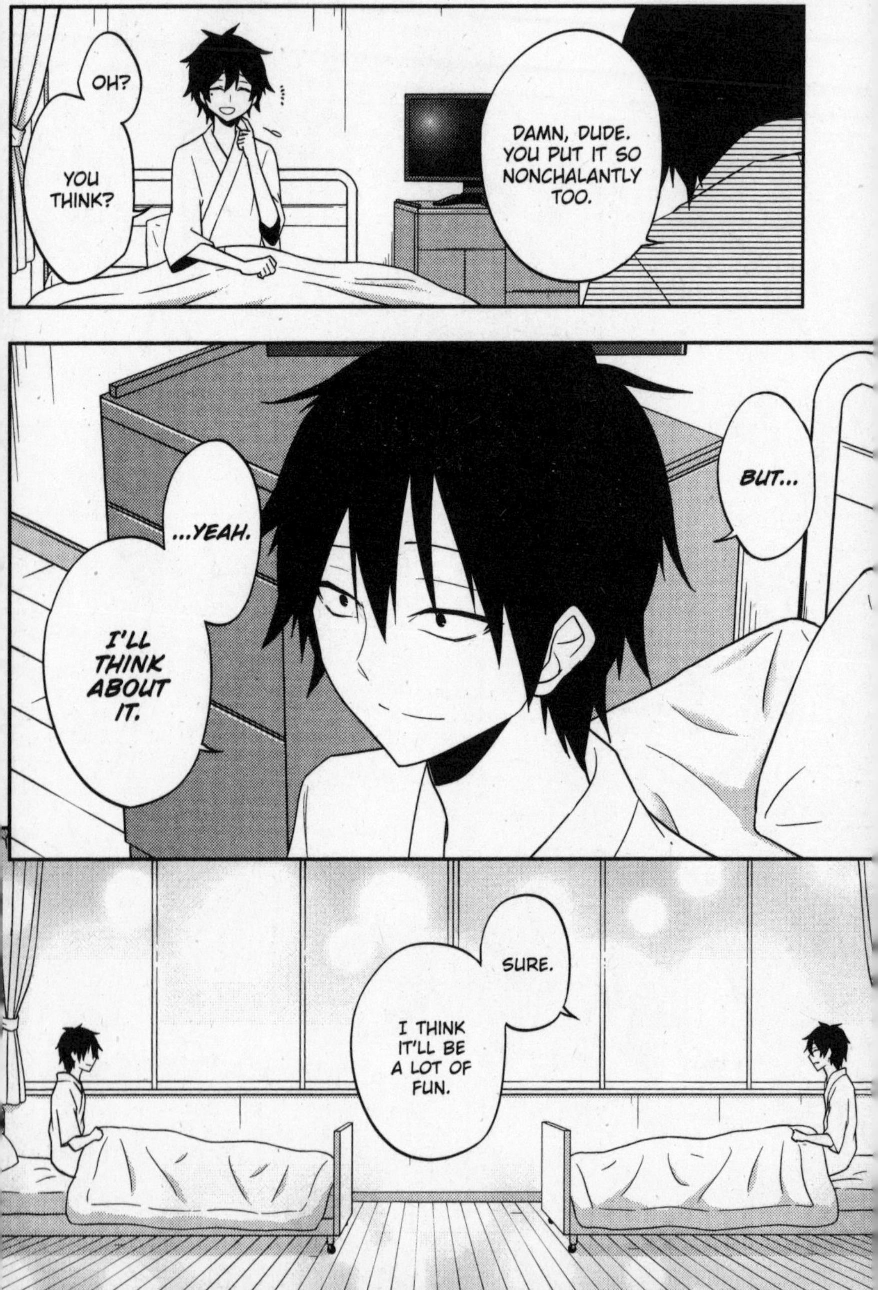
DAMN, DUDE. YOU PUT IT SO NONCHALANTLY TOO.
OH?
YOU THINK?
BUT...
...YEAH.
I'LL THINK ABOUT IT.
SURE.
I THINK IT'LL BE A LOT OF FUN.

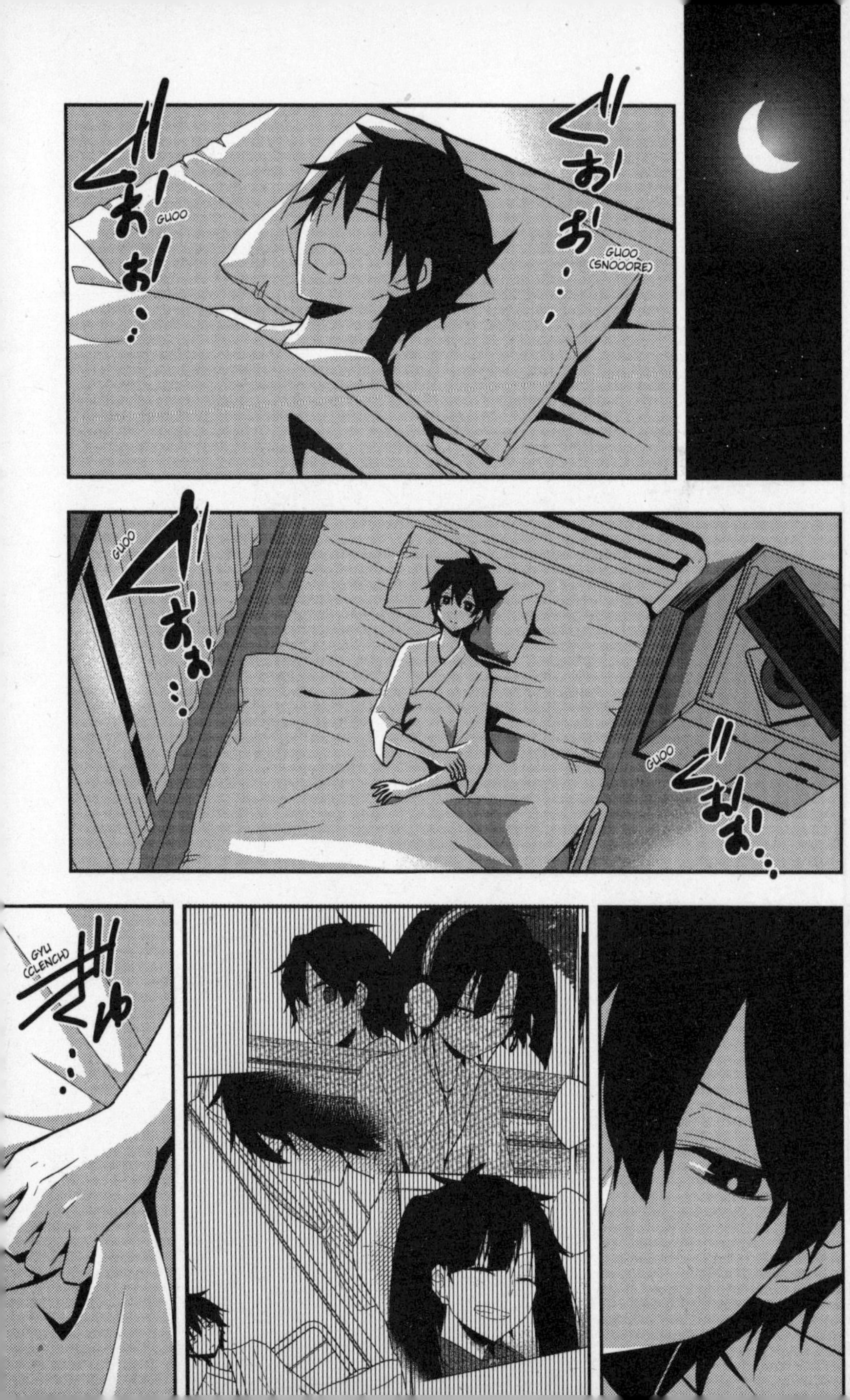
GUOO
(SNOOORE)
GUOO
GUOO
GUOO
GYU
(CLENCH)

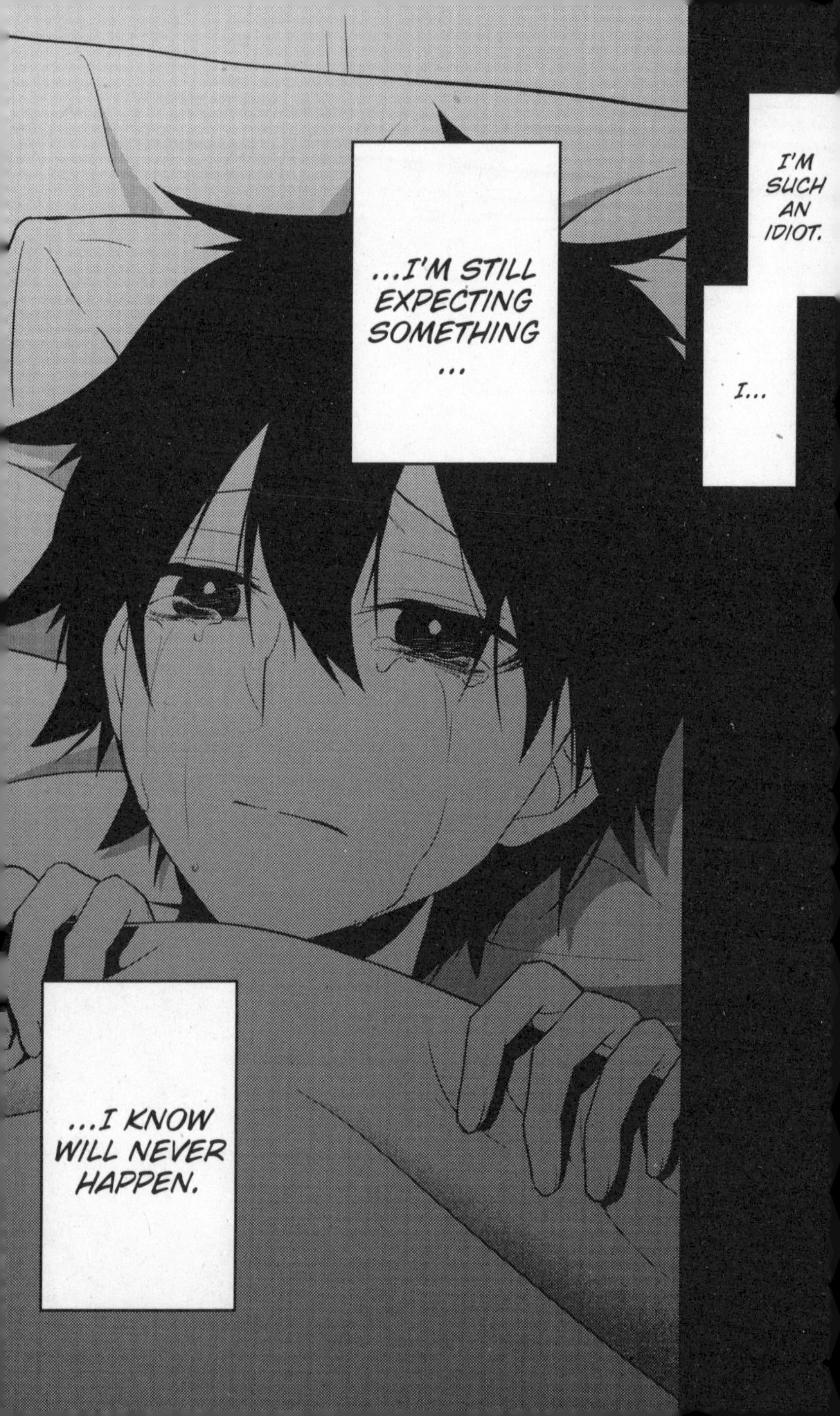
I'M SUCH AN IDIOT.
I...
...I'M STILL EXPECTING SOMETHING ...
...I KNOW WILL NEVER HAPPEN.

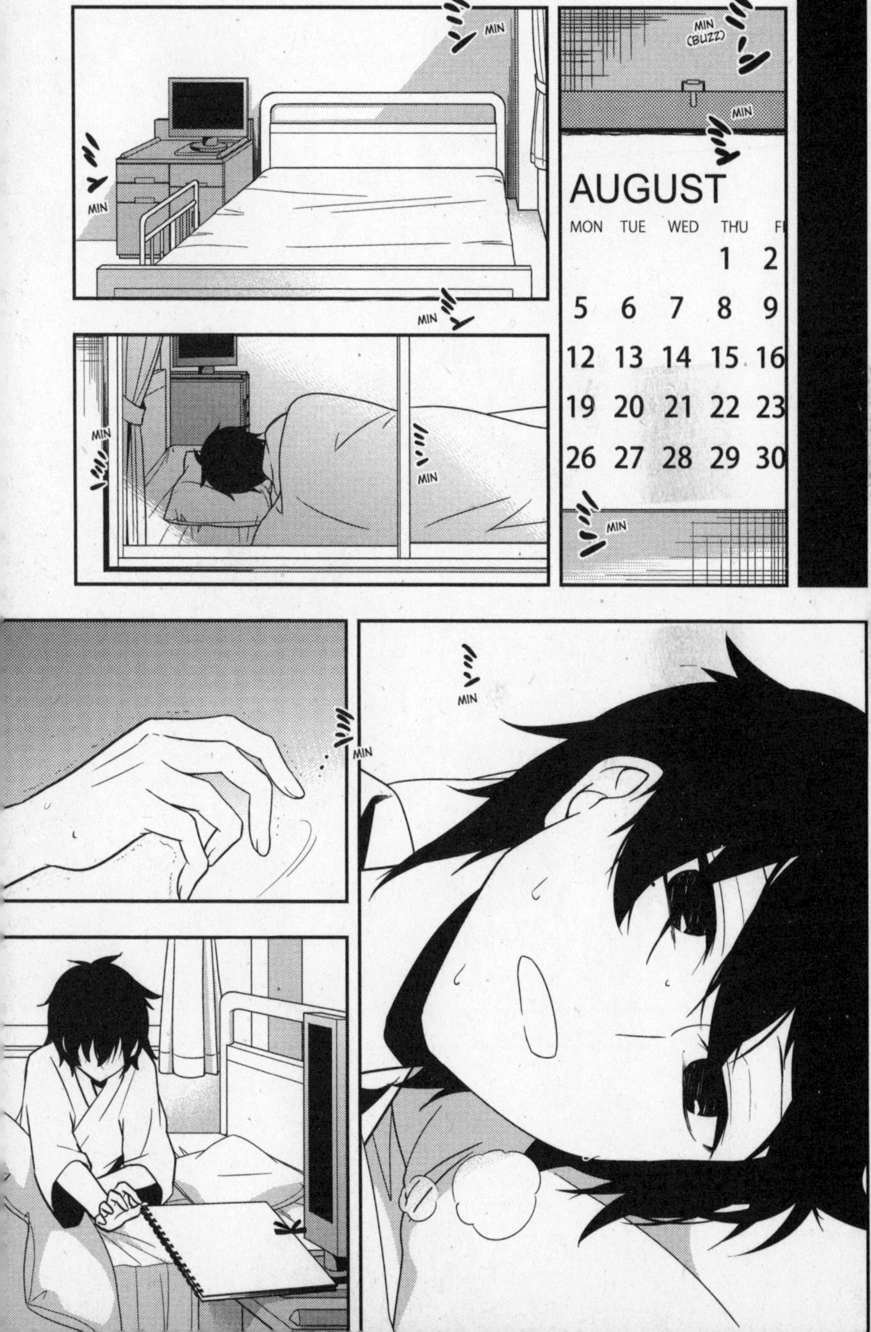
MIN (BUZZ)
MIN
AUGUST
MON TUE WED THU F
1 2
5 6 7 8 9
12 13 14 15 16
19 20 21 22 23
26 27 28 29 30
MIN
MIN
MIN
MIN
MIN
MIN
MIN
MIN

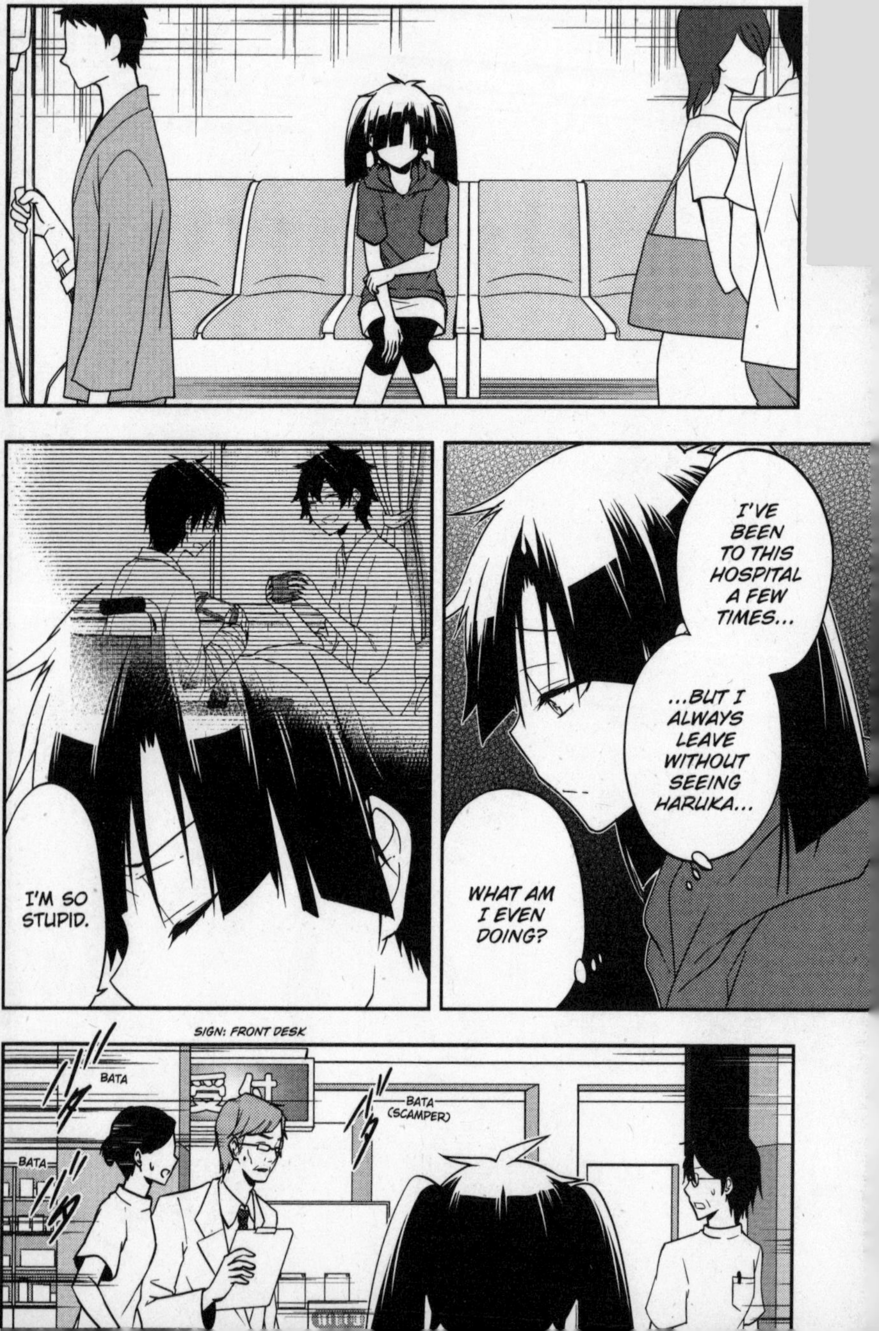
I'VE BEEN TO THIS HOSPITAL A FEW TIMES...
...BUT I ALWAYS LEAVE WITHOUT SEEING HARUKA...
WHAT AM I EVEN DOING?
I'M SO STUPID.
SIGN: FRONT DESK
BATA (SCAMPER)
BATA
BATA

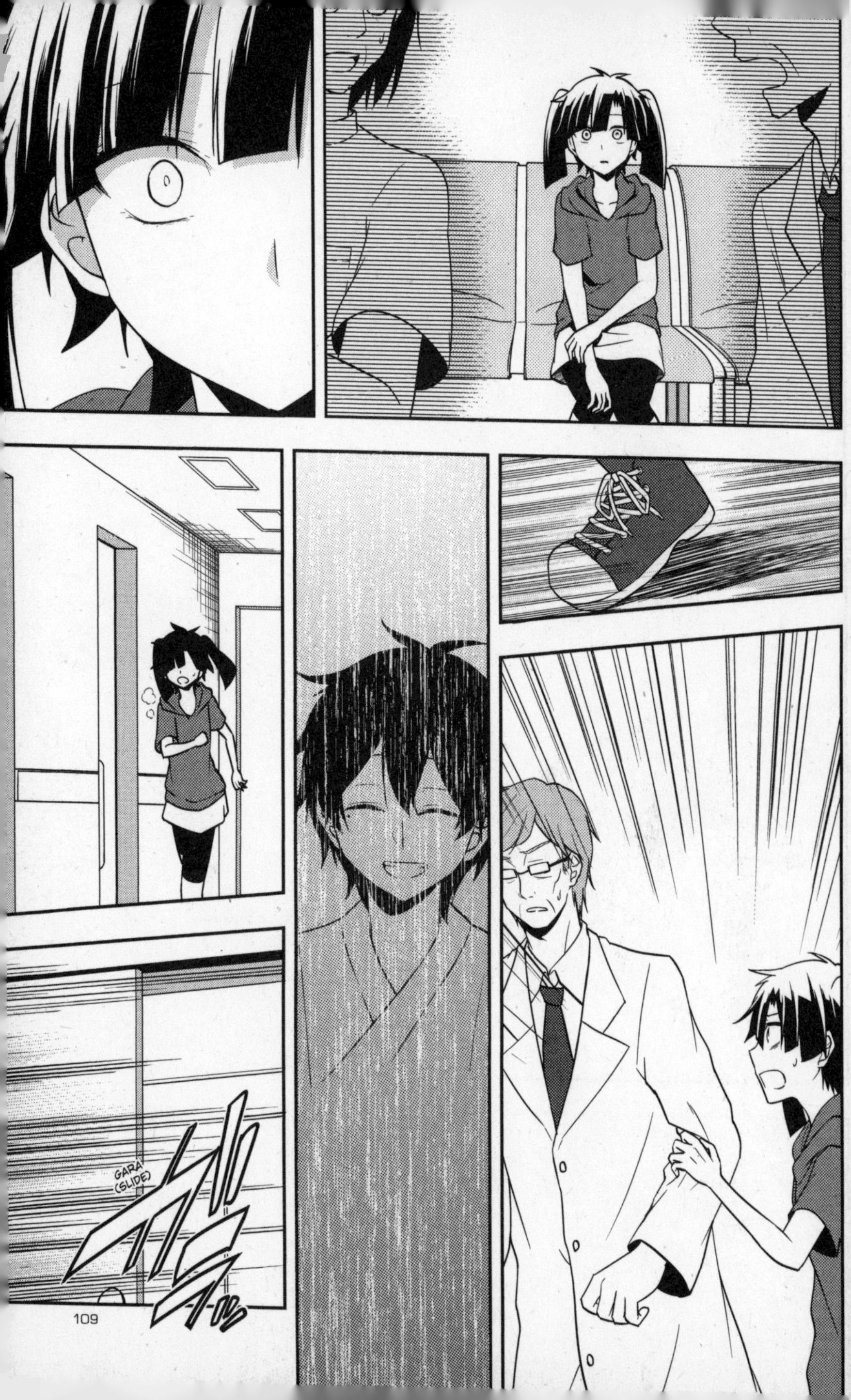
GARA
(SLIDE)

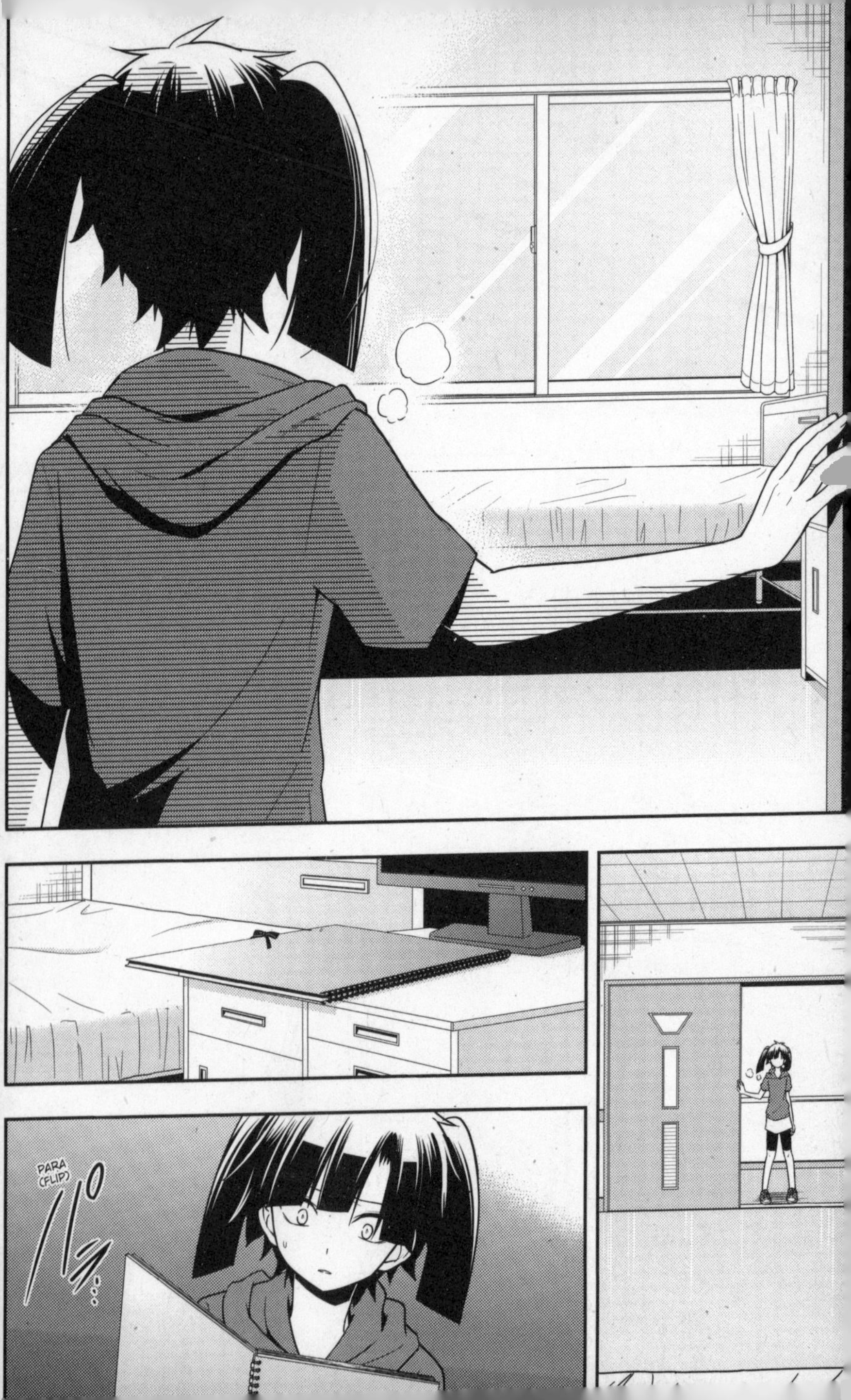
PARA (FLIP)

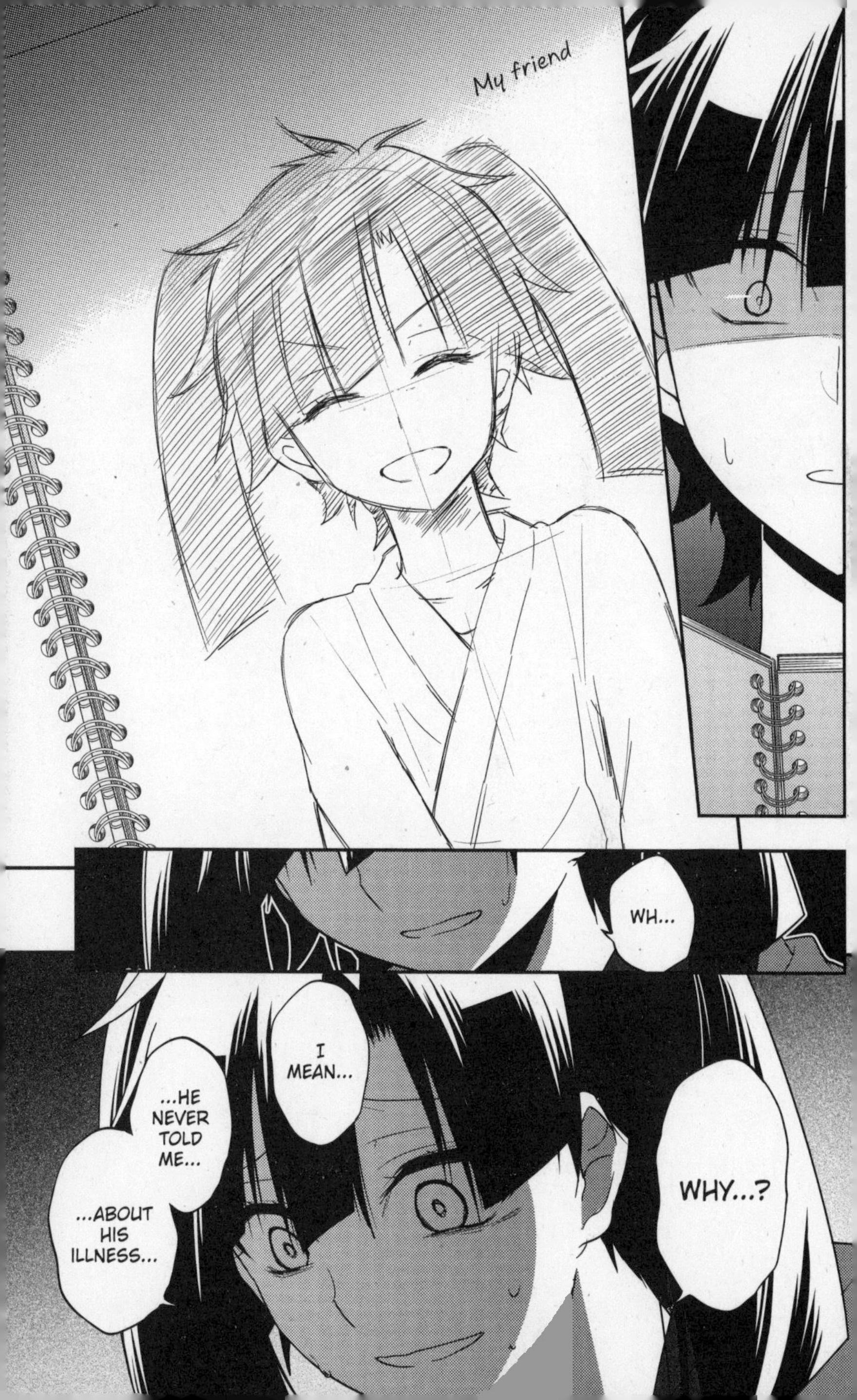
My friend
WH...
WHY...?
I MEAN...
...HE NEVER TOLD ME...
...ABOUT HIS ILLNESS...

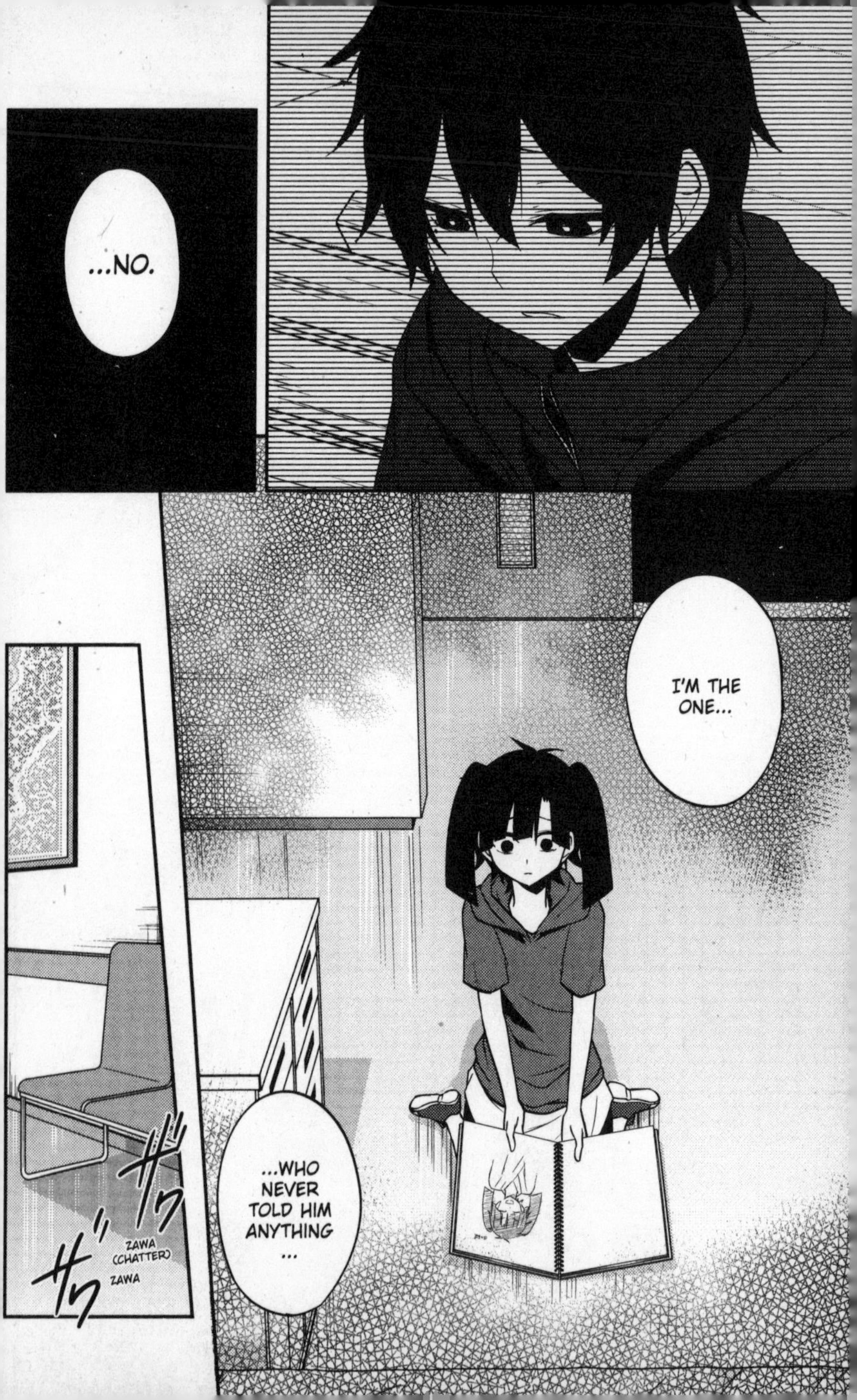
...NO.
I'M THE ONE...
...WHO NEVER TOLD HIM ANYTHING ...
ZAWA (CHATTER) ZAWA

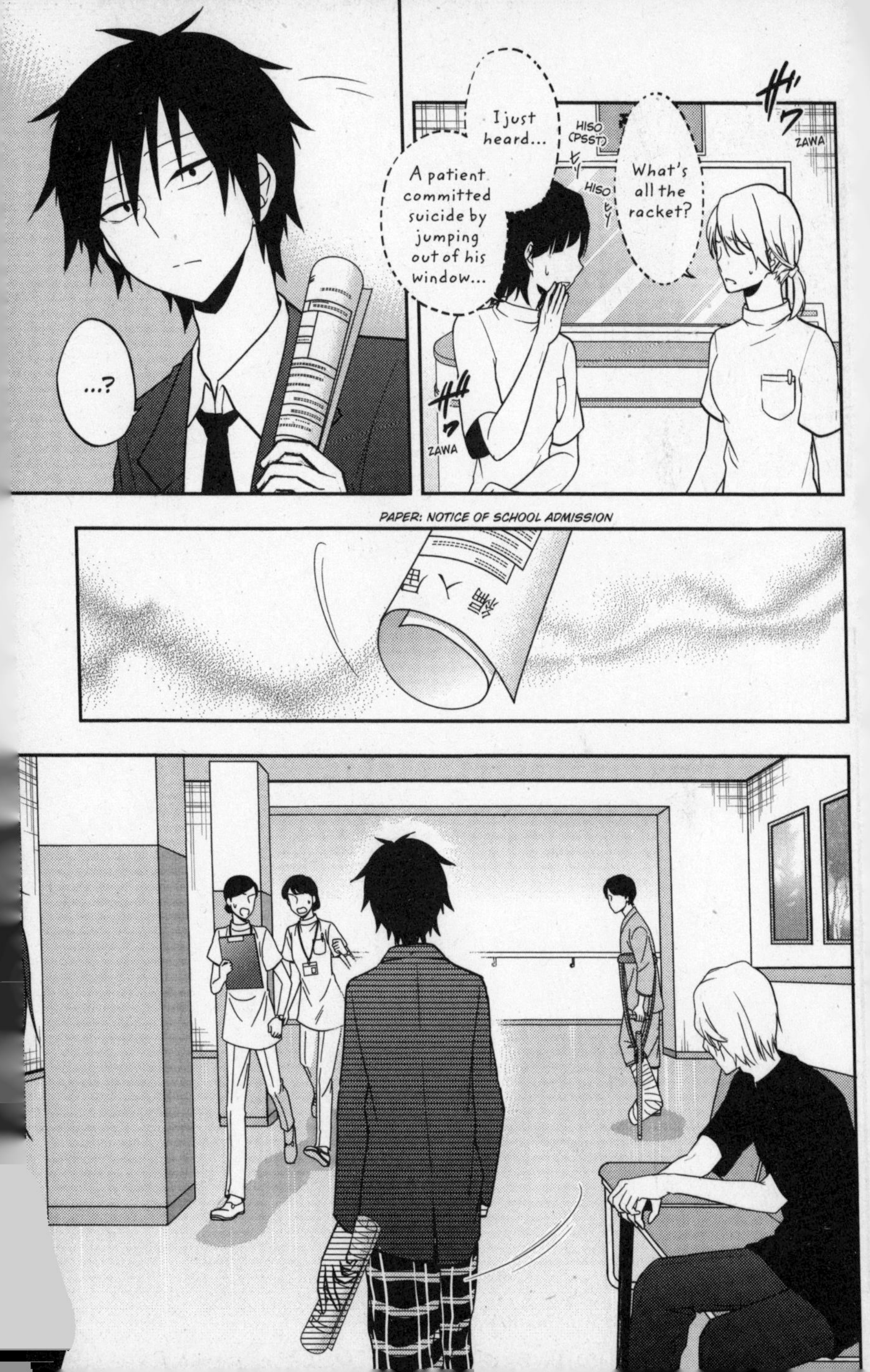
ZAWA
What's all the racket?
HISO (PSST)
I just heard...
HISO
A patient committed suicide by jumping out of his window...
ZAWA
...?
PAPER: NOTICE OF SCHOOL ADMISSION

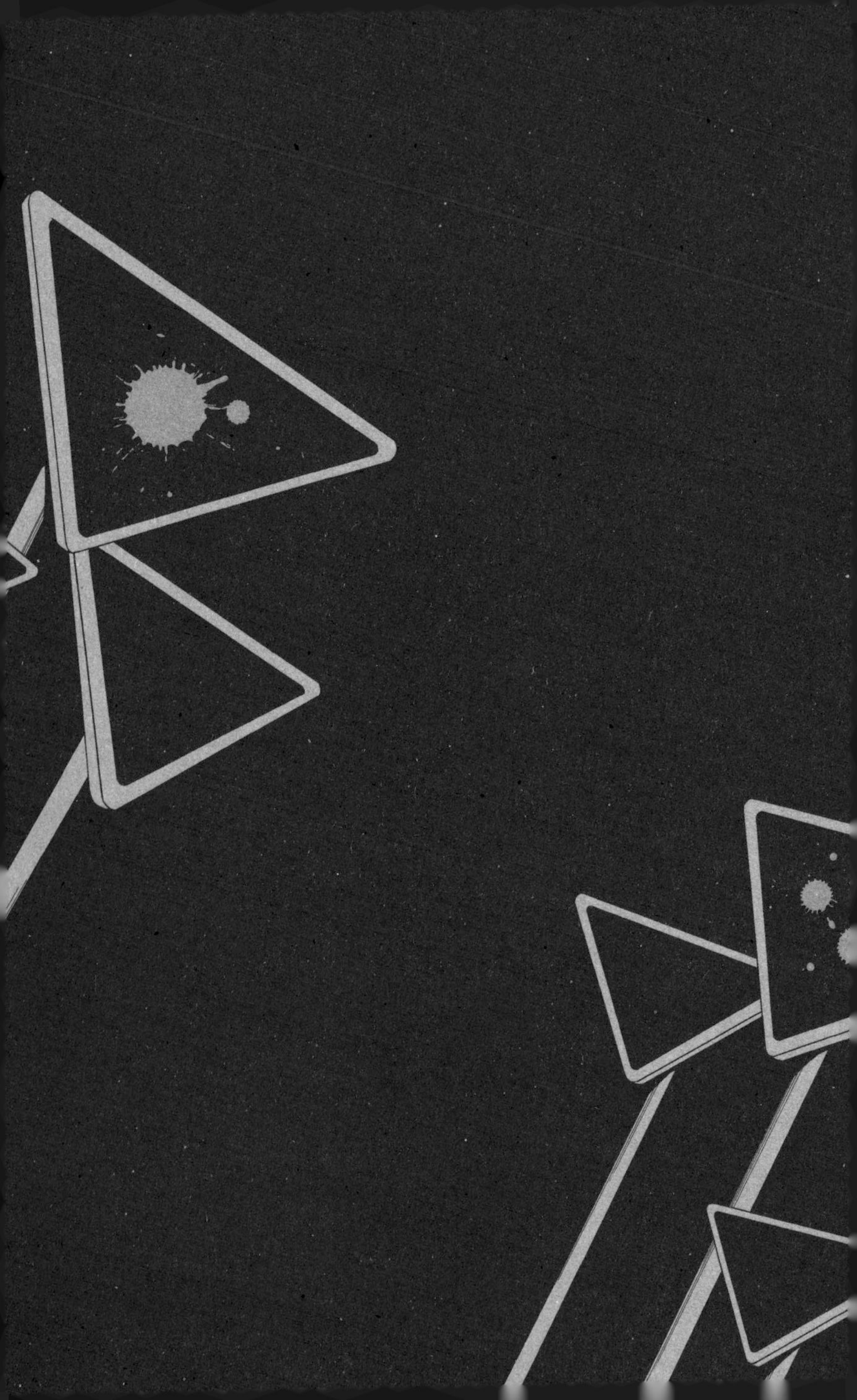

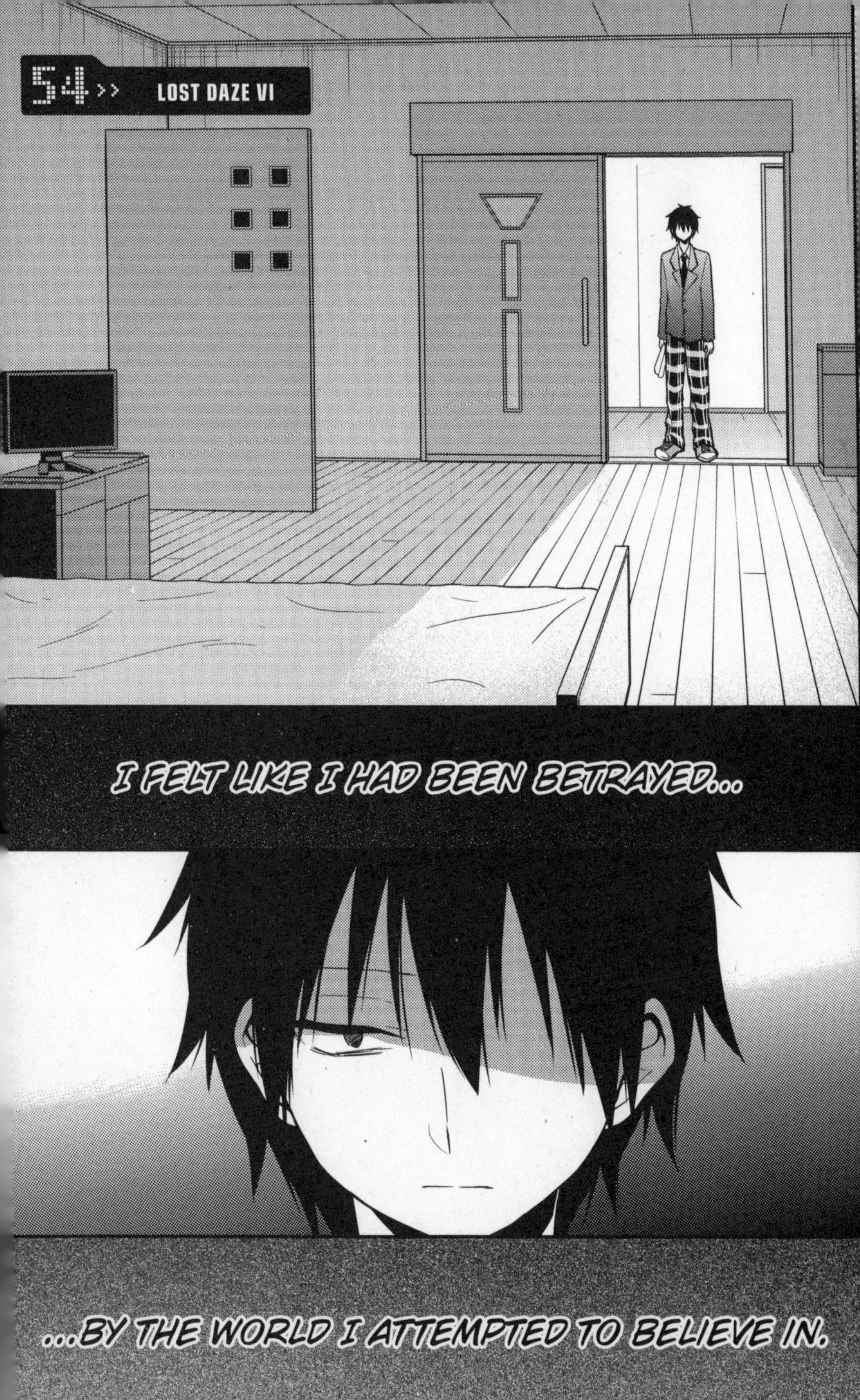
54 >> LOST DAZE VI
I FELT LIKE I HAD BEEN BETRAYED...
...BY THE WORLD I ATTEMPTED TO BELIEVE IN.

PAPER: NOTICE OF SCHOOL ADMISSION
チッ
CHI (TICK)
チッ
CHI
チッ
CHI
チッ…
CHI
9 M 3 D FRIDA
ガッ
チャ…
GACHA (KACHAK)

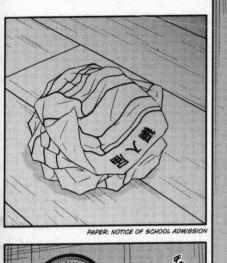

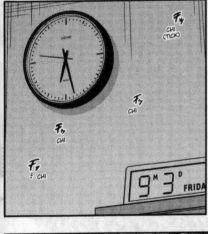

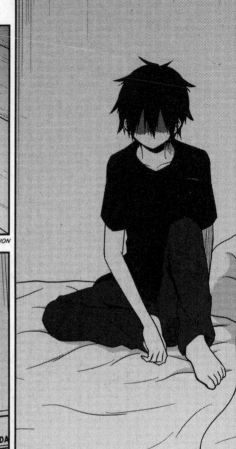

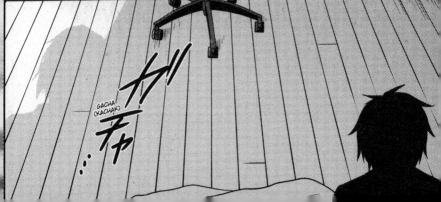

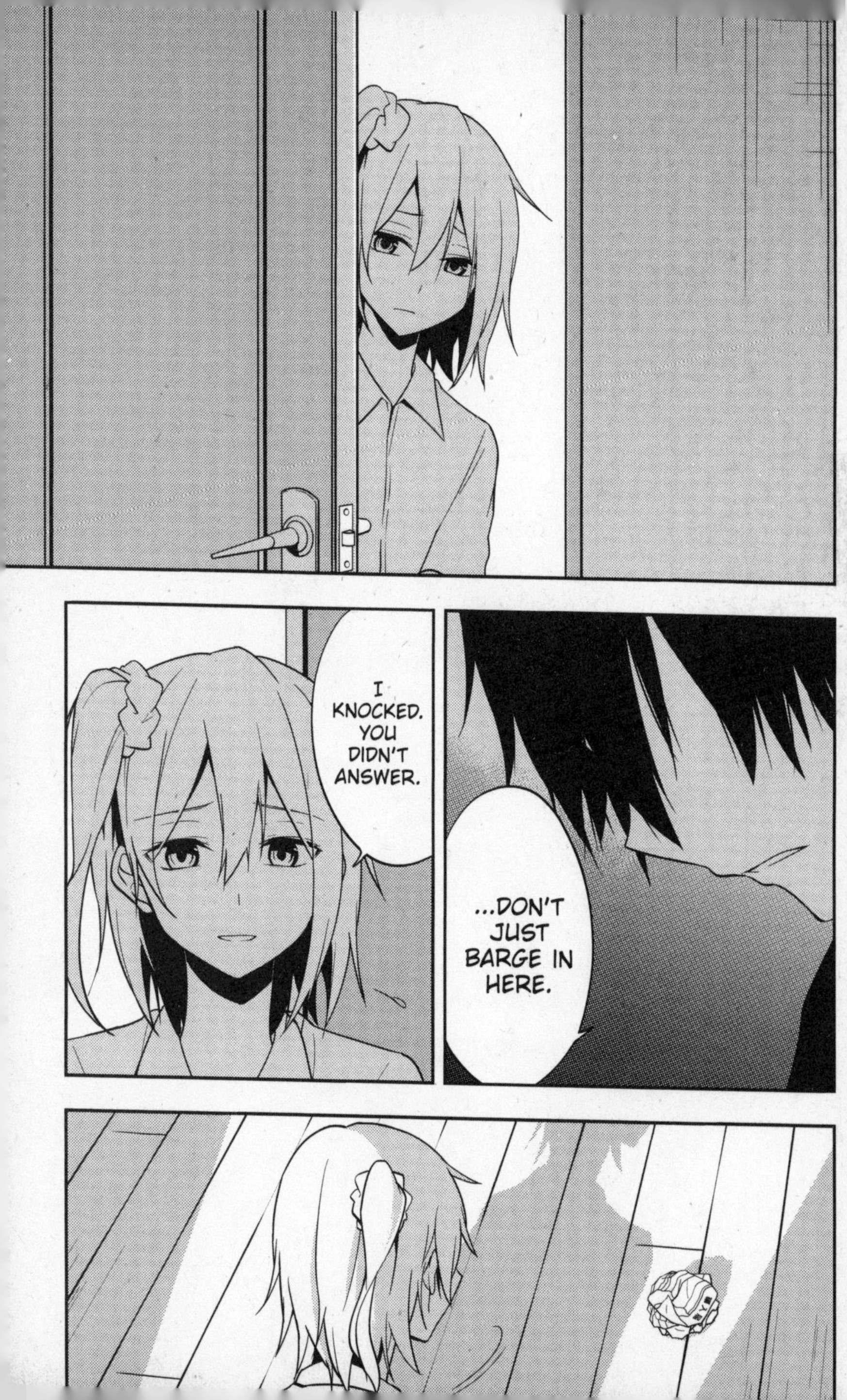
...DON'T JUST BARGE IN HERE.
I KNOCKED. YOU DIDN'T ANSWER.

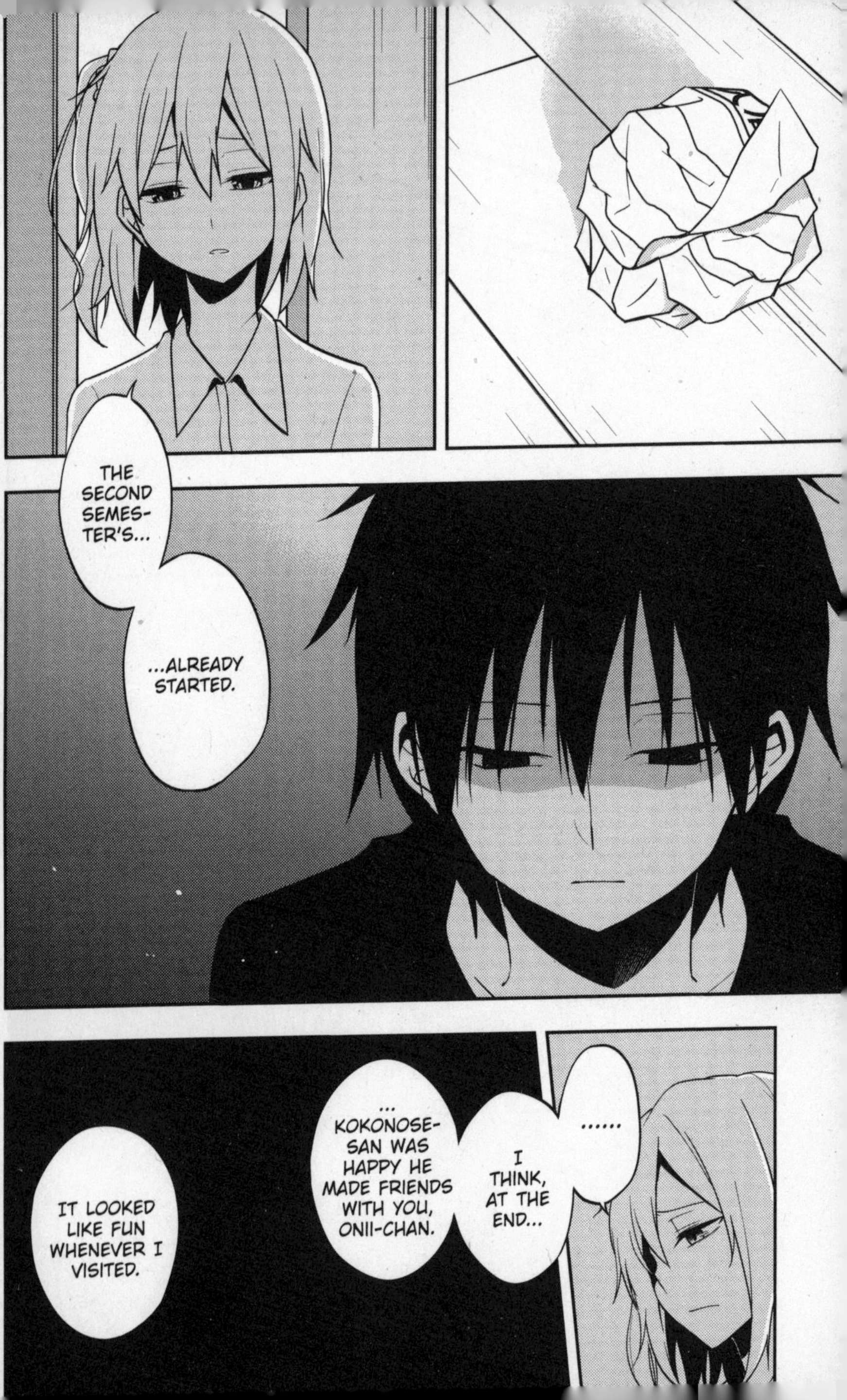
THE SECOND SEMESTER'S...
...ALREADY STARTED.
......
I THINK, AT THE END...
... KOKONOSE-SAN WAS HAPPY HE MADE FRIENDS WITH YOU, ONII-CHAN.
IT LOOKED LIKE FUN WHENEVER I VISITED.

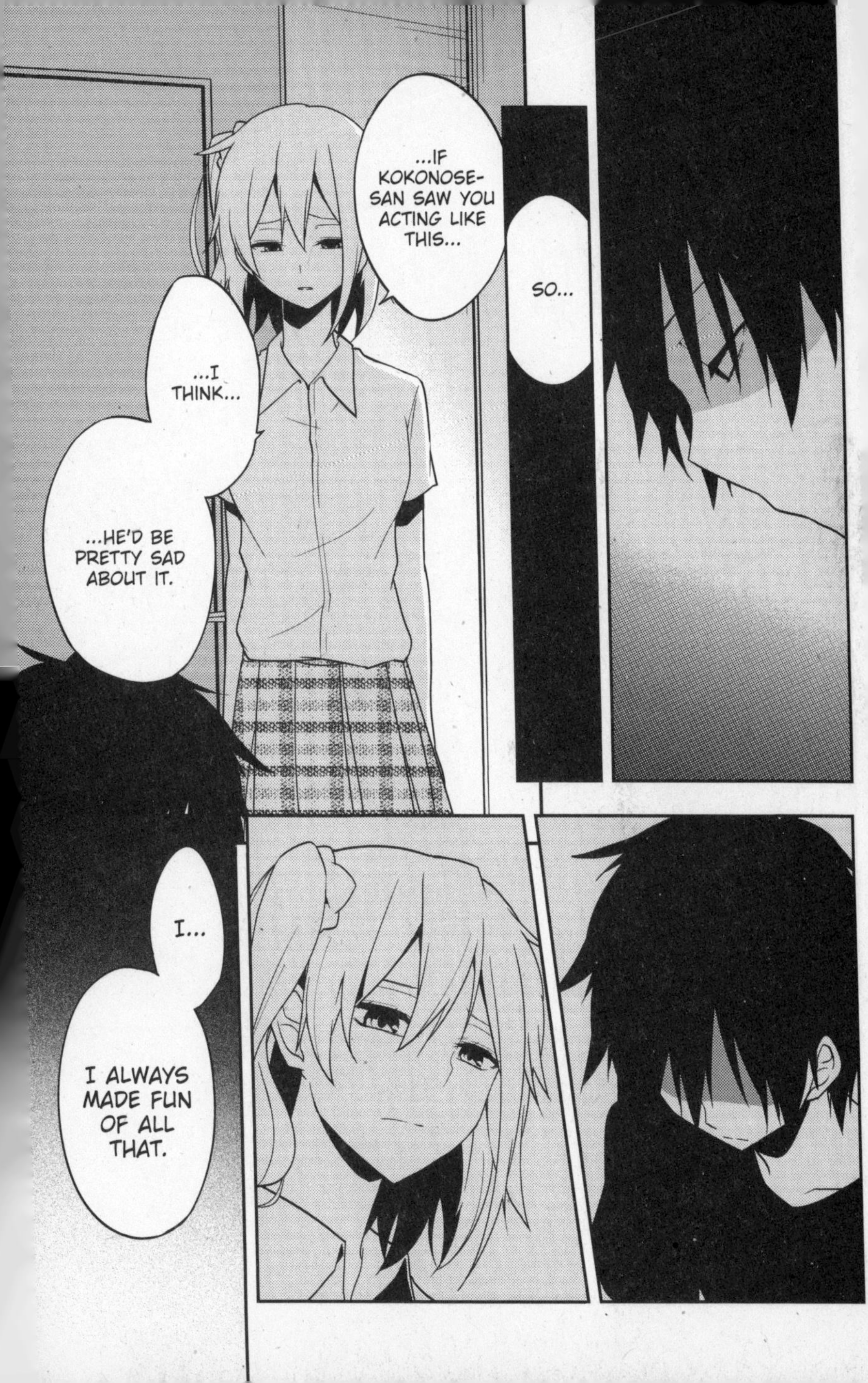
SO...
...IF KOKONOSE-SAN SAW YOU ACTING LIKE THIS...
...I THINK...
...HE'D BE PRETTY SAD ABOUT IT.
I...
I ALWAYS MADE FUN OF ALL THAT.

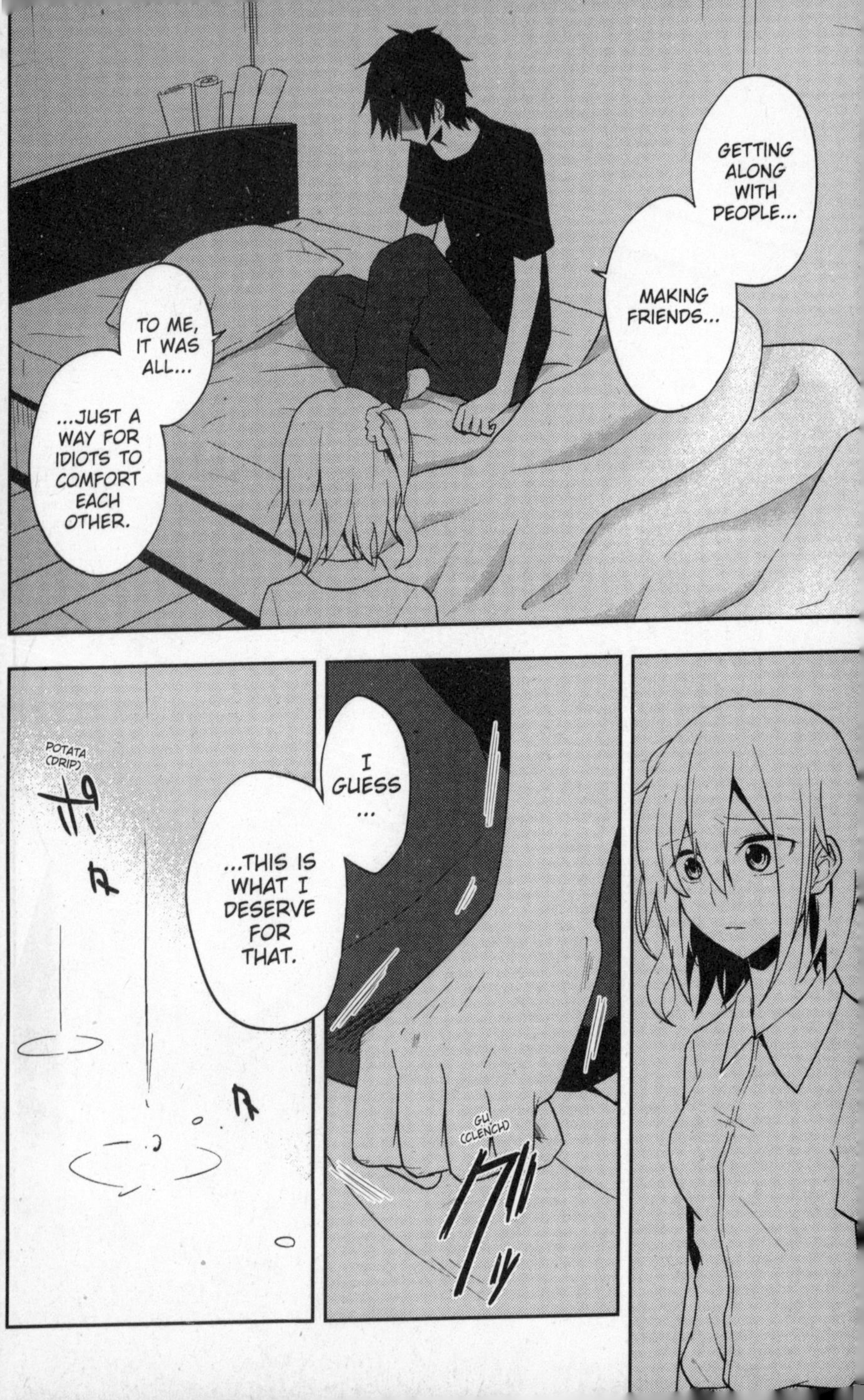
GETTING ALONG WITH PEOPLE...
MAKING FRIENDS...
TO ME, IT WAS ALL...
...JUST A WAY FOR IDIOTS TO COMFORT EACH OTHER.
I GUESS...
...THIS IS WHAT I DESERVE FOR THAT.
GU (CLENCH)
POTATA (DRIP)

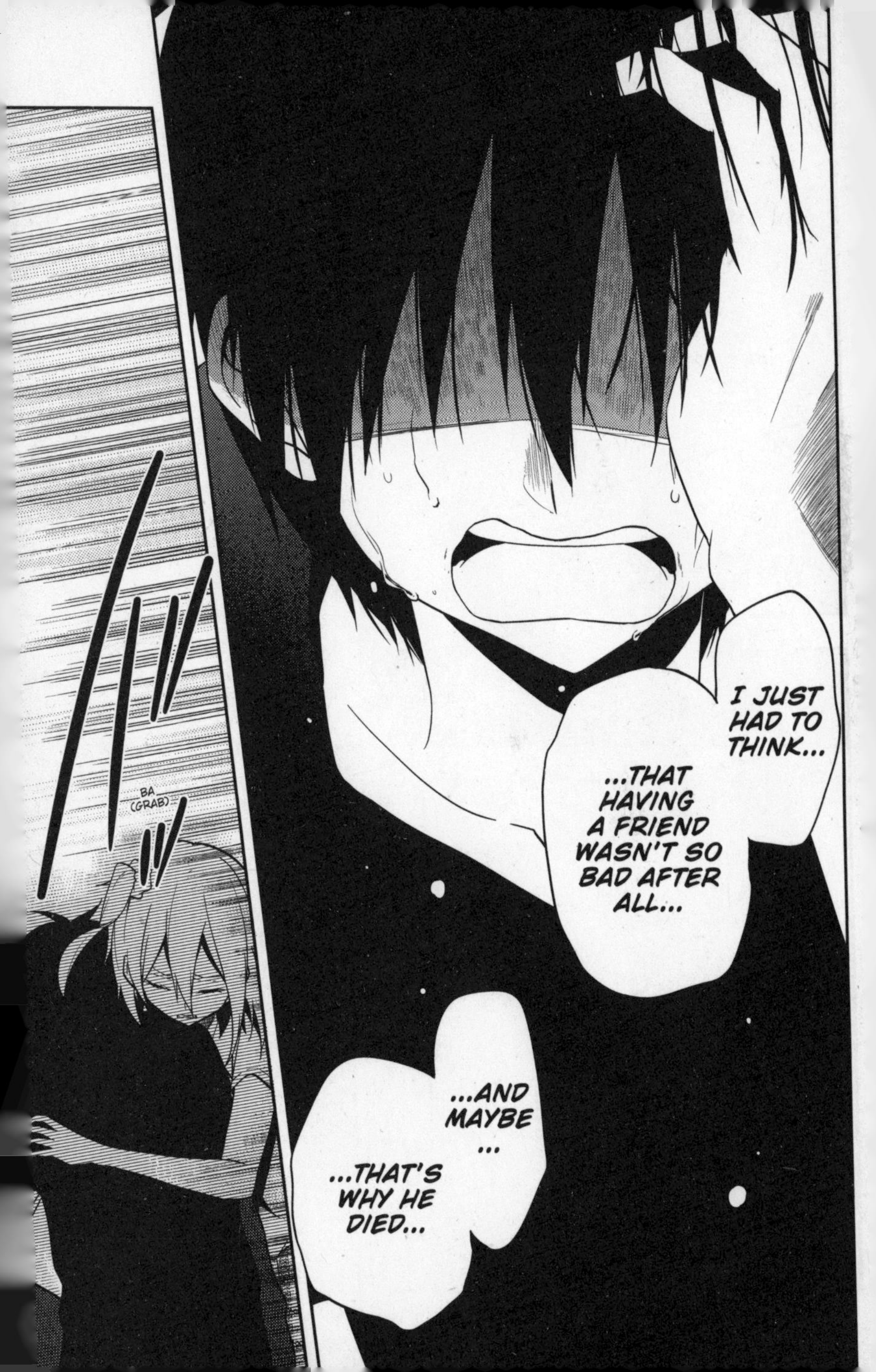
I JUST HAD TO THINK...
...THAT HAVING A FRIEND WASN'T SO BAD AFTER ALL...
...AND MAYBE ...
...THAT'S WHY HE DIED...
BA (GRAB)

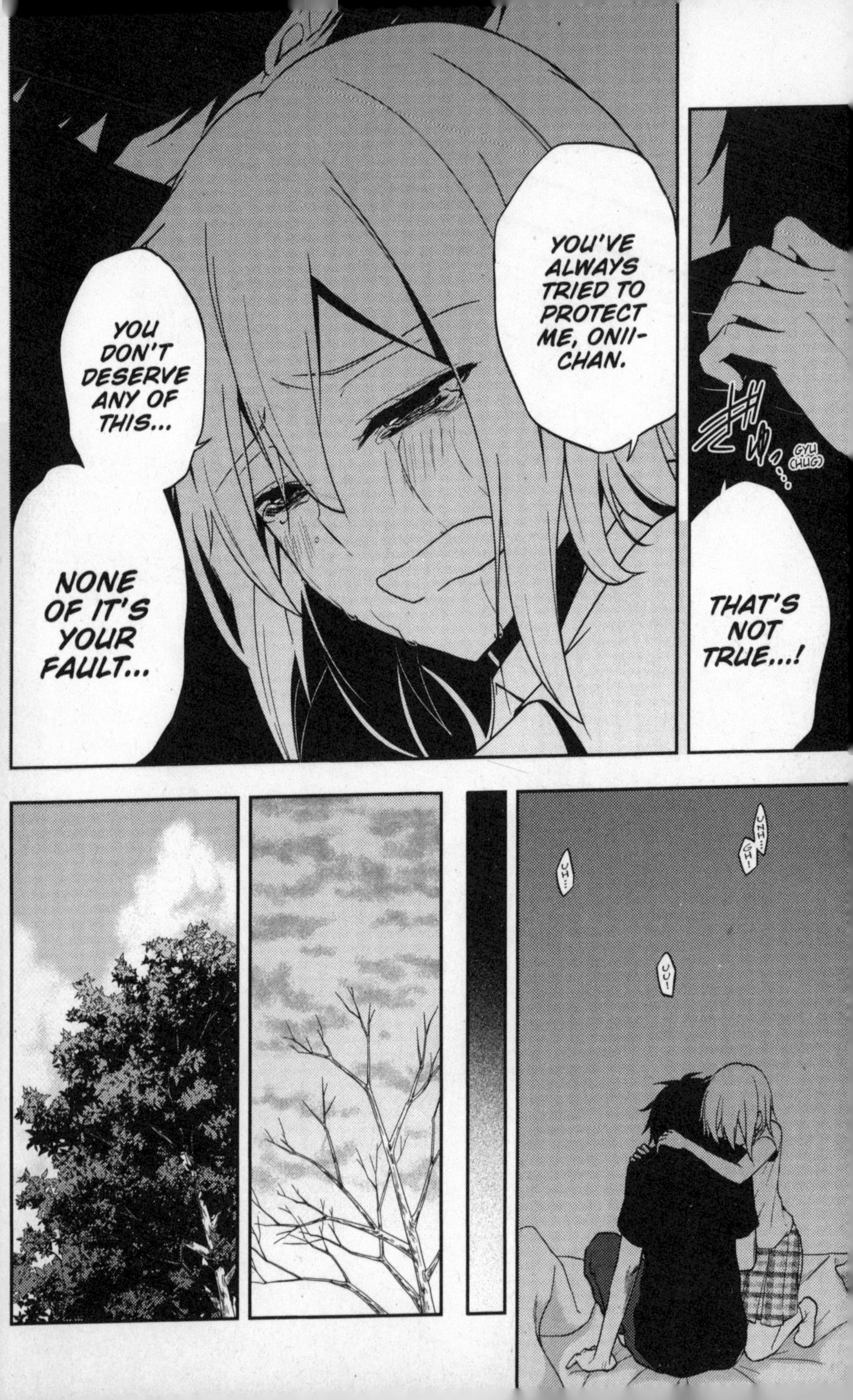
GYU (HUG)
THAT'S NOT TRUE...!
YOU'VE ALWAYS TRIED TO PROTECT ME, ONII-CHAN.
YOU DON'T DESERVE ANY OF THIS...
NONE OF IT'S YOUR FAULT...
UNH... GH!
UH...
UU!

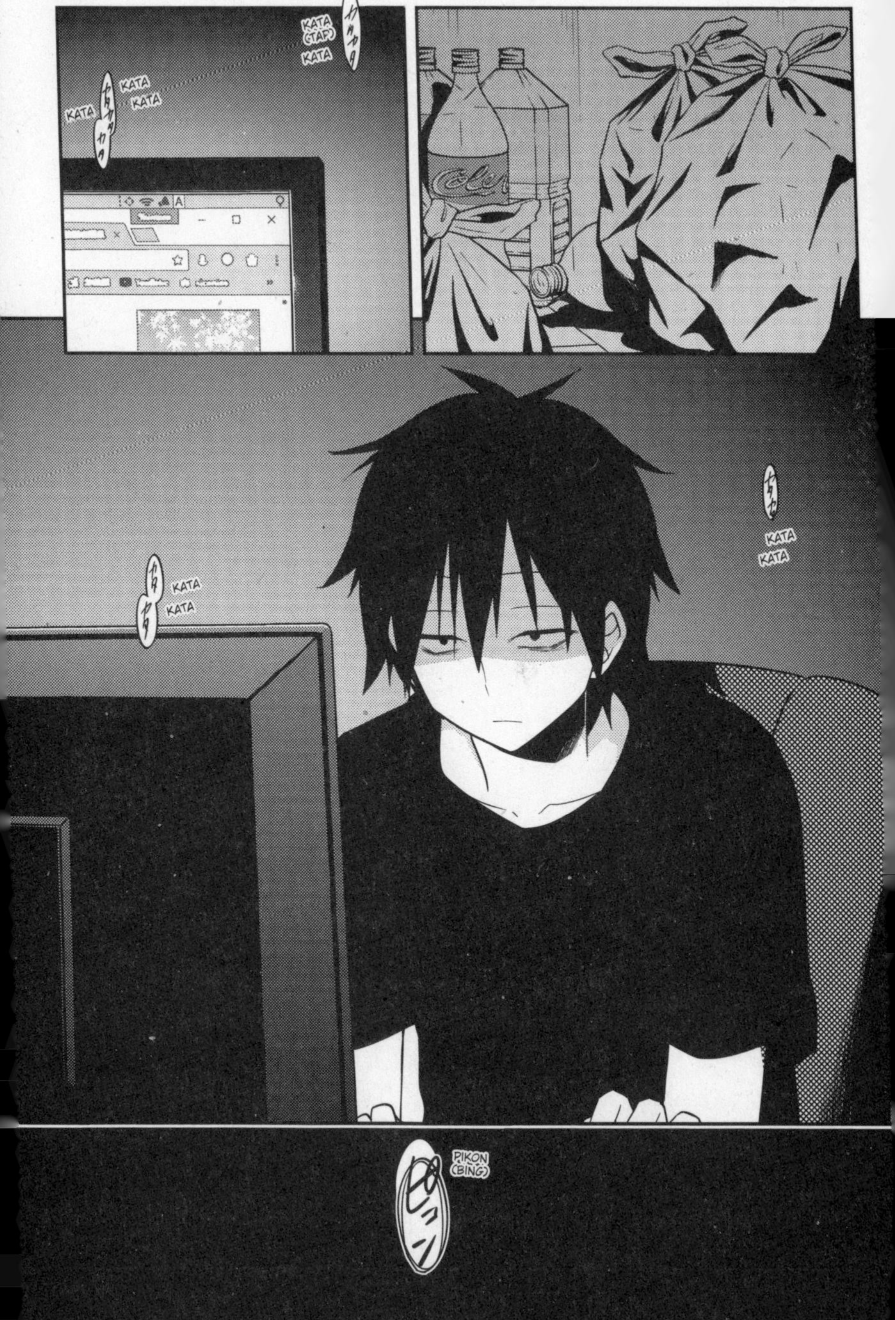
KATA (TAP) KATA
KATA KATA KATA
KATA KATA
KATA KATA
PIKON (BING)

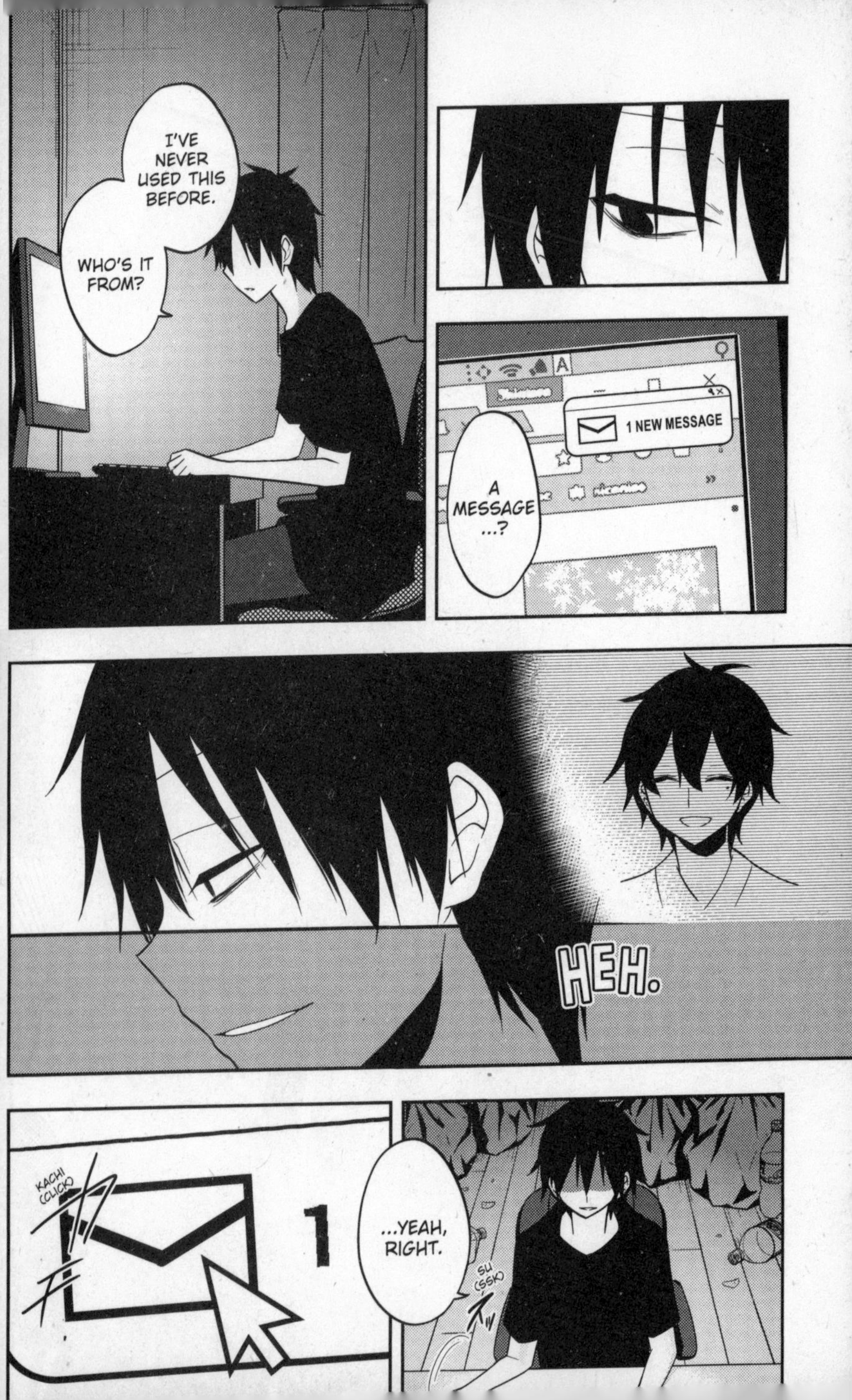
1 NEW MESSAGE
A MESSAGE ...?
I'VE NEVER USED THIS BEFORE.
WHO'S IT FROM?
HEH.
...YEAH, RIGHT.
SU (SSK)
1
KACHI (CLICK)

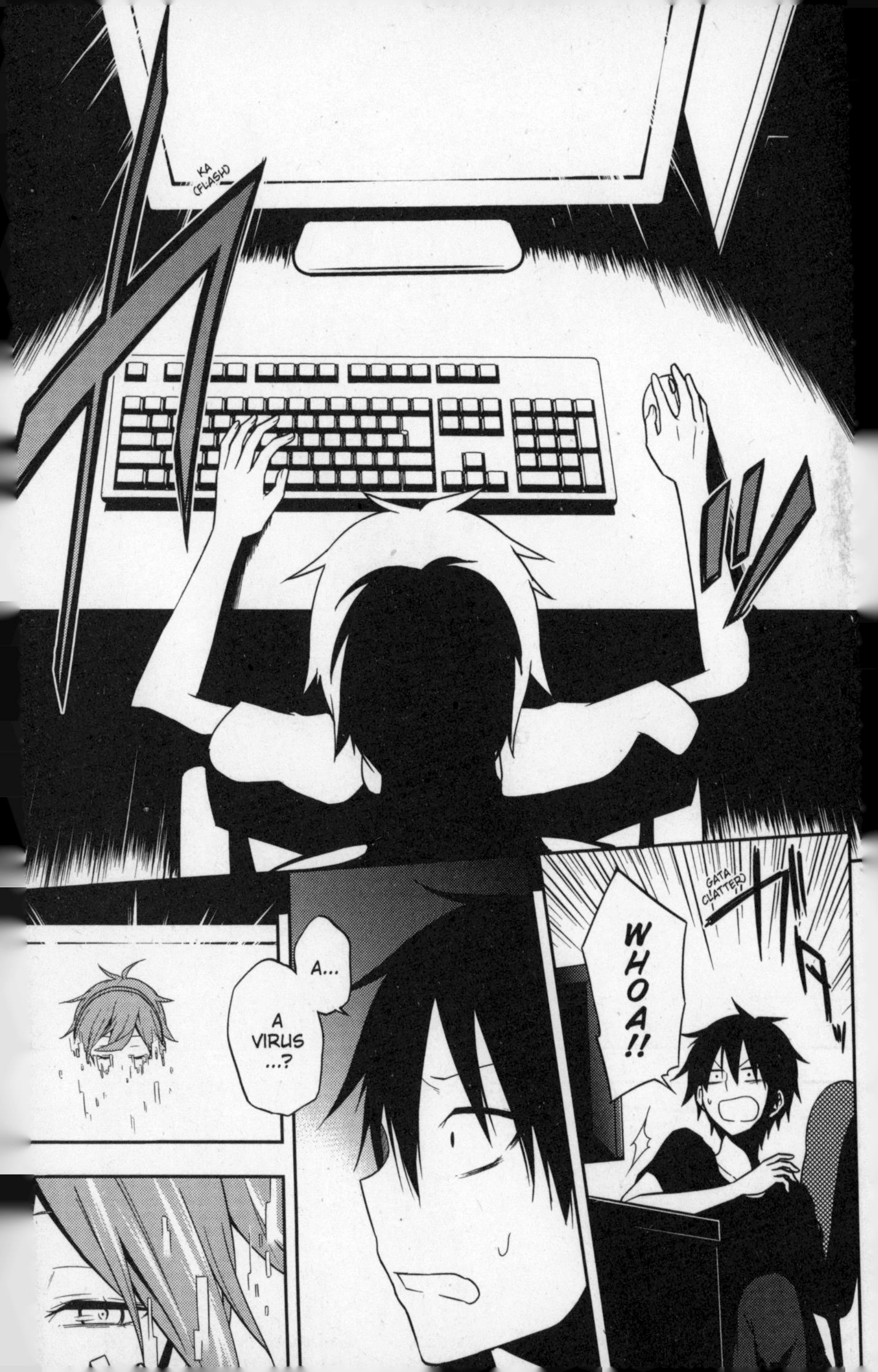
KA (FLASH)
GATA (CLATTER)
WHOA!!
A...
A VIRUS ...?

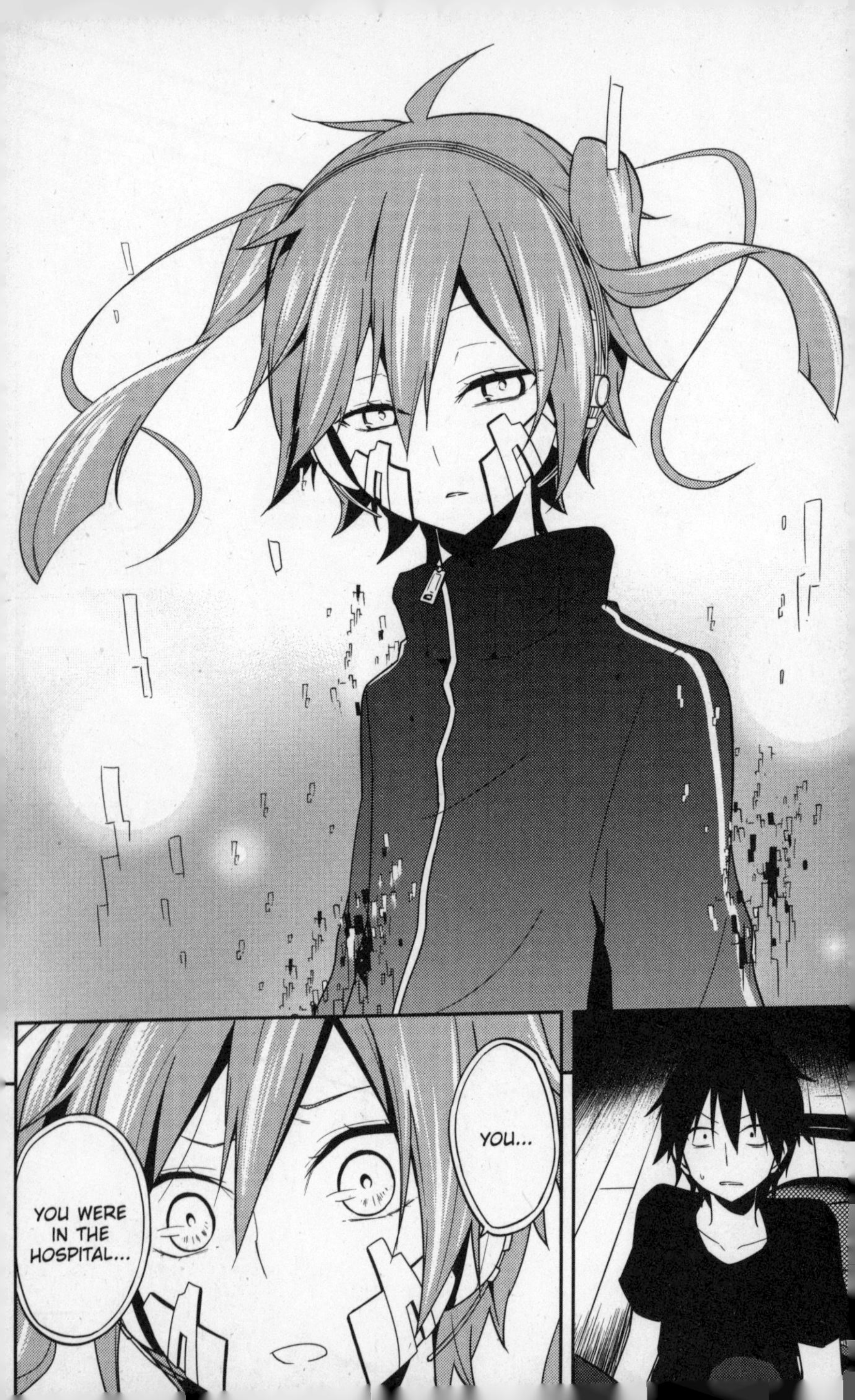
YOU...
YOU WERE IN THE HOSPITAL...

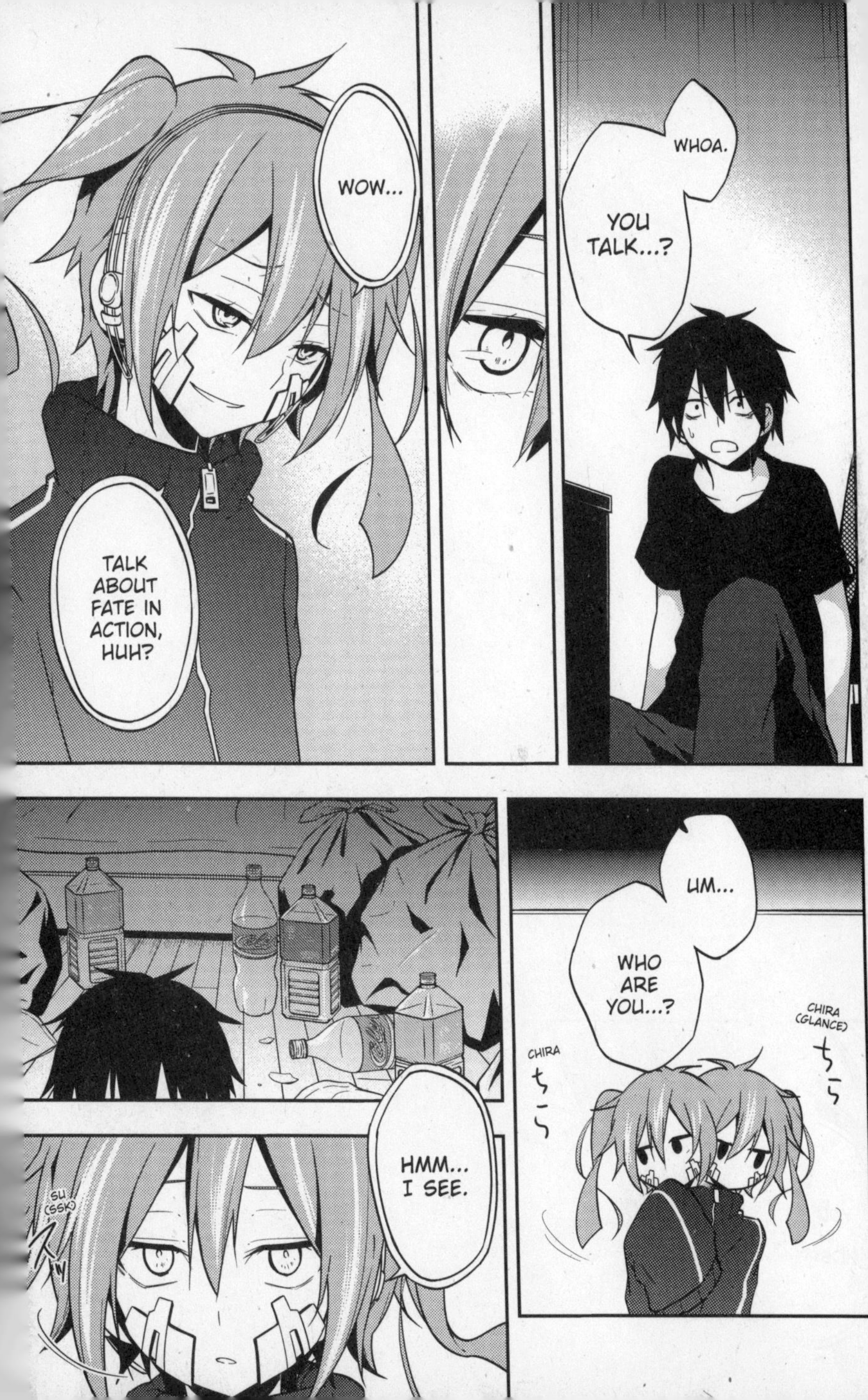
WHOA.
YOU TALK...?
WOW...
TALK ABOUT FATE IN ACTION, HUH?
UM...
WHO ARE YOU...?
CHIRA (GLANCE)
ちら
CHIRA
ちら
HMM... I SEE.
SU (SSK)

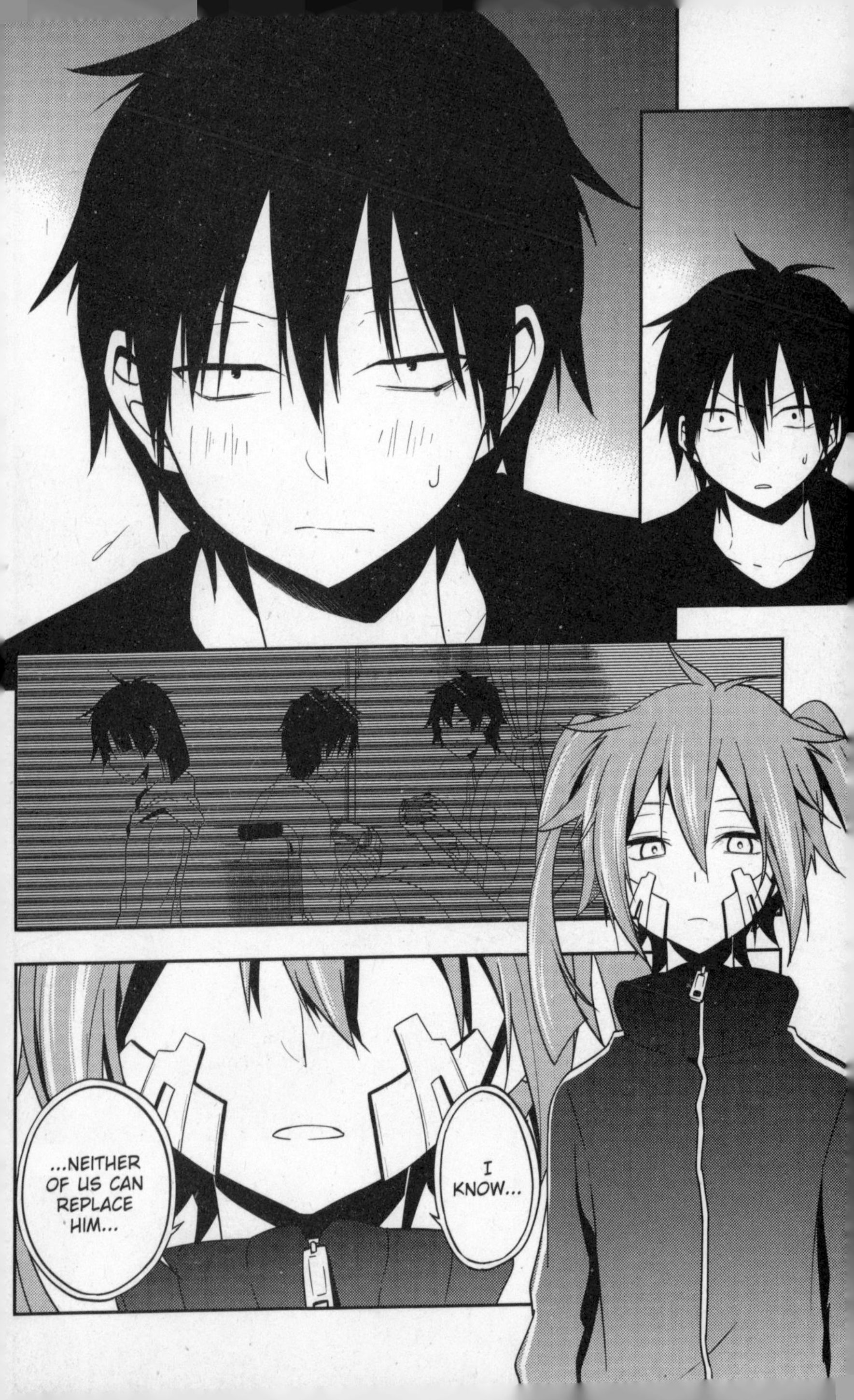
I KNOW...
...NEITHER OF US CAN REPLACE HIM...

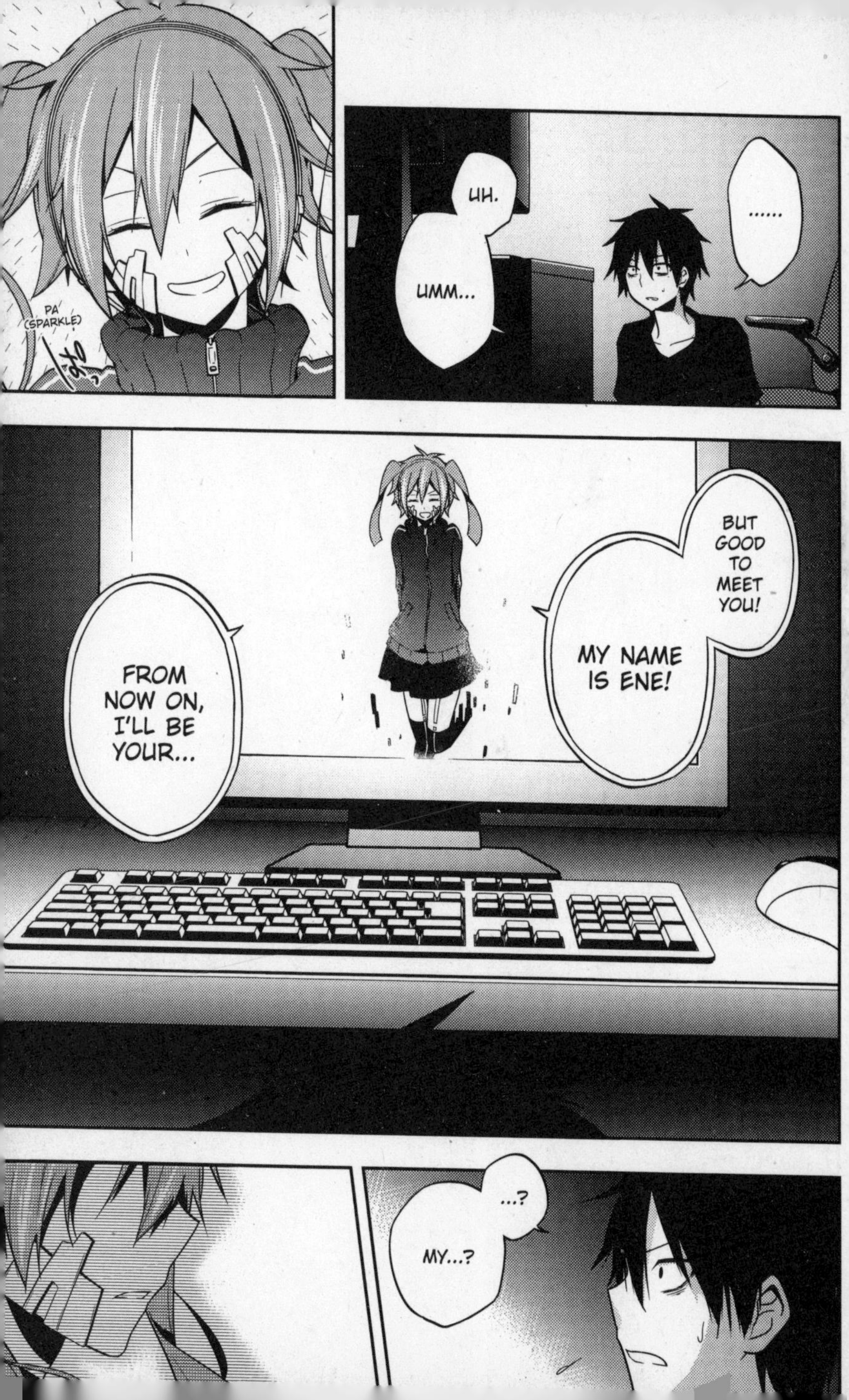
......
UH.
UMM...
PA (SPARKLE)
BUT GOOD TO MEET YOU!
MY NAME IS ENE!
FROM NOW ON, I'LL BE YOUR...
...?
MY...?

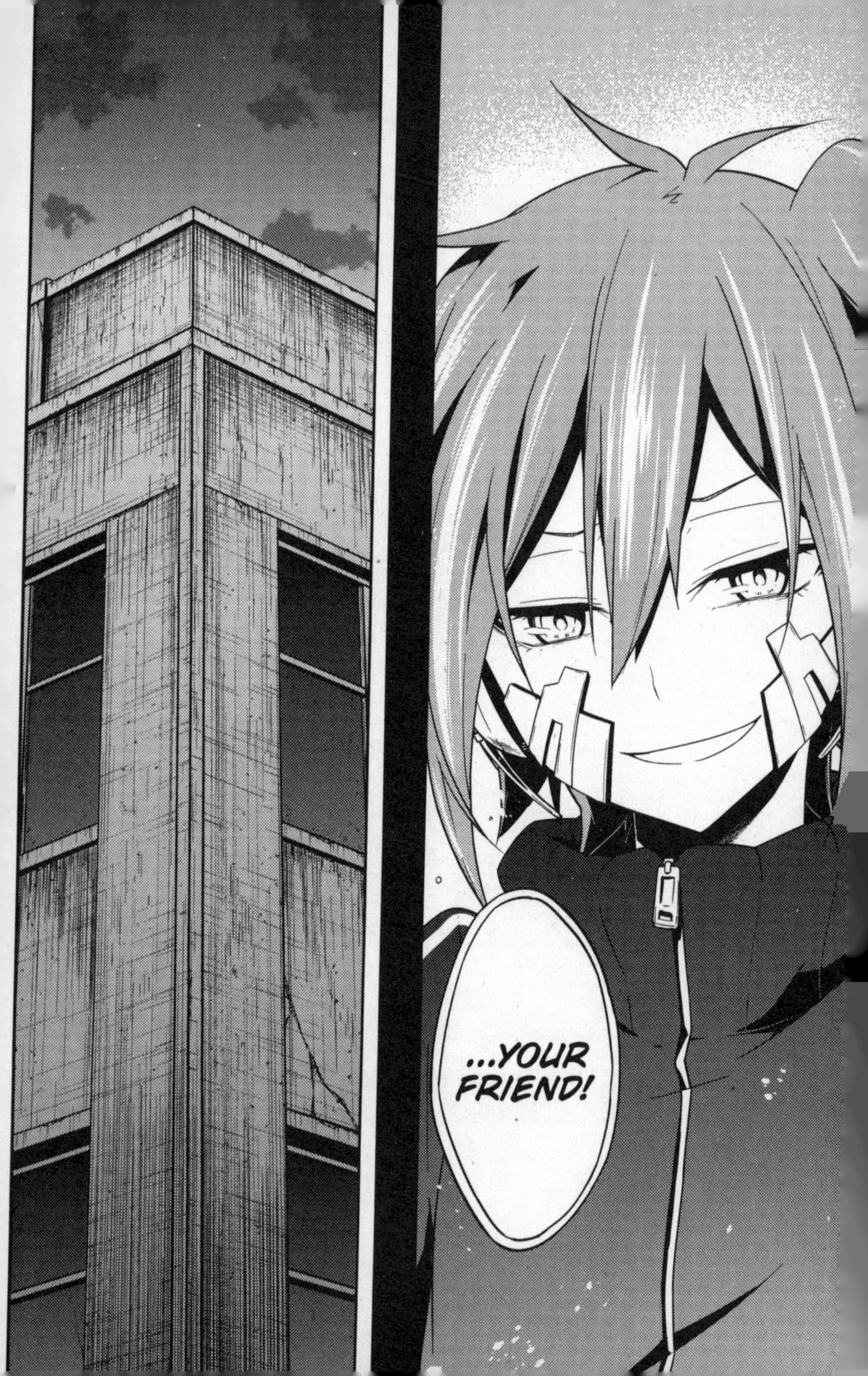
...YOUR FRIEND!

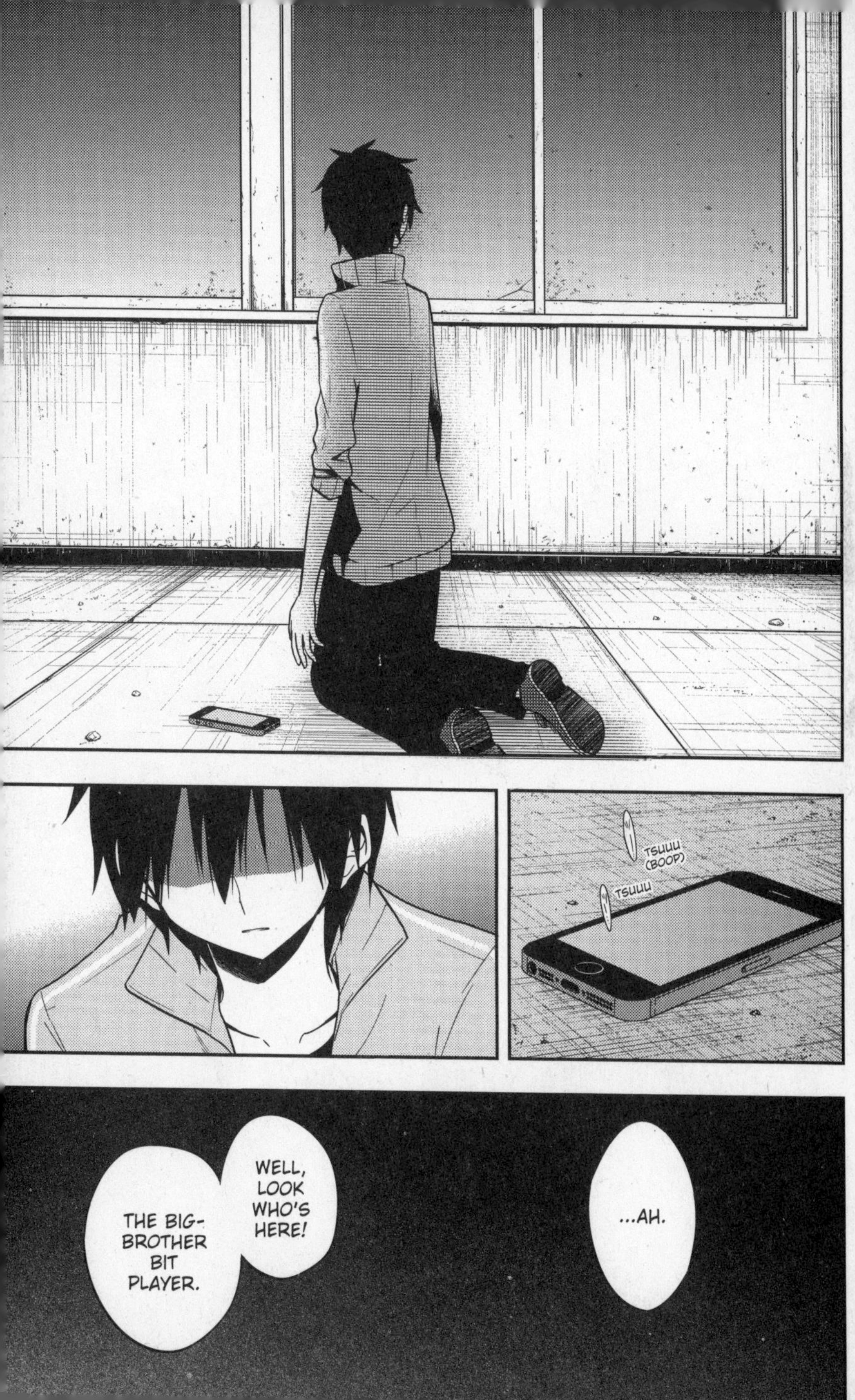
TSUUU (BOOP)
TSUUU
...AH.
WELL, LOOK WHO'S HERE!
THE BIG-BROTHER BIT PLAYER.

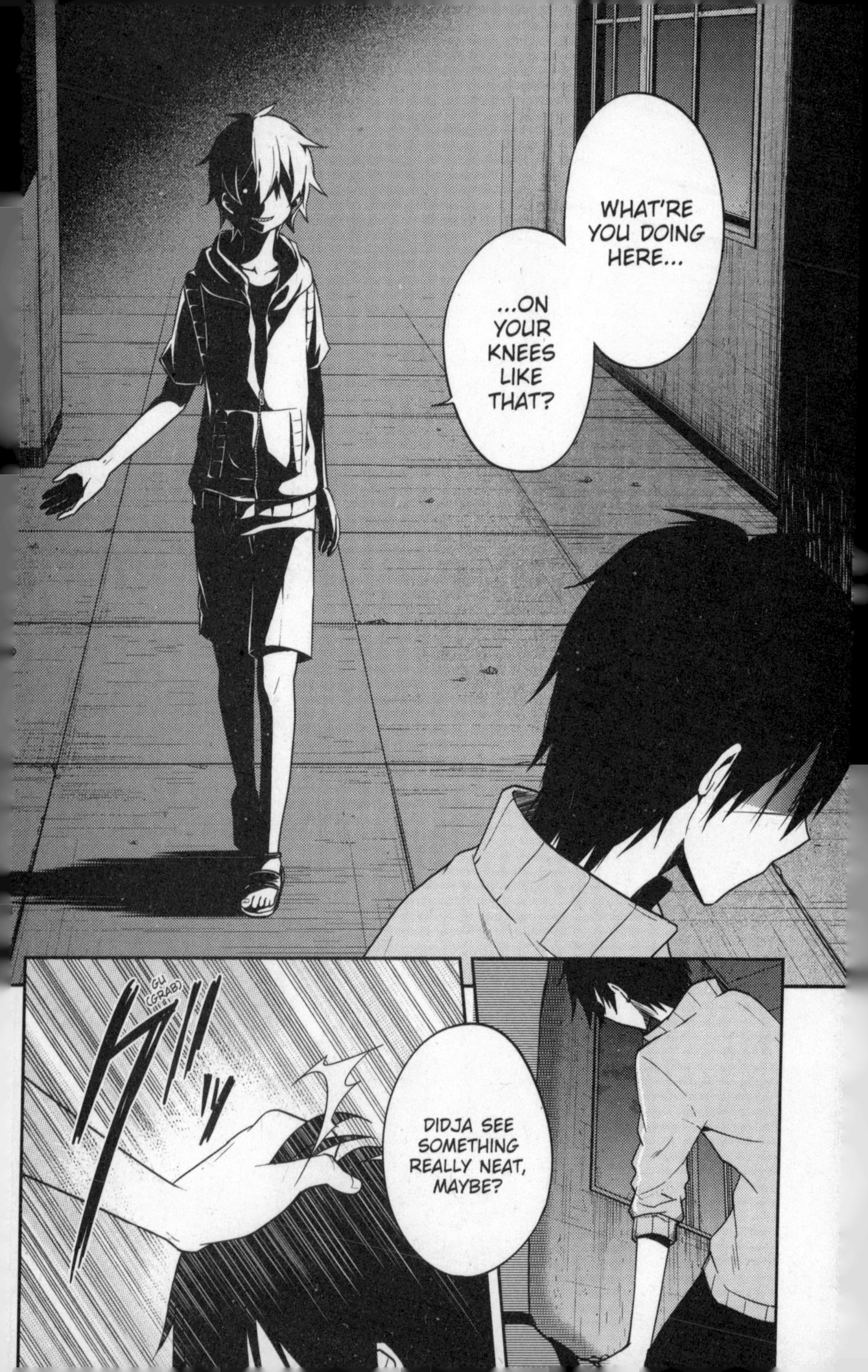
WHAT'RE YOU DOING HERE...
...ON YOUR KNEES LIKE THAT?
DIDJA SEE SOMETHING REALLY NEAT, MAYBE?
GU (GRAB)

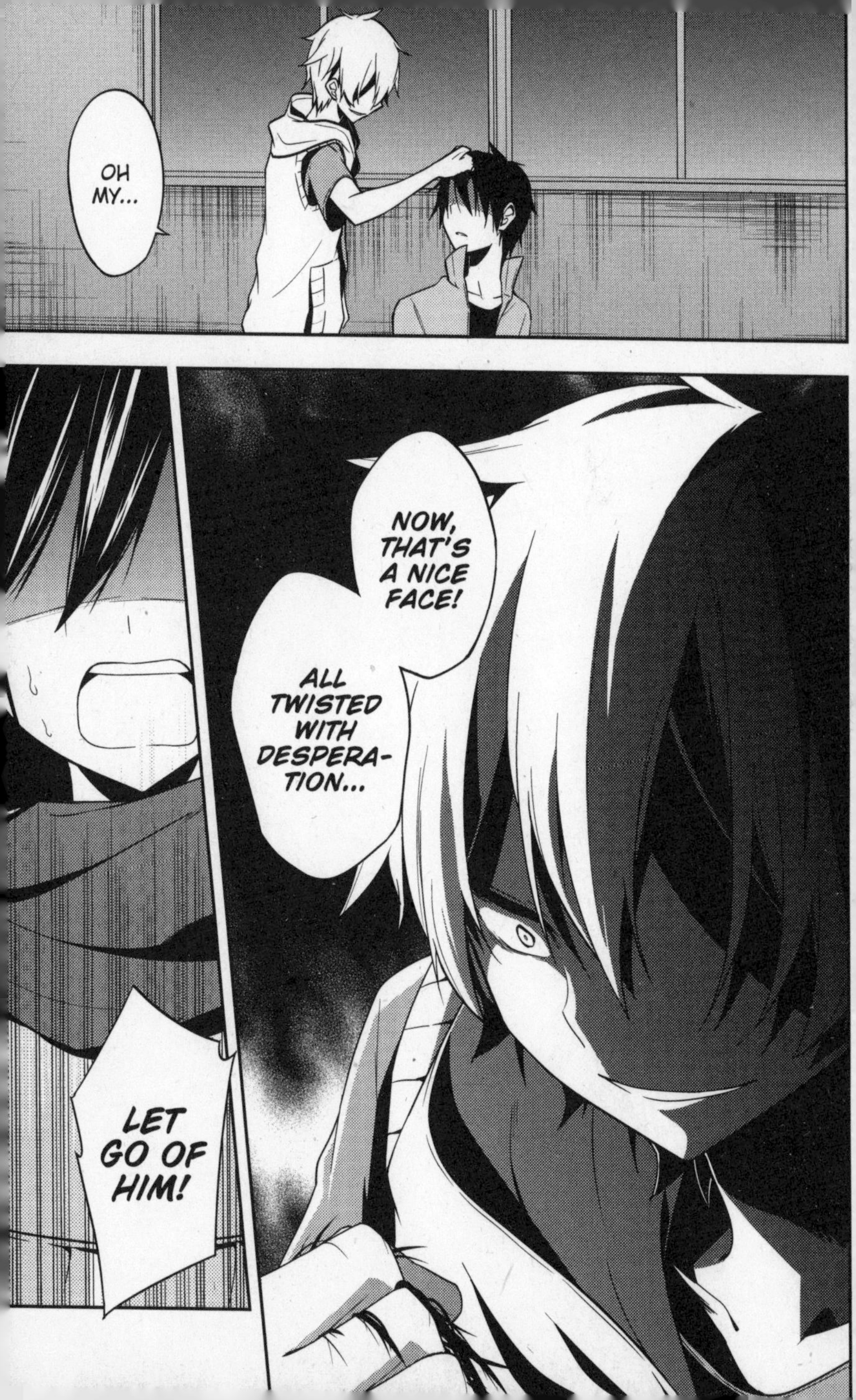
OH MY...
NOW, THAT'S A NICE FACE!
ALL TWISTED WITH DESPERA-TION...
LET GO OF HIM!

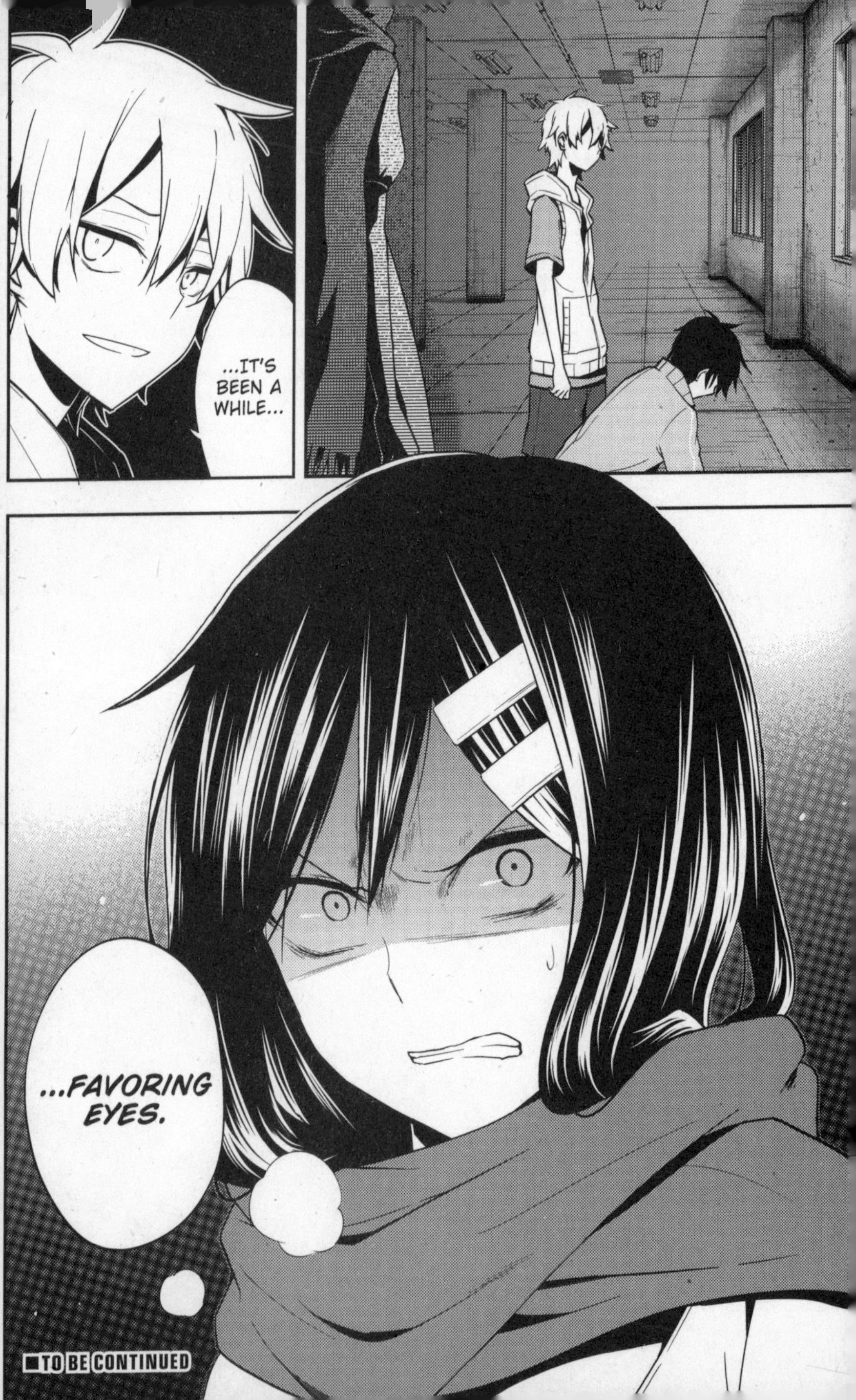
...IT'S BEEN A WHILE...
...FAVORING EYES.
TO BE CONTINUED

KAGEROU DAZE

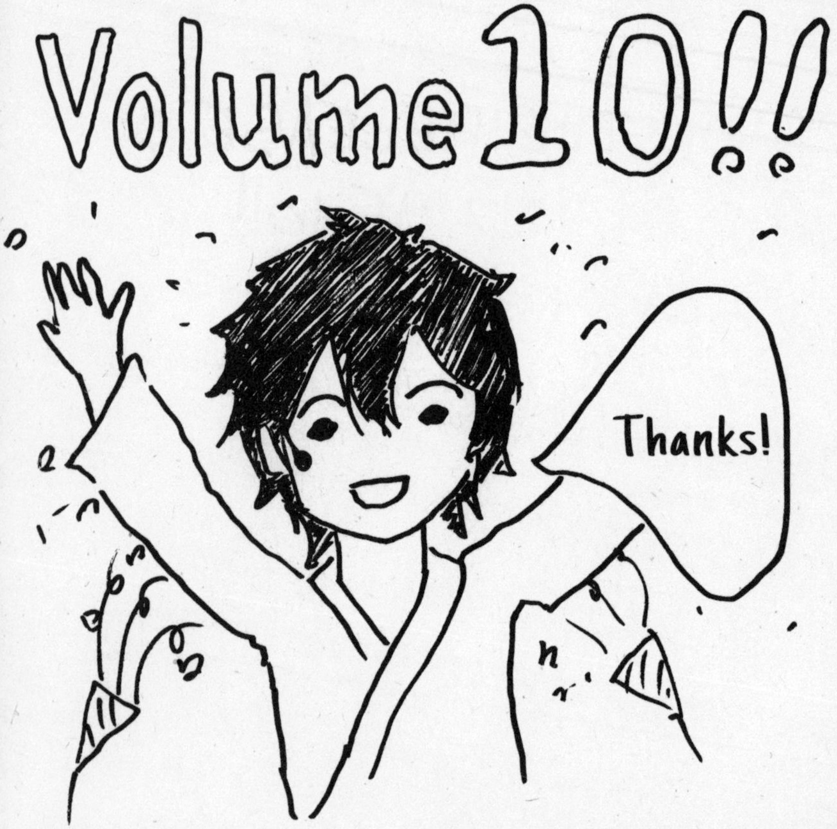
Volume 10!!
Thanks!

This is Jin, the writer. We've now made it to the illustrious ten-volume mark in the *Kagerou Daze* manga. It's all thanks to Mahiro-sensei's hard work and the support all of you provide. Here's hoping that you'll continue to wonder how the story will turn out. I'll keep working hard on it.

Jin

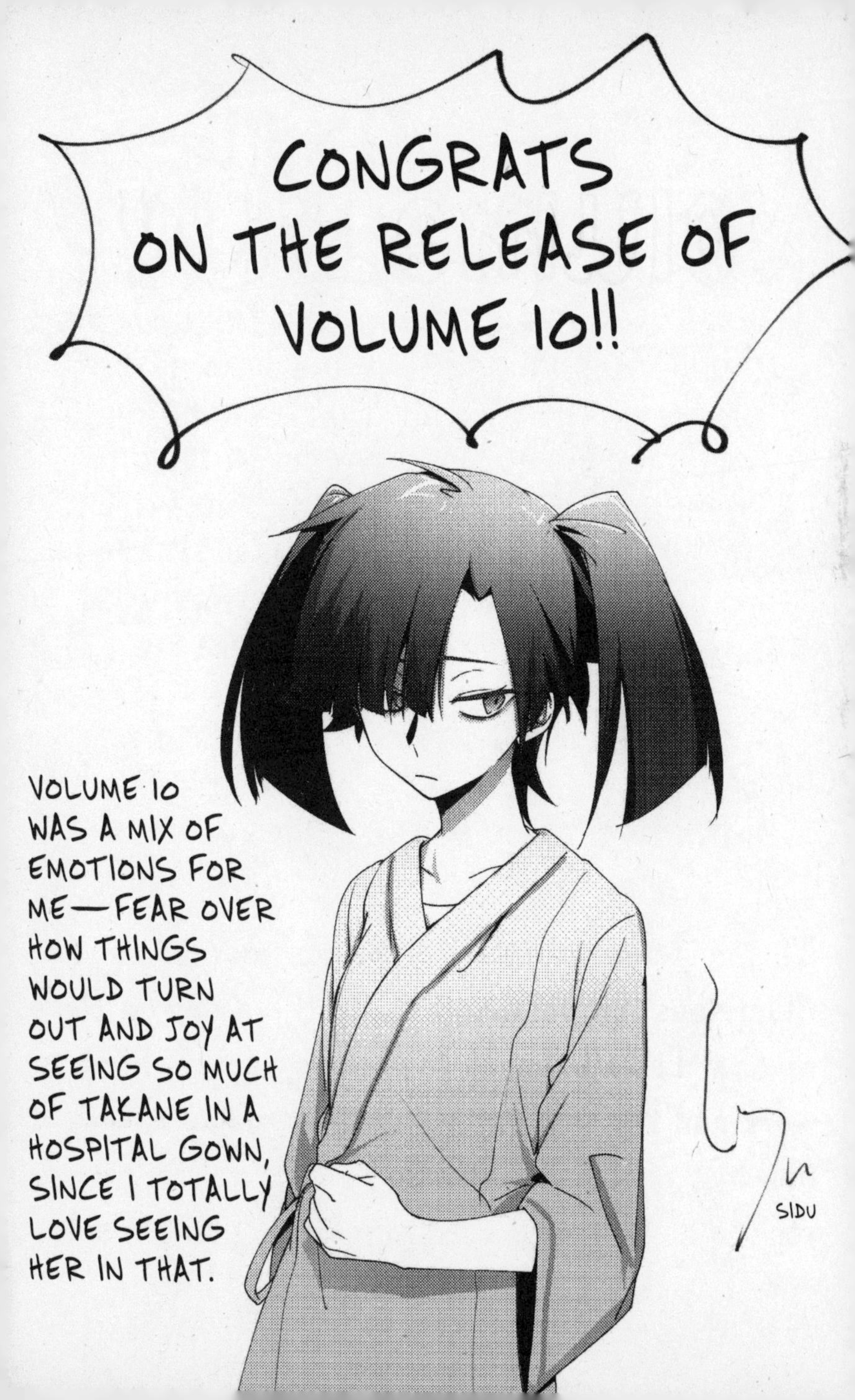
CONGRATS ON THE RELEASE OF VOLUME 10!!
VOLUME 10 WAS A MIX OF EMOTIONS FOR ME—FEAR OVER HOW THINGS WOULD TURN OUT AND JOY AT SEEING SO MUCH OF TAKANE IN A HOSPITAL GOWN, SINCE I TOTALLY LOVE SEEING HER IN THAT.
SIDU

WE'RE FINALLY AT VOLUME 10!!

WHEN THIS SERIES BEGAN, NEVER IN MY DREAMS DID I IMAGINE WE'D HIT DOUBLE DIGITS IN THE VOLUME COUNT! BASED ON THE TALKS I HAD WITH MY EDITOR BEFORE WE BEGAN, WE FIGURED A YEAR AND A HALF... MAYBE TWO YEARS? IT FILLS ME WITH JOY TO BE INVOLVED WITH A STORY THAT SO MANY PEOPLE LOVE! THINGS HAVE BEEN GETTING PRETTY DARK LATELY, BUT HOPEFULLY WE'LL SEE THE CHARACTERS SMILING AGAIN BEFORE LONG. HERE'S HOPING I SEE YOU IN THE NEXT VOLUME!

佐藤 まひろ

MAHIRO SATOU

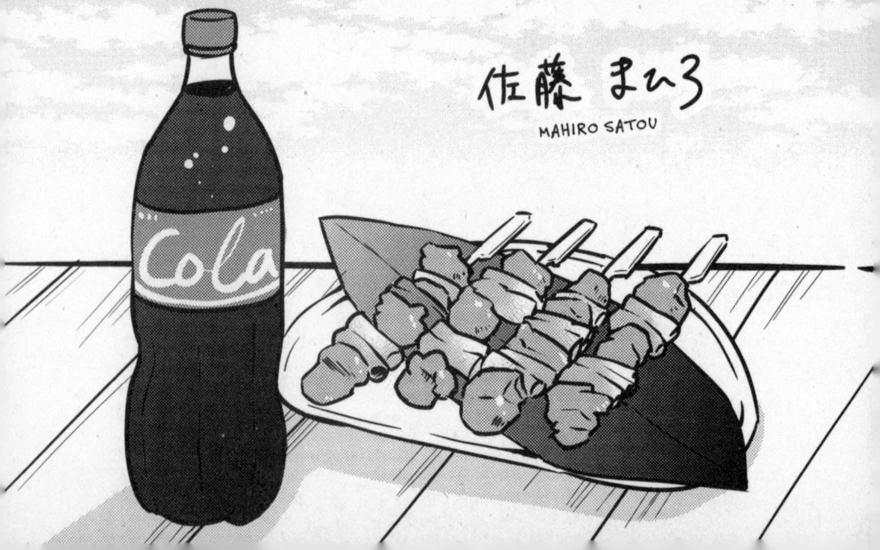
Cola

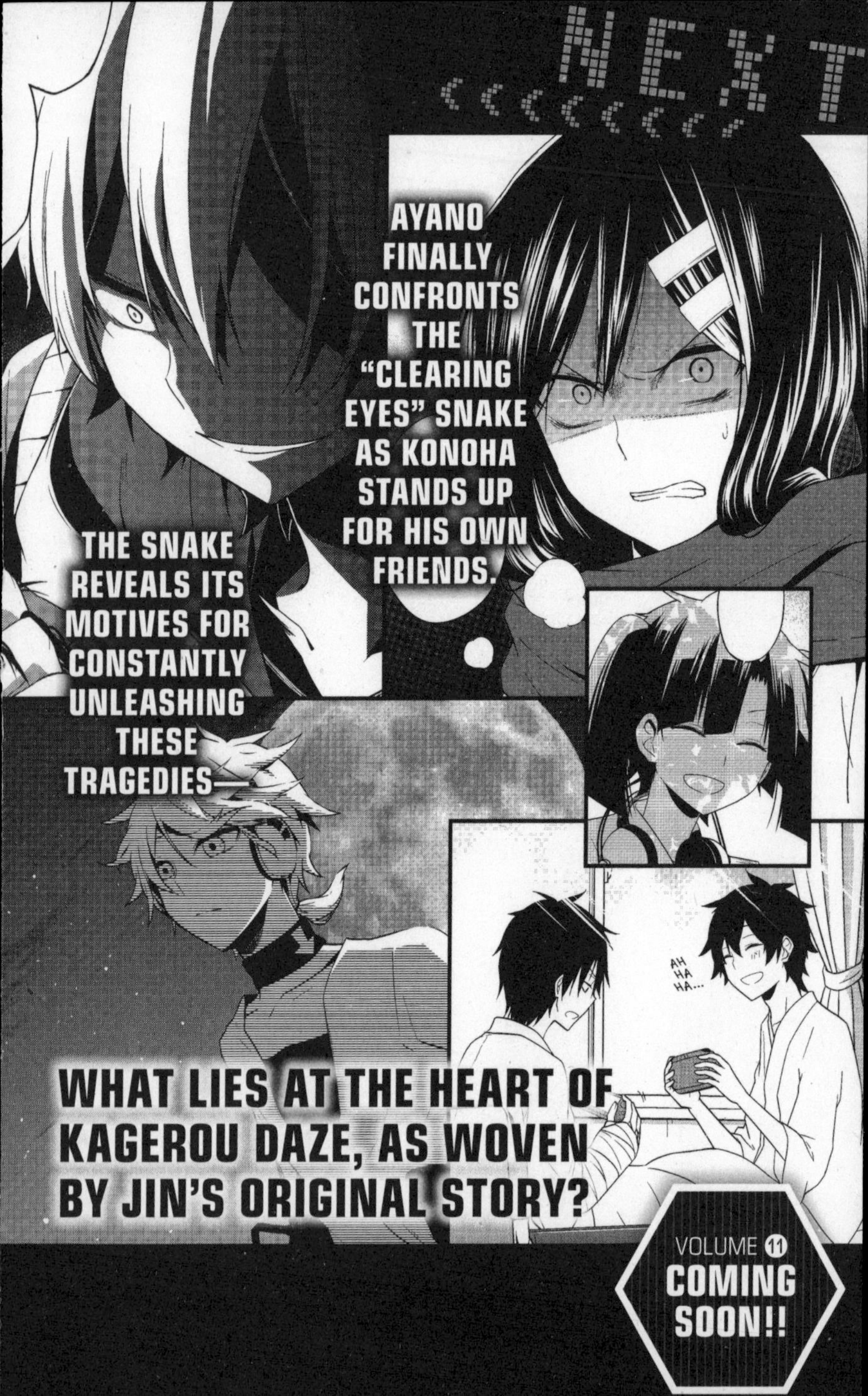
NEXT
AYANO FINALLY CONFRONTS THE "CLEARING EYES" SNAKE AS KONOHA STANDS UP FOR HIS OWN FRIENDS.
THE SNAKE REVEALS ITS MOTIVES FOR CONSTANTLY UNLEASHING THESE TRAGEDIES—
AH HA HA...
WHAT LIES AT THE HEART OF KAGEROU DAZE, AS WOVEN BY JIN'S ORIGINAL STORY?
VOLUME 11 COMING SOON!!

KAGEROU DAZE

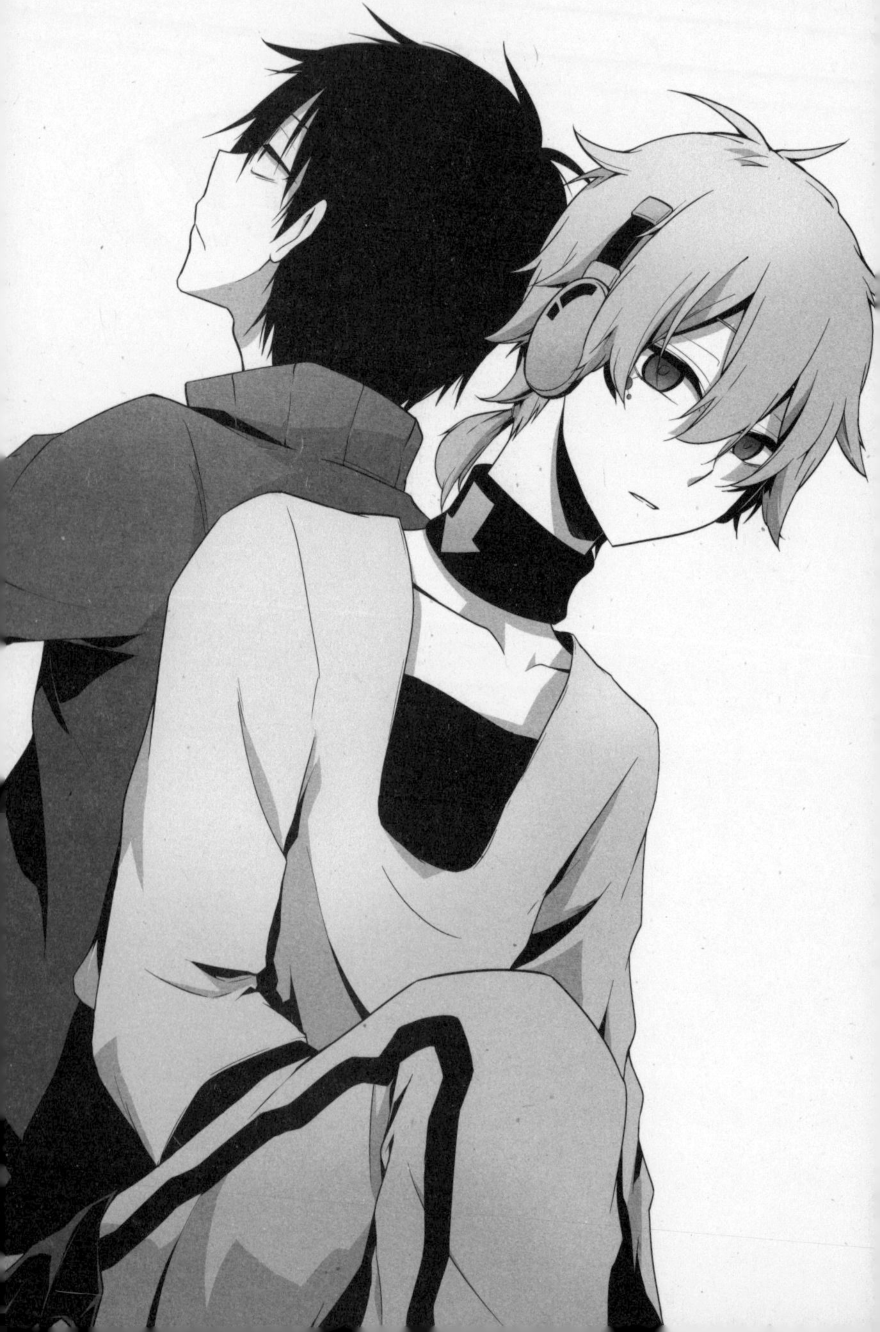

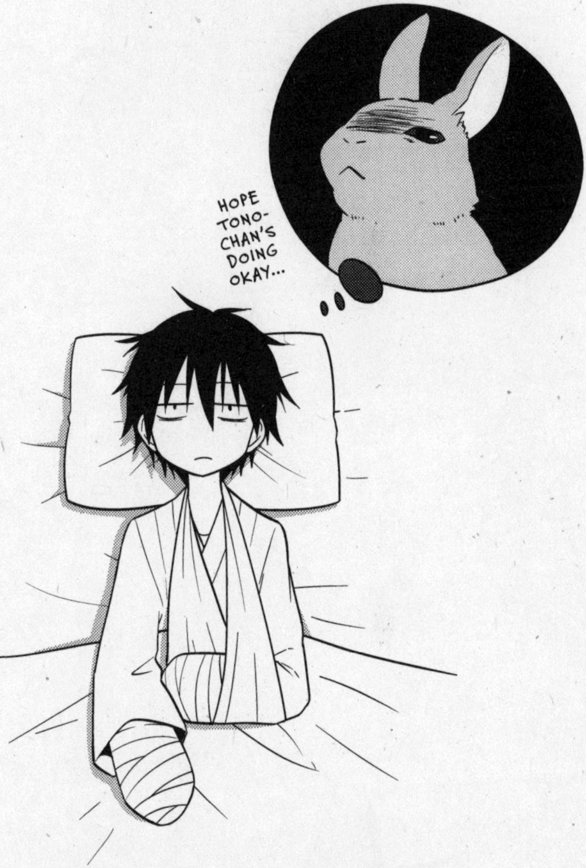
HOPE TONO-CHAN'S DOING OKAY...

KAGEROU DAZE

MAHIRO SATOU
Original Story: JIN
(SHIZEN NO TEKI P)
Character Design: SIDU, WANNYANPOO

Translation: Kevin Gifford   •   Lettering: Abigail Blackman

KAGEROUDAZE Vol. 10
© Mahiro Satou 2017
© KAGEROU PROJECT / 1st PLACE
First published in Japan in 2017 by KADOKAWA CORPORATION, Tokyo.
English translation rights arranged with KADOKAWA CORPORATION, Tokyo through TUTTLE-MORI AGENCY, Inc., Tokyo.

English translation © 2018 by Yen Press, LLC

Yen Press
1290 Avenue of the Americas
New York, NY 10104

Visit us at yenpress.com
facebook.com/yenpress
twitter.com/yenpress
yenpress.tumblr.com
instagram.com/yenpress

First Yen Press Edition: June 2018

Yen Press is an imprint of Yen Press, LLC.
The Yen Press name and logo are trademarks of Yen Press, LLC.

The publisher is not responsible for websites (or their content) that are not owned by the publisher.

Library of Congress Control Number: 2016297061

ISBNs: 978-1-9753-2751-4 (paperback)
       978-1-9753-5427-5 (ebook)

10 9 8 7 6 5 4 3 2 1

WOR

Printed in the United States of America